The Age of Systems in the Thought of Ivan Illich

The Age of Systems in the Thought of Ivan Illich

Jean Robert

Translated by Edoardo McKenna

equinox

SHEFFIELD UK BRISTOL CT

Published by Equinox Publishing Ltd.

UK: Office 415, The Workstation, 15 Paternoster Row,
Sheffield, South Yorkshire S1 2BX

USA: ISD, 70 Enterprise Drive, Bristol, CT 06010

www.equinoxpub.com

First published in Italian as *L'età dei sistemi: Nel Pensiero dell'ultimo Illich* by Museodei by Hermatena 2019. This first English edition published by Equinox Publishing Ltd 2026.

British Library Cataloguing-in-Publication Data

A catalogue record for this book is available from the British Library.

ISBN-13	978 1 80050 886 6	(hardback)
	978 1 80050 887 3	(paperback)
	978 1 80050 888 0	(ePDF)
	978 1 80050 889 7	(ePub)

Library of Congress Cataloging-in-Publication Data

Names: Robert, Jean, 1937-2020 author | McKenna, Edoardo translator
Title: The age of systems in the thought of Ivan Illich / Jean Robert ; translated by Edoardo McKenna.
Other titles: Eta dei sistemi. English
Description: Sheffield, South Yorkshire ; Bristol, CT : Equinox Publishing Ltd, 2026. | "First published in Italian as L'eta dei sistemi: Nel Pensiero dell'ultimo Illich by Museodei by Hermatena 2019. This first English edition published by Equinox Publishing Ltd 2026." | Includes bibliographical references. | Summary: "Jean Robert was a close friend and intellectual interlocutor of Illich. This engagement with Illich's "last thoughts" is also Robert's last book. As such, it is the final fruit of a life devoted to serious conversations in the company of friends"-- Provided by publisher.
Identifiers: LCCN 2026022915 (print) | LCCN 2026022916 (ebook) | ISBN 9781800508866 hardback | ISBN 9781800508873 paperback | ISBN 9781800508880 pdf | ISBN 9781800508897 epub
Subjects: LCSH: Illich, Ivan, 1926-2002 | Philosophy, American--20th century | Philosophers--United States | Technology--Philosophy | Technology--Social aspects
Classification: LCC B945.I454 R6313 2026 (print) | LCC B945.I454 (ebook)
LC record available at https://lccn.loc.gov/2026022915
LC ebook record available at https://lccn.loc.gov/2026022916

Typeset by Isabelle Cedotti

Contents

Foreword

We live in a technological age. By 'technology,' we commonly mean instruments or tools designed for human purposes and available for use at will. Everything man-made fits this frame: a plow, a hospital, a search engine. But such a view obscures the depth of our current entanglement with the world we have made. From the roads and sewers beneath our feet to the food that fills our stomachs, the screens that mediate our relationships, and the algorithms that scaffold our thoughts, few today can survive outside technology-as-womb.

The issue is not merely the dominance of the built world over the natural environment. As Ivan Illich argued, there is a crucial difference between tools that assist or extend human capacities and those that disable or replace them. A car is not just a faster bicycle; it incapacitates the feet. It is a deformation of language to say, 'I went to the market,' when I was carried there in an automobile. But enveloping and disabling artifacts do not fully define the present. That we shape tools that then shape us is well known—since McLuhan, if not Thoreau. Yet, artifacts were not always designed to reconstitute perception of the world and oneself. For example, rail travel still restructures our sense of speed and landscape, but trains were not designed for that purpose.

Today, however, cybernetic systems are designed primarily to structure experience. The iPhone is well named: it is a device that not only constitutes a screened experience of the world, but also the 'I' who is subjected to that experience. Online courses do not merely transmit knowledge; they direct the learner through a sequence of clicks, modules, and assessments that constitute her as a consumer of prepackaged content. In such artifacts, the user does not operate the device so much as function within it. This raises a fundamental question: can we still speak of using technology when our behaviors are elements of the product design?

Rooted in his long collaboration and friendship with Ivan Illich, this book—Jean Robert's last—offers his most sustained meditation yet on the nature, limits, and fate of the instrument. Robert does not merely extend Illich's thesis concerning the passing of the age of tools. He reconsiders it in the context of all Illich's work, testing it through etymological excavations, historical contrasts, phenomenological vignettes, and vivid metaphors, in a style that is both suggestive and precise. Moving from Illich's theological sources through the histories of vernacular gender, the gaze, and the alphabet, Robert's book clarifies one of Illich's most searching—and least appreciated—lines of inquiry.

Robert was uniquely suited to explore this terrain. Few in Illich's circle matched his architectural training, linguistic fluency, and ease with both European intellectual traditions and Latin American vernacular life. He also shared Illich's commitment to defending a world built in proportion to the 'human' scale. We met Jean Robert in the late 1980s during his sojourns at Penn State University, where he joined a small itinerant circle that gathered around Illich each year. What began as a collegial acquaintance ripened into something more like discipleship—less loyalty to dogma than admiration for a way of being. Jean refused lazy explanations, demanded exactitude in language and etymology, and insisted that key texts be read aloud until their rhythm and breath became audible. His writing, too, invites the ear as much as the eye. Some things did not change over the quarter century we knew him: the shock of white hair atop a ruddy face, the lean frame that unfurled to an imposing height, and, above all, the fiery intellect devoted to defamiliarizing the present.

This was the opposite of an antiquarian's delight in rummaging through the past. If Illich's early work is known for critiques of institutional monopolies—of schooling, medicine, and transportation—his later work excavated the grammar of technological society: the displacement of vernacular gender by economic sex, the evaporation of water into H_2O, the formation of the textual mind, and the transmutation of tool-users into managed functions within systems. Robert emphasizes the rarity of this style of historical investigation, which goes to the heart of how both he and Illich studied the present. Robert invokes the idea of eversion—turning a glove inside out—to describe the kind of disjunction they saw when viewing the present in the mirror of the past. But equally, they believed that the past remains, in shards and fragments that could orient stances to the present.

This book continues that ethos. It is centered on an original insight of Ivan Illich. The instrument refers to an artifact that is distinct from its user, whose intention it transfers without distortion. As such, the instrument is not a natural category but a social construct. Illich located its rise in twelfth-century theology, where the concept of instrumentum described priests and the sacraments as tools of God.

What is made can also be unmade. A hammer is distinct from the hand; it can be taken up or laid down at will. By contrast, a system integrates the user as a managed input. A facial-recognition machine that opens doors for you but not for me is a banal but telling example. Elsewhere, Robert calls 'pseudo-tools' those artifacts that seem like instruments but lack their distality. They appear subservient but, in fact, instrumentalize the human. Illich's thesis was not just that systems are eclipsing tools, but that the two are incommensurable. Systems do not follow tools in a linear history of progress. Rather, the system inaugurates a fundamentally different relationship, if any, between the human and device. It names artifacts that are disproportionate to human capacities and purposes.

This book is not a manifesto. It is a witness to a fading epoch and an invitation to think anew about the means we live by.

Samar Farage and Sajay Samuel
State College, PA

Preface[1]

When Ivan Illich was in his teens, a fortune teller told him that he was going to invent a 'science that does not exist.' As a grown man, he kept himself abreast of the different facets of 'industrial society,' of which he had been one of the most coherent critics. As such, he undertook research endeavors that focused on 'the axioms underlying our social theorems,' 'the topology of the late modern mind,' 'historical somatics' (a history of the self-perceived body in past eras), a history of the gaze, and the social history of alphabetic culture, which together did amount to a new science.

The present book has the ambition of introducing some of the ideas which Illich developed, either orally or in writing, over the last twenty years of his life. They concern examining and understanding the present with the eyes of a historian; 'historicizing' the guiding principles and the certainties that shape the late modern mind. After the early 1980s, two new intuitions began to inspire Illich:

1. Unquestioned certainties were not purely conceptual or 'scientific' but relied, in fact, on tangles of conceptions and perceptions, of concepts and precepts. The historian Barbara Duden, a member of the 'West German Women's Movement,' whom Illich met in Berlin around 1980, alerted him to the aphorism devised by the anthropologist Mary Douglas in the context of her 'theory of the two bodies'—'the social body determines the way in which the physical body is perceived, which in turn supports a specific view of society' (Douglas, 1970, p. 72). After 1980, Illich undertook with Barbara Duden a wide-ranging program for the exploration of physical perceptions and of their contribution to the crystallization of what contemporary man held to be true.
2. Illich's second intuition took shape in stages: after the 1970s, mankind was faced with an 'epistemological landslide,' which he believed to have been caused by the

1 This manuscript is a translation by Edoardo McKenna of Jean Robert's *L'età dei sistemi nel pensiero dell'ultimo Illich* (Museodei by Hermatena, Bologna, 2019).

weakening of a certainty that was initially theological, and later techno-logical: namely, the certainty that some objects were made to obey a certain kind of intention, be they divine or, at a later stage, human.[2] These objects are what we nowadays know as tools, and what medieval Latin designated with the word *instrumenta* (*instrumentum* in the singular).

After the twelfth century, scholastic philosophers developed a more precise definition of *instrumentum* by adding a fifth cause (*causa instrumentalis*) to Aristotle's four causes (*materialis, formalis, finalis, efficiens*). Thereafter, tools became an instrumental cause, and the 'technological age' that was about to begin is more adequately defined as the instrumental age. Illich hypothesized that this instrumental age had entered its decline in the years between 1970 and 1980. The epistemological upheavals that have followed each other after the end of the twentieth century constitute a 'farewell to tools' which we are still unable to express properly. We still use the words 'tools' or 'technologies' to describe artifacts that, in fact, do not serve human intentions.

Many of Illich's readers and friends sink in an embarrassed silence when questioned about those two daring hypotheses. In the present book, I intend to clearly differentiate what might be true (and what I consider to be as such) from what may be refuted for lack of empirical evidence.[3]

Illich was one of those thinkers who pushed themselves to the limit, and who did not try to identify the solid stepping-stones in a fjord, but rather the shaky one right in the middle that enabled them to think the unthinkable.

Illich argued that certain modern circumstances and notions constituted a complete break with the past. The fracture between orality and literacy and between gender and sex are two examples of such a break. Modernity refuses to take stock of the radicality of such ruptures. Instead of taking full measure that a hyper-alphabetized society is bereft of any link whatsoever to

2 See Chapter 1.

3 See Chapter 4.

orality, reference is usually made to 'oral *literatures*.' What Illich claimed about the alphabet can also be said of the idea of sex in economic society: it is a reality inconceivable before its birth and therefore impossible to forget after its emergence. Alphabetized people have become so incapable of understanding the oral world's specificity that whenever they attempt to do so, they colonize it with hopelessly alphabetical concepts such as 'oral *literatures*.' Likewise, modern societies are dominated by what Illich called 'economic sex.' He claimed that *sex* was fundamentally different from *gender*, in the same way that societies organized in accordance with economic laws based on the axiom of scarcity could not be compared to subsistence societies, which could experience indigence, but not scarcity. Subsistence *economies* is just as erroneous a notion as oral *literatures*. By the same token, 'gender studies' reconstruct the concept of gender, though it has historically vanished, based on the evidence provided by a sexed society.

The present introduction is a map, a compass, and an instruction manual of sorts. Its footnotes will confine themselves to indicating the book chapters where the topics briefly touched upon here are discussed in greater detail. Hereafter, this introduction will focus on clearly defined issues linked to the second half of Illich's journey, as a thinker engaged in deciphering modern concepts in the mirror of the past. Whenever I have reason to evoke the years before 1980, I shall endeavor to do so with both feet firmly planted in that bygone past while keeping my gaze fixed on the present.

One individual man, two projects

While it is undeniable that there was only one Illich, as Thierry Paquot claimed,[4] that same man was responsible for more than one project! One could for instance mention the two projects listed below:

1. In the 1970s, at the time of CIDOC and Cuernavaca, he developed a project to study the services institutions un-

4 See Chapter 3.

der the light of reason, a 'reason' that was supported by scientific principles. His accurate study of the available data on educational, transportation, and health institutions demonstrated that they (sometimes) accomplished the opposite of what they promised and were consequently often counterproductive. To take up the metaphor of spindles and weaving looms, criticism (which was often substantiated by studies carried out by the same professionals who sponsored those very institutions) was of the way certain important concepts were 'woven,' without considering the thread's nature and the stuff of which it was made.

2. In the 1980s Illich began to examine the stuff, the *hylè* (as the Ancient Greeks were wont to say) of which the thread of the conceptual weaving was made. In the same way that each specific region has its own kind of *mud*,[5] each era had its own perception of the primeval stuff of which its things were made: the soil,[6] the elements of its material culture, and especially the body and its flesh.

Previously: The years of Illich's mediatic fame

The 1970s were, conversely, the years in which Illich was a famous personality. At the time, his criticism of industrial society made explicit an intuition that was shared by many critical spirits the world over: the institutions that provided services (education, transport, medical health) were *counterproductive* and delivered the opposite of what they promised. Illich proceeded to *prove* his point sequentially in relation to the institutions that provided services in the fields of education, transport and health, and he was widely read. Schools brought about absent-mindedness, transport led to a paralysis, while medicine made bodies ill, and above all impaired their ability to self-protect. At that time, his books were translated into dozens of languages, and their circulation was in the range of five or six digits.

5 See Chapter 2.

6 See Chapter 2.

CIDOC and Cuernavaca

In those years, Illich's name was associated with an institute known as CIDOC (the Center for Intercultural Documentation),[7] which had its seat in one of Mexico's provincial cities, Cuernavaca, and which was to become a pilgrimage destination for many intellectuals from all over the world,[8] who were beginning to understand that 'things cannot go on like this.' In that period, Illich himself believed it was important to start preparing the great debates that were to mark the end of the twentieth century without further ado.

Those debates, however, never took place. In order to do so, they would have required what Jacques Ellul called a 'burst of freedom.' The late 1970s were characterized by a backwash of fatalism and conformism, which I believe was due to the spread of the systems theory's notions, their acceptance as metaphors of society, and the intrusion into our language of neologisms that helped to modify the self-perception of those who employed them: *input-output*, flight data recorder, population curve, the human body as immune system.

What else was CIDOC, if not a place of freedom whose visitors did not wish to become integrated into the system? It may seem a paradox that Ivan Illich's personal friends and CIDOC's visitors included a thinker such as Heinz von Förster, who acted as secretary for the Macy Conferences (during which concepts that constituted a sharp break with conventional notions on causality were developed in the 1950s), and who introduced the term *cybernetics* (derived from a Greek word that means helmsman, pilot). At a conceptual level, questioning the concept of causality and replacing it with that of program represented, in effect, a farewell of sorts to the concept of instrumental cause, the backbone of the age of the tools.

CIDOC was a 'free university' with no exams or diplomas, a *think tank* where industrial society's concepts and guiding principles of the 1970s could be discussed contrastively, and

7 See Chapter 1.

8 See Chapter 2.

where everybody became in turn teacher and student. Valentine Borremans, who directed it, encouraged all auditors-students-professors to shed the yoke of what she called *industrial ethos*, according to which the rich were the vanguard of a way of life that was fated to be adopted by everybody, a grotesque delusion that has nowadays been so thoroughly belied by facts that only the most cynical can still support it.

The industrial *ethos*

Ethos is a Greek word whose etymology is related to the English word *gait*, which designates one's *own* posture and way of walking. The industrial *ethos* is a gait in which each new step requires renouncing one's autonomy. The corridors of the Montparnasse–Bienvenüe station of Paris' underground system force me to walk a great deal, but my muscular efforts are a kind of ghost work that only serves the purpose of supplying the local transport agency with new passengers. If *autonomy* is the ability to act with one's own means within the context of accepted restrictions, its opposite, namely *heteronomy*, is a Hobbesian surrender of the right to exercise one's freedom in favor of the progressive elimination of all limitations. It follows that one of the topics debated in the conversations that took place at CIDOC concerned *limitations*,[9] which were defined at a political level and accepted in a convivial fashion.

One of the seminars convened by Valentine Borremans revolved around the topic of *the technological imperative*: whichever technological advance turned out to be achievable in whichever part of the world, it had to be made available to the ruling *elites* regardless of the price that the majority of the world's population was forced to pay.

A society based on heteronomy, which to exist needs to tolerate the destruction of autonomy

Since there can be no ethics without autonomy, one has the ethical duty of containing the renunciation of one's autonomy. In

9 See Chapter 4.

the 1970s, Illich believed that industrial society was a society in which the conditions of existence were progressively being eroded, thereby freeing the horizon for the pluralistic invention of post-industrial societies. Ten years later, there was the finalization of the constitutive elements of a form of social cybernetics that threatened to consign to the oblivion of history the tool placed at the service of *human intentions.*[10]

Taking a step back: 1976, the closing down of CIDOC

The closing down of CIDOC, which took place in 1976 during a memorable celebration, forced Illich to reconsider his way of living. The proceeds from the sale of his books dropped significantly, especially after a misunderstanding that was shrewdly exacerbated by a handful of feminist professors from Berkeley, who strove to shift the debate onto an ideological ground where he flatly refused to follow them.[11]

Illich then decided to earn his living by becoming a wandering philosopher or a beggar, as he himself stated on many occasions. Neither one nor the other produced any useful values, nor did they have the pretension to *justify* the right to suckle milk from their *alma mater*. Since he had nothing to lose, Illich defined rigorously the conditions of his engagement with university education:

- no more than a three-month term per year at each university;
- complete freedom to choose topics; that is to say, the rejection of any imposed curriculum and of any incorporation under the aegis of specific disciplines or programs;
- a refusal to give marks or diplomas to his students;
- his teaching commitments were to be limited to one afternoon per week.

What was not stipulated by contract and cannot be seen as anything other than a disinterested gesture on his part was the fact

10 See Chapter 4.

11 See Chapter 5.

that Illich made his own home, his small library, and his cellar available to those who attended his lectures and their friends. The weekly *living room conversations* (which sometimes lasted many days) at his place in Foster Avenue caused a sensation at the Pennsylvania State University (Penn State). After a decade of such initiatives, Bremen's local authorities awarded him a prize and symbolically presented him with the keys of the city, just as they had done a few years earlier in tribute to the poet Paul Celan.[12]

By means of his 'underlying attitude' and 'predisposition' (the Ancient Greeks' *hexis*) to voluntary self-restrictions that afforded *eutrapelia* (the spirit of joyful sharing within self-defined boundaries), Illich implemented a project aimed at the subversion of university education, with the ultimate goal of shifting it from its usual seat, the classrooms, and setting its center of gravity in friendly houses equipped with a living room, a kitchen in which to cook spaghetti, a good supply of decent wine, and located close to a well-stocked library. The house in Forster Avenue, which owed a lot to the kind of hospitality that Barbara Duden was capable of offering, embodied the very idea of a friendly house.

Faith in the power of conversation[13]

Illich envisaged conversation as the original repository of the birth of the thought. As a distinguished representative of the most refined alphabetic tradition, who was able to read more than ten languages, that utterly alphabetized man was convinced that thought—or philosophy—arose from conversations; i.e., from oral improvisations among friends. As a believer who praised Semitic prophets for their intuition of a conversing God, Illich saw an illustration of the 'perversion of what is best which the worst represents' in the progressive disincarnation of the act of reading (the spacing of words on the page after the end of the twelfth century, and the page's growing dematerialization from

12 See Chapter 3.

13 See Chapter 7.

parchment to paper, and later to immaterial screens).[14]

An unsettling hypothesis: The end of the age of the tools[15]

The historian Illich (who still counts as the only historian who has ever been alert to it) expressed his conviction that the last years of the twentieth century represented a radical break, one of the greatest rifts in the whole history of the world, that had been born out the faith in the Incarnation of the Word: the Western world. In his view, it was the end of the age of the tools. One of the warning signs in that sense was allegedly the intrusion in common speech of the terminology associated with a new 'pop science,' which had been generated by the concepts of cybernetics and systems analysis after their escape from their scientific domains of origin. This invasion of 'plastic' words, which deprived speakers of the power to shape the meaning they intended to give to their words, coincided with the instability that marked the end of the Glorious Thirty, the three decades of economic growth that occurred after the end of the Second World War.

The first symptoms of the end of the age of the tools

Around 1970, before the massive impact of cybernetic and systemic concepts on people's mentality, it was already possible to detect some signs of the twilight of the industrial ethos. Is it not about time, Illich wondered, to write an epilogue for the industrial age? In order to find an answer to that question, it became necessary to place at the center of the debate the concept of one object, the *instrumentum*, which was defined at the time of its appearance in the Middle Ages as 'mechanic,' a word whose etymology Hugh of Saint Victor ascribed to Greek *moichos* (the adulterer).[16] Once it was cautiously accepted in the twelfth cen-

14 See Chapter 7.

15 See Chapter 4.

16 In his imagined dialogues with Dindimus (an Indian wiseman), Hugh of Saint Victor (*cf.* Illich, 1991) introduced him to the concept of tool, which was beginning to spread especially thanks to *De variis artibus* (1128), penned by Theophilus Presbyter, which for the first time presented craftsmen's tools as if they could be separated from their users' hands. That approach seemed to somehow suggest giving one's body to the

tury, the *instrumentum* became, in the following century, one of those objects that exemplify an era, which Paul Veyne defined as *objets biscornus* (weird and unpredictable objects). Since the fourteenth century, at the very earliest, underneath every discussion on 'technology' and its advances, the 'tool' object, which is polymorphous and, in the industrial age, constantly evolving (and perhaps also on the brink of extinction), has summarized the essence of an age in which 'the tool was the answer to all questions.' Illich came to understand that industrial society and its fate could be interpreted through the tool's metamorphosis.

What differentiated the 1970s from the 1980s *in Ivan Illich's thought* was the fact that during the first decade he still saw the tool as one of history's unchanging elements. It was necessary to wait until the 1980s for Magritte's 'this is not a pipe' to be applied to the tool, when Illich understood its deep *historicity*. Just try to imagine a computer bearing the caption: 'this is not a tool.'

A change in the *lumen sub quo*

During the 1980s, the light under which the topology of the late modern mind could be examined changed. In the 1970s, that light had been, or had seemed to be, the light of Reason itself. At that time, the certainties on which our social theorems relied were axiomatic. For instance, the postulate according to which scarcity defined certain objects as 'economic goods' was the foundation of the laws of economics and made the adjectives economic and scarce essentially synonymous. If the law of supply and demand is to preserve at least a modicum of ties to common sense, it must necessarily imply a sense of satiety: supply should thus reduce demand by satisfying it. What is generally observed, however, is in fact the opposite: far from satisfying demand, supply often makes it only worse. Suffice it to consider motorized transport: each new transformation of the urban soil into a road track will in the future cause further demand for

first comer. The English expression 'sowing wild oats' (which in Italian would translate as *correre la cavallina*) aptly depicts the vague feeling of impropriety caused by the new tool. It is perhaps what Hugh had in mind when he hypothesized that the word *mechanics* derived from Greek *moichos*, the adulterer (*cf.* Illich, 2005, p. 73).

an even greater number of roads, bypasses, suburban ring roads and elevated highways. Faced with the evidence that supply does not reduce demand, but actually makes it grow, Illich began to raise questions that were quite different from the ones he was pondering at the time of CIDOC. He began. for instance, to ask: why do economic goods progressively lose their ability to satisfy the senses? Because economic goods were quantifiable and disincarnated values. The senses conversely aspired to wellness, or rather to a kind of 'well-being' that was utterly carnal.

Now that almost seventeen years have elapsed since Ivan Illich's death, what is no longer an instrument but is still called technology[17] is able to generate 'non-things' which are made of the stuff's shadow, and which threaten to swallow up in a boundless virtuality all that Illich defined as 'residues of reality.'

To distinguish them from tools, Illich adopted the conventional term 'system' to designate those artifacts that provided access to a virtual mode. Very few people at the time understood their nature as 'black holes'—their ability to absorb everything that fell in them, and to detach themselves from every kind of reality, thereby making them *mutterlos* (as Illich used to say in German): motherless, without a generating matrix. 'Systems' have the pretension to tell us who we are, they shape our perceptions of the world and of ourselves, and in so doing turn us (as well as our flesh and its history) into a functional sub-system. If we accept to be defined as an immune system, then we, and our bodies, will eventually become a sub-system of a worldwide biomedical system.

I cannot conclude the present introduction without at least trying to dispel a misunderstanding that is quite commonplace among my French readers and friends. The light under which Illich intended to examine the topology of the modern mind in the 1980s was not the same as the one which he had publicly projected on the counterproductivity of services institutions ten years before. The change in his perspective, nonetheless, had nothing to do with a slip into irrationality.

In short: the present book endeavors to present Ivan Il-

17 See Chapter 4.

lich's ideas on those objects that in common parlance are sometimes still known as 'tools,' but for which scholars have devised more prestigious categories: Technics and (under the influence of US terminology) Technology.

Seduced by Technology

We are trapped in the net with which every era tries to snatch pieces of reality and organize them in a coherent image of 'what is real.' Foucault spoke of the episteme of a historical era. After 1980, Illich wanted to study the certainties (made up of concepts and perceptions) that shape the topology of the late modern mind. Since he was a *philosopher of the tools*, he wanted to radically distance himself from the extant consensus on 'what is real in relation to the field of technology,' which was of fundamental importance for the episteme of our age. He believed that the combination of the two Greek words *technē* and *logos* (techno-logy) could only be understood in their literal meaning: a discourse (*logos*) on what the Greeks called *technē*, the skills, the art, the stratagem, the contrivance.

The 1980s: Concepts and perceptions

Was Illich a sociologist, an economist, a historian, a philosopher, or a theologian? To the eyes of those who believe that those categories structure thoughts and designate professions capable of imparting the one true knowledge in a given field, Illich might have seemed to be a Jack-of-all-trades and an amateur. Those who knew him and saw him at work considered him to be a passionate researcher who rebelled against all restrictions, particularly in a specialized field characterized by hypertrophic scientific aspirations. After lifting a stone under which he had seen something move (such as, for instance, the possibility of a history of the *sensory perception* of the body that went beyond the images with which anatomy and physiology portrayed it),[18] he was able to examine that something from different angles, including those of official science, without

18 See Chapter 6.

ever becoming compliant with their dogmas. Since he could not accept the certainties of the topology of the modern mind, and he was at the same time incapable of conceiving himself as living in the past (which was no more), he lived, as he stated himself, in a *double ghetto*.[19]

If I were asked to describe in one sentence the cooperation lasting more than two decades between the historians Ivan Illich and Barbara Duden, I would quote the following one: 'The spindles on which the sensory perceptions of an age were spun were buried in the soils of history far more deeply than the looms on which its conceptual certainties were woven.' Those are the words of archaeologists of perceptions and historians of ideas. Since the general object of their studies was the topology of the modern mind, its exploration required them to walk on both legs. Indeed, around 1980 Illich regretted having until then carried out his analysis of modern ideas in an exclusively conceptual fashion, thereby walking with only one eye open or on just one leg.[20]

Thereafter, he focused his attention on the aggregates of sensory evidence and of the generally inherited ideas that constitute the foundations of the topology of the modern mind. Together with his friends and colleagues, he undertook a sort of archaeological exploration of those certainties. He embarked with them on research on the five physical senses, and (especially with Barbara Duden's help) on the history of the inner perception of the body, as well as on Antique optics and the transformation of the gaze into a tool after the eleventh century.[21]

Illich defined as the age of the tools the period that ranged conceptually from the twelfth to the twentieth century, and 'technologically' from the fourteenth century to the years 1970–1980. The rise and fall of the tool as 'the key that opened all doors' delimit an age in which those aged fifty or more still have one foot. The instrumental age was that of the instrumental means, a metaphorically luminescent object which, not unlike Borges' Aleph, enabled the whole world to be seen under its

19 See Chapter 5.

20 See Chapter 3.

21 See Chapter 6.

light. It is in that sense that I shall consider Ivan Illich as a historian of the tools, and the present book as a tribute to a historian of the tools who is still little known in that capacity.

A countermove: Research on sensory perceptions

I do not perceive myself as you see me. The eye is not the most ideal organ to perceive the 'darkness under my skin' that is my flesh.[22]

Together with the historian Barbara Duden, Illich opened new paths and explored new lands, which he named as if they could really become new intellectual disciplines. For instance, with their decision to designate the body by its Greek name, *sōma* (the felt body), rather than by a derivation of the Latin word *corpus*, which always evokes a whole seen from the outside, Illich and Duden undertook sustained research, which they called *historical somatics*, on the self-perception of the body in some of the past ages. It was research on perception, or rather on the *self-ception* of what is the most concrete element in existence, the *concretissimus*, namely the flesh. Their intuition brought to light unforeseen objects of study, which did not entail immediate subservience to pre-established scientific disciplines. Is it not sometimes possible to weave new disciplines out of the weeds that grow among the rocks on the beaten path? It was not a case of invention for its own sake. Ivan Illich and Barbara Duden aspired to shed new light on the topology of the modern mind. It was therefore a search for the *lumen sub quo*, for the light under which that topology was to reveal its true nature.

A synoptic exposition of the concept of tool

The present book's fourth chapter shall tackle the most complex, hypothetical, and possibly debatable of the reflections Illich made after 1980, which I am going to summarize in eight points:

1. Under the name of *instrumentum*, a few Scholastic texts

22 See Chapter 6.

of the twelfth century introduced a radically new approach to what we now call a utensil, a 'tool.'

2. Those texts presented the *instrumentum* as a means to implement divine, and later human, intentions.
3. A new type of causality, the *instrumental cause*, was attributed to that new kind of utensil; there was a *line of continuity* between the instrumental cause of the twelfth, thirteenth and fourteenth centuries, and the notion of *productive forces* that emerged in the nineteenth century.
4. The new tool was no longer either one of the body's organs or an extension of one of the body's organs or limbs. Instead, it found itself placed at a distance from its users' body, a condition which Illich called *distality*.
5. Distality was *a constitutive element of the relationship* between the tool and its user's hand.
6. The concept of tool afforded a detailed analysis of the nature of the relationship between the tool and its user's hand and body. Conversely, the concept of technology was a veil that concealed this relationship.
7. At the end of the twentieth century, that relationship changed to such an extent that the artifacts subsumed under the category of 'Technology' lost the characteristic features of what were once called 'the tools.'
8. The main characteristic feature among the ones they lost concerned the fact that the instrumental relationship had *human* intentions.

Illich the historian meant to observe the rise of the tools in the twelfth century with his feet well planted in that time, but with his gaze fixed on the present

Illich did not intend to speak of the change which the civilization that filled the world with tools is currently undergoing in the same way as did the historians of technology. The latter always tended to do so retroactively and only took into consideration those elements of the past that had repercussions on modernity. They were solidly rooted in the present, and it was from the present that they turned their gaze to the past, to detect what looked like the present and possibly even anticipated it. Illich wanted to do the exact opposite. He wanted to soak himself in the concepts and perceptions of a past age until he could feel he had actually put down roots in it—as far as it was possible, of course. From there, he wanted to turn his gaze to the present. He strove to see the present in light of the past. And he consequently chose the age in which the concept of *instrumentum* was developed.

What did he find in his sources? He found tools, he found the concept of instrumentality (the adverb *instrumentaliter* in Thomas Aquinas), and he found the concept of instrumental cause. However, he never found the word 'technology,' and seldom the word *technē*.

All of the above emanated a light that he intended to project on the present. He therefore wished to observe the present time in light of the actual concepts of tool, body, hand, as well as of their potential relationships. The grandiose word 'Technology' did, in fact, the opposite of what Illich intended to accomplish. It was a modern concept that, when projected on the past, made the latter illegible.

Illich, a theologian who became a historian and a philosopher of the tools

The present book strives to provide an answer to one question. The most recent writings (be they books or articles) on Ivan Illich avoid (or at any rate avoid tackling directly) an issue which I see as central in his work, namely that of the tools. Illich was a theologian, a philosopher, and a historian, and especially a *historian of the tools*. He placed great emphasis on the historian's ability to make accessible topics that were generally seen as theological, such as 'the corruption of what is best that generates the worst' which a French editor chose as the title for his edition of the last conversations between Illich and David Cayley[23] (Illich and Cayley, 2005). One of the mysteries of evil is that the culture which was born from faith in the Incarnation of the Word has

23 A journalist from the Canadian Broadcasting Corporation, who interviewed Illich on two or three occasions (*cf.* Cayley, 1992; Illich, 2005; Illich and Cayley, 2005).

become the most disincarnated of all documented cultures, as if the heights of love which the Incarnation afforded has been matched by a symmetrical abyss of disincarnation and indifference toward the others.

Although the reflection was inspired by theology, the historian soon replaced the theologian and stated: after the twelfth century, it is possible to document some of the steps taken toward the disincarnation of the word (with no capital letters and understood as a mere word). It was, for instance, on those very steps that the four or five books and articles which Illich devoted to the social history of the alphabet intended to shed light,[24] with no recourse to theology, and in a way that was accessible to both believers and agnostics. In those writings, Illich drew his readers' attention to a few moments in history when significant steps were taken on the path of progressive disincarnation represented by the 'march toward modernity.' One of those moments was the generalization of silent reading after the thirteenth century.

The gaze and the alphabet become tools

This book ends with a chapter on the 'instrumentation'[25] of the gaze (which leads to an account of vision based on the model offered by video cameras), and the 'instrumentation' of the alphabet.

24 See Chapter 7.

25 Translator's Note: Illich employed the English word 'instrumentation' with the meaning of 'transformation into a tool,' and 'application of an instrumental conception.' Since the Italian '*strumentalizzare*' usually means 'using something to one's advantage, to exploit, to manipulate,' given the lack of a word that expresses the meaning intended by Illich, the word '*strumentalizzazione*' is going to be employed throughout between inverted commas, thereby implying the meaning specified above.

Chapter 1: A Great Historian of the Tools Who is Still Misunderstood

I. Ivan Illich: Theologian or Thinker of Technology?

A man firmly anchored in Western tradition 'takes a step back' from it

In 1951, Ivan Illich—considered by Cardinal Giovanni Montini (the future Pope Paul VI) to be an extraordinary theologian, and encouraged by the cardinal to remain in Rome, where he had studied philosophy and theology with a special focus on **ecclesiology,**[1]—left for the United States. His intention was to immerse himself in the study of the work of Albert the Great (1206–1280) under Jacques Maritain's supervision at Princeton University.[2]

In New York, he discovered the Puerto Ricans and their neglected, almost clandestine condition as the repositories of a tradition they dared not express in public. One evening, at a family friend's home, he quickly sensed the aura of prejudice, misunderstanding, and fear surrounding the public perception of that recent wave of immigration.[3] Illich devoted the following days to mingling with the inhabitants of the neighborhoods in which New York's Puerto Rican immigrants were most dense-

1 'My favorite subject was ecclesiology' (Cayley, 1992, p. 112). See also Illich, 2005, p. 142: 'One of ecclesiology's sub-branches is the study of liturgy; and liturgy may of course be studied as the history of the rites, of popular processions and of the blessings, or as the aesthetics of altar furnishings... But that is not how liturgy becomes part of ecclesiology. Liturgy becomes part of ecclesiology only when rites are envisaged as the womb from which and within which the Church takes its shape in the present time.'

Editor's Note: The author's reference to Illich 2005 is to the English edition of *Rivers North of the Future*. However, having translated that book into French (see reference to Illich and Cayley 2005), he deviates sparingly from the original. We have kept his wording.

2 There are various works that provide a detailed overview of Ivan Illich's biography. Here I shall mention only a handful, which are available both in French and Italian: Cayley, 1992; Illich and Cayley, 2005; Paquot, 2012; Rey, 2014 (especially Appendix 2, pp. 253–261).

3 For a lively and well-documented account of the years Illich spent among New York's Puerto Rican immigrants and then in Puerto Rico itself, see Paquot, 2012, pp. 15–18.

ly settled. Something in their gazes, faces, and attitude struck a note with him. Illich's roots lay in the cosmopolitan Viennese culture of the 1930s, which the war had destroyed. But rather than consigning that loss to oblivion, he had preserved that world in his heart. It now seemed to him that New York's Puerto Ricans were keeping alive in their hearts a far from extinct culture which they practiced within their families and with their neighbors in the barrio, but which they could still not display to North American society.

Driven by an instinctive fondness for people who had been drawn away from their traditions, Illich gave up his project to pursue medieval studies and expressed his wish to be posted to a Puerto Rican parish to the Cardinal of New York, Francis Spellman; he was thus assigned to the Church of the Incarnation in Upper Manhattan.

Once he had mastered the intricacies of the Puerto Rican variety of Spanish, Illich confronted the cultural segregation affecting his parishioners. For more than four years, he relentlessly demanded that the US Church actively engage itself to welcome those newcomers. To give visibility to the community overlooked by the wider Anglo-American society, in 1956 he organized a large open-air social gathering on a plot of land belonging to Fordham University. His initiative—to which the Puerto Ricans invited New York's inhabitants to become acquainted with their community—took place on St. John's Day and managed to gather about 30,000 people, thereby supplying vibrant proof of the existence of a Puerto Rican settlement in the very heart of Manhattan.

Puerto Rico: The gateway to Latin American culture, and much more besides

In that same year, Illich was appointed prorector of the Catholic University in Ponce, in Puerto Rico.[4] He stayed on the island for

4 Translator's Note: Before Illich took up his post on the island, he traveled the length and breadth of it to familiarize himself with its customs and language. For an account of Illich's experience in Puerto Rico, see the statement written by Father Joseph P. Fitzpatrick, S. J. in 1991, which is available online at: https://files.goliard.xyz/ixtus/LiIxtus3.htm

four years, during which he made a few significant encounters: first and foremost with Puerto Rican culture, which opened the doors for him to the wider Latin American world, but also with a number of important personalities, such as Everett Reimer, an early critic of compulsory schooling,[5] and Leopold Kohr, an Austrian professor of economics based in Puerto Rico[6] who theorized the concepts of optimum size and proportionality, of which more will be said below. Illich left the island in 1960 due to disagreements with its ecclesiastical hierarchy over the stance adopted by two of the local bishops, who threatened to excommunicate any parishioner ready to vote for the 'wrong' party.[7]

Since he intended to become acquainted with the 'deep' side of Latin America, he boarded a plane for Santiago de Chile and spent the next four months moving northward, either on foot, by bus, or hitchhiking, until he reached Caracas in Venezuela, having covered about 3,100 miles.

During his journey, Illich was greatly impressed by the fervor of the popular displays of faith he witnessed in the various countries through which he traveled. He recognized in them the voice of the Gospel, which reached him through a language and gestures quite different from those to which he, as a European, was accustomed. He was conversely surprised—

5 *Cf.* Reimer, 1971. Illich's conversations with Reimer in Puerto Rico greatly contributed to shaping the structure of Illich's critique on compulsory schooling. See also Illich, 1971, Italian translation, p. 17: 'My interest in public education owes a lot to Everett Reimer, whom I met in Puerto Rico in 1958. Right from our first encounter I had no doubts whatsoever as to the importance of making compulsory education available to everybody.'

6 On this specific aspect, see Rey, 2014, whose third chapter 'Proportion is beautiful' (pp. 84–102) constitutes an excellent introduction to Leopold Kohr's thought; Leopold Kohr, for his part, helped to establish the popularity of Fritz Ernst Schumacher, the author of *Small is Beautiful*.

7 *Cf.* Cayley, 1992, p. 42. As Illich told Cayley, in 1960 two of the island's bishops 'basically stepped into the local political arena by threatening to excommunicate whomever would vote for a certain political party that did not oppose the sale of condoms in drugstores.' The stance adopted by those bishops therefore threatened 'to let a religious issue creep into American politics... I felt it was my duty to do something about it as most people did not seem to take the matter seriously, and the few who did, did not appear to be willing to take action. In consequence of having set off that situation I became a catalyst for everybody's hatred, and I was fully aware of the fact that I had precluded myself any future chance of carrying out any kind of public activity in Puerto Rico without triggering off the memory of that political action of mine.'

and even shocked—by the apparent deafness of some of the US missionaries he met along the way. He had the impression that, for them, the Gospel could only be heard through the voice of the North American Church, and he labeled them *ecclesiastical conquistadores*. He was later to state that their monocultural preaching—despite the tentative Spanish into which they had learned to translate it—paved the way for Coca-Cola and capitalist exploitation.

From a philosophy of missionary humility to a critique of development

In 1961, Illich founded the Center for Intercultural Formation (CIF) in Cuernavaca, Mexico, affiliated with New York's Fordham University, and officially entrusted with the training of missionaries and lay collaborators bound for Latin America. This institute was in fact set up as an answer to the increasingly pressing issues raised by the newly introduced practice of recruiting volunteers in rich countries to send them to poorer ones as missionaries or aid workers.[8] The first session enrolled thirty-five lay people and twenty-seven male and female members of religious orders; CIF offered two sessions per year, each lasting four months. Illich never tired of telling his pupils, over and over again, that in the countries where they were to carry out their missionary duties, they would not be met with a pastoral vacuum to be filled: on the contrary, they would find expressions of faith which, though often disconcerting, were nonetheless very deep. Their pastoral approach was consequently to be 'vernacular'[9] and respectful of those very expressions; whenever faced by things they could not comprehend, they were to hold their peace. The memory of the culturally monolingual missionaries

8 'There was the *Peace Corps*, and then there was that *awful* letter penned by John Considine—who had even managed to convince Pope John XXIII to undersign it—which ordered the North American bishops to send one tenth of their staff to Latin America in order to save it from Communism!' (Cayley, 1992, p. 17).

9 Translator's Note: As Cayley explained, 'Illich endeavored to instill into that word the meaning of the Latin *vernaculum*, which applies to anything that is indigenous and domestic—what is homemade, or raised, grown and produced locally (Illich, 2005, p. 21).

Illich had met on his journey through Latin America led him to 'torture his students' (as the Bishop of Cuernavaca, Sergio Mendez Arceo, used to say), to rid them of their habit of confusing the Gospel with the shape of their own Church.

Todd Hartch, a Protestant convert to Catholicism, has spent years documenting CIF's foundation and its subsequent evolution from a training center for missionaries and aid workers to a place where a philosophy of missions capable of providing solutions to the issues raised by the modern world could be devised and developed, thereby leading to a critique of development. Hartch combed the archives of Harvard University, the University of Notre Dame, Indiana, Fordham University, and The Catholic University of America in Washington, D.C. (Hartch, 2015). His study mainly focused on what he termed—in my view rather inaccurately—Illich's 'Catholic phase' between 1961 and 1967, as well as on the eight years during which, after Illich was summoned to Rome in 1968 by the Congregation for the Doctrine of the Faith (an institution once known as the Inquisition), he was actively engaged at the *Centro Intercultural de Documentación* (CIDOC), a lay 'think tank' where he wrote and discussed the texts that brought him fame. CIDOC was closed down for good in 1976; by that stage, Illich's mission was over. Hartch's book also offers a few biographical notes on the years preceding 1961.

One of that book's great merits is the clarification it offers on the legend surrounding Illich—a legend he himself sometimes spread to explain situations too complex for those ignorant of the mysteries surrounding the Church as an institution—namely what Illich called *it* ('the Church as It'), as opposed to the *she* ('the Church as She') in which he believed.[10] When I first met him in the early 1970s, I was one such ignoramus. Illich used to summarize his CIF project by evoking the image of an open tap threatening to flood the room, which it was advisable to turn off. Hartch's book shows just how much effort and how many

10 Translator's Note: As Cayley explained (see Illich, 2005, p. 21), Illich considered the 'Church as She' to be 'the Church that was the repository of the tradition and the community's living body', whereas the 'Church as It' was 'the Church as a secular power that served only itself.'

clashes—as well as how many laughs—it took to reach decisions which, in hindsight, may appear self-evident. Illich's relationship with John Considine, his direct superior in the ecclesiastical hierarchy and his benefactor for an extended period, was by no means as simple as Illich described it to the radio journalist David Cayley of the Canadian Broadcasting Corporation.

In light of the critique of development that Illich formulated in the 1990s, together with a group of collaborators,[11] everything points to an interpretation of the Church's missionary project as a development program to which Illich cautiously contributed from 1961 until his summons to Rome in 1968. As Cayley himself clarified:

> The year of CIF's establishment was the same in which President Kennedy launched his 'Alliance for Progress,' an ambitious aid program for the development of Latin America. It was also the year in which Pope John XXIII urged the North American Church to send 10% of the religious staff at its disposal on a mission to Latin America, as well as the year in which the *Peace Corps* was set up. The notion of 'development' as a coherent and transmissible cure for 'underdevelopment' had been gaining currency ever since Truman mentioned that concept in his inaugural address in 1949. Now the 'decade of development' was ushered in, and Illich set up his center with the express purpose of subverting it. He ridiculed the Peace Corps, called the Alliance for Progress 'an alliance for the progress of the middle classes,' and sowed doubt in the minds of the missionaries who flocked to him to learn Spanish.

11 In the early 1990s, Illich turned out to be an especially insightful critic of the international development plan for the poor countries which was placed under the leadership of the rich ones. Seventeen authors summoned together by Illich, some of whom met for the first time, agreed to envisage development as a mixture of quite heterogeneous ingredients. For instance, there could be no development plan without also taking into account notions of equality, needs, quality of life, poverty, participation, planning, population, production, and progress. Every author endeavored to explore one of those ingredients. Illich, for his part, took care of the 'needs,' while Barbara Duden concentrated on 'population,' Majid Rahnema on 'poverty' and 'participation,' Jean Robert on 'production,' and Vandana Shiva on 'resources.' One of the last preparatory meetings took place in Puerto Rico. The ensuing book, edited by Wolfgang Sachs, was published under the title *The Development Dictionary. A Guide to Knowledge as Power*, and has been translated into fifteen languages.

> Illich considered 'development' to be a sort of war on subsistence that would eventually replace a tolerable shortage of goods and services with a far more painful condition, which he described as 'modernized poverty' (Illich, 2005, pp. 237–238).[12]

Illich believed the very idea of letting the Church climb on development's bandwagon to be blasphemous. Where were the surrender of power, the humility, and the experience of depending on somebody else's goodwill typically associated with the oral acquisition of a foreign language? Most of the North American missionaries learned to translate their certainties into an unidiomatic form of Spanish, which they drew from limited manuals of 'linguistic engineering' under the guidance of an instructor who shared those very same certainties.

Illich's critique of a missionary project cloaked in development earned him the status of a 'radical Catholic' (Du Plessix Gray, 1971). He never laid any claim to such a definition, however, and in fact intended to dispel lies by laughter (which, all things considered, was no less ambitious an aspiration, though far more courteous). Most of all, he wished to cultivate hope: what we now must wait for, he once told Cayley,

> is the resurrection of the Church; and when I say that I believe in the resurrection of the dead and in eternal life, I mean that to me the resurrection of the dead is the same as the resurrection of the Church (Illich, 2005, p. 189).

While Todd Hartch praised Illich's intellectual and pedagogical talents, and the quality of CIF's publications, he also believed that dampening his students' missionary enthusiasm had been a mistake. David Cayley has written a long review of Hartch's book (Cayley, 2015). The Church, which Illich reprimanded for having supported a kind of economic development that forced the poor to embrace the desires and needs of the rich as their own and to imitate them, was the Church as It, 'the greatest bureaucracy in the world' and a huge transnational organi-

12 The last conversations between Ivan Illich and David Cayley were broadcast by the CBC and were later published in English as *The Rivers North of the Future* by Anansi Press.

zation. The missionary project advocated by that bureaucracy was a Trojan horse for the operations of other transnational organizations, in a subcontinent which the ecclesiastical *conquistadores* seemed determined to turn into a cultural wasteland. In his review, Cayley defended Illich from Hartch's accusation of having hidden his deeper motives. Illich sought a common ground with both his audience and his readers, regardless of whether they were believers or not. His knowledge of ecclesiology—a sort of sociology of the Church *ante litteram*—told him unequivocally that modern institutions derived, for the most part, from the Church of the second Christian millennium. He wanted to *demonstrate* this without hiding the fact that he was a believer and a historian, but also without exercising that authority which within the Catholic Church is usually associated with the qualification of theologian.[13] Indeed, he spoke in his capacity as a historian, and the facts he wished to illustrate—such as the drift towards the growing disincarnation of a society founded on faith in God's incarnation—needed no theological *nihil obstat*.

From the tool of medieval theology to industrial technology

On Father John Considine's urging, Pope John XXIII hitched the Catholic Church's wagon to the Alliance for Progress launched by Kennedy in 1961. Right from the outset, CIF endeavored to rescue the Church from development's quagmire. In the chapter entitled 'From the tools to the systems,' included in the book devoted to David Cayley's last conversations with Ivan Illich, Illich makes the following statement:

> Some time ago I had a conversation with Father John Considine, the priest from the Maryknoll Society who convinced Pope John XXIII to get the Church involved with the Alliance for Progress. Those missionaries' idea was to help those poor people; and helping them meant endowing them with means

13 Illich was quite eager to state: 'My decision, which I pondered at length, [was] not to act any longer as a theologian in the fold of the Roman Catholic Church, whose very name designates a precise institutional and juridical role. Luckily nobody can accuse me of being a theologian. I am not one, nor do I wish to act as one' (Illich and Cayley, 2005, p. 170).

> and instruments they did not possess — electricity, penicillin, adequate legal protection, and knowledge conceived in an instrumental fashion. It was something that was taken for granted. Placing between brackets, at an epistemic level, concepts such as 'tool,' 'instrument,' 'device,' 'technique,' is just as difficult as placing between brackets ethical norms and regulations (Illich, 2005, p. 204).[14]

This passage holds, in a nutshell, the first attempt at an answer to one of the questions I would like to pose time and again in the present book: *why did a man who was at first interested in a philosophy of missionary humility end up focusing his reflections, from the early 1970s to the late 1990s, on the tools (more commonly known as techniques and technology) and their effects—first material, then symbolic?*

The 1970s were marked by the end of the *Trente Glorieuses* (the Glorious Thirty), those years of carefree growth during which it was normal to think that the next day would be better, and the one after that better still. The year 1968 tolled the death knell for a future portrayed as a stairway to the stars, each step of which was to lead to something 'more:' more wealth, more greatness, more power, more health. Three of Illich's polemical works dating to the 1970s (*Deschooling Society*, *Energy and Equity*, and *Medical Nemesis*),[15] which he later described as *pamphlets*, questioned the three main institutional pillars of industrial society: education, transport, and health services, seen as *tools* to promote learning, mutual presence, and health.

I would now like to reformulate the question I wish to pose: why did a man who was a deep believer and a man of the Church who had exercised his ministry become, at a moment when faith in development had not yet been openly belied by facts, a critical philosopher and a historian of the tools—of what is more

14 See also Illich, 1971a: 'Right from our center's inauguration I especially stressed two of our objectives. First, we meant to make every possible effort to prevent the damage which the Pope's demands threatened to wreak from being too extensive. Secondly, we were set on acquiring a sufficiently extensive influence that would enable us to convince the relevant authorities to desist from implementing such a program' (translated from the French edition, see Illich and Cayley, 2005, p. 78).

15 See Illich 1971; 1973; 1975.

commonly known as Technique or Technology? When he issued his *pamphlets*, Illich, who envisaged tools as a means to an end, believed that society's institutions were also tools of sorts: schools were tools for learning; roads and means of transport were tools for bringing people closer to one another; hospitals were tools for treating illnesses. At the time of his activity at CIDOC, Illich pointed out that the effects of industrial society's institutions and tools went, in fact, against their stated purpose: schools quelled the desire to learn, transport infrastructure actually prevented people from meeting, while hospitals and other 'health services' gave rise to new pathologies. In other words, the tools for education, transport, and health were *counterproductive* in industrial societies because they had overstepped a certain threshold in terms of their size and power. Consequently, there was only one possible solution: setting political restrictions on their size and power.

Throughout the 1980s, Illich began to realize that industrial society's institutions did not only do the opposite of what they promised, but actually went even further: they defined their clients or patients *by imposing an identity on them.*

From the time he spent at CIF down to his last days, Illich never ceased his reflection on the tools and the institutions.

At the beginning of the 1970s, he stressed the institutions' instrumental nature and their counterproductivity. Over that decade, he proceeded to study their material consequences (i.e., what they did), and starting in 1980, he began to concentrate on the symbolic ones (i.e., what they said). It was at that stage that he realized that it was impossible to go on envisaging institutional services as tools, as the intentions which seemingly pervaded them were becoming increasingly murky, while the terms that defined their purposes were more and more contradictory; the capital letters to be found in words such as Education Services, Communication Services, and Health System did nothing other than conceal their lack of precise denotation.

In the same period, Illich began to speak of the *historicity of the tools*, thereby emphasizing the theological origin of the Western *concept* of tool from the twelfth century onward. He consequently posited the surprising hypothesis of the beginning of the end of the 'era of the tools' that was to obtain in the 1980s.

At the end of the 1970s, Illich's critique of the tools and of the institutional instruments relied on certainties that neither the author of *Tools for Conviviality* nor his readership had yet called into question: the concept of tool was still seen as universal, and the institutions themselves were still deemed to be tools. Nonetheless, at the beginning of the 1980s, what had hitherto appeared as solidly stable as the earth under our feet suddenly turned into quicksand. Far from being universal, the concept of tools turned out to be an historical construct, and the great movements behind its history were discovered to actually define eras. Contemporary time, therefore, could perhaps mark the end of the era of the tools.

Until around 1980, tools preserved a link of sorts to the human hand, even in their industrial form. Thereafter, however, that link was severed, especially as far as institutions were concerned. Institutions deprived of any relationship—real or metaphorical—with the human hand could no longer be seen as tools. What was to replace tools was as yet impossible to describe, even though it was already possible to outline some of its conceptual premises. The notion that tools could be held by a hand, or at least controlled by it, and that they served a human purpose, had been formulated in the twelfth century and had held sway in the West since the fourteenth century, but was now on the wane. If that scenario was correct, Western culture had lost its main drive, and the whole of the Western world was consequently on the verge of an epistemic upheaval of remarkable proportions.

The ideas that Illich developed as a historian of the tools are difficult to understand unless one bears in mind that, starting from what he saw as the end of the era of the tools in the 1980s, he relentlessly harked back to the time of its inception, some six to eight centuries before. In 1999, in a conversation subsequently published in *Science, Technology and Society*, he stated that 'the present time is a farewell to the tools' (Illich, 1999, p. 5), thus making explicit his intuition that the era of the tools had come to an end. In several essays appearing during the 1990s, he developed the hypothesis that the beginning of the era of the tools had been marked by a far-reaching modification of the notion of causality around AD 1150. At approximately that time, a fifth cause, the *causa instrumentalis*, had been added to Aristotle's four causes, and ended up replacing them altogether. This reflection, however, was theological before it became 'techno-logical.' Illich subsequently called *instrumentality* a trait common both to what are still known as 'tools' and to certain sacramental implements.[16] Toward the end of his life, his meditation on the potential convergence between theology and technology took on a dramatic—or rather 'apocalyptic'—nuance. If the concept of the *instrumental tool* was historically based, and if the notion of *instrumentality* became axiomatic only from the fourteenth century onward, it was conceivable that its nature could subsequently be lost—thereby marking the end of the 'era of the tools' and depriving Western (and Westernized) societies of one of their fundamental postulates. If, as Illich predicted, that process has already been underway for some thirty years, we are now facing one of the greatest changes within Western culture as it has been known for the past seven or eight centuries:

> If it is indeed true that 'tool' is a concept which can be assigned to a specific era and seen as typical of a well-defined period—a period in which the concept of tool, or technology, as it is more often described, becomes the most unquestionable of our daily certainties—the possibility arises to do what I have endeavored to do over the past fifteen or twenty years: namely to claim, or at least to posit the hypothesis, that at some stage in the 1980s, the technological society born in the fourteenth century came to an end (Illich, 2005, p. 77).

Illich's reflection on this topic over thirty years has turned him into one of the great theorists and historians of the tools, of

16 In his reply to Cayley's questions on the issue of technology, Illich made a reference to Theophilus Presbyter (who wrote the first medieval treatise on the tools in 1128): 'Fifteen years ago, I first came across Theophilus Presbyter while reading Lessing, who discovered his manuscript two centuries ago.' The reason behind his interest, as Illich explained, was that 'I suspect that the concept of instrument and the theological concept of sacrament are closely connected... I believe there is a link between the idea of tool, which does whatever you want it to do, and that of sacrament, which is a symbol God allows mankind to dispense, but which does in fact what God wants to accomplish, more or less independently of the ability, the power, the intention, or even the humility of the priest who administers it. These two concepts are typically Western, and it is quite pointless to speak of the perception of the tools *per se* outside the context of Western history or before 1215' (Cayley, 1992, p. 133).

techniques, and of 'technology' (literally, a 'discourse on technics'). In his mind, did techno-logy replace theology—or did medieval theology actually lie at the roots of Western technology? This dual question, which I shall address from a number of different perspectives below, constitutes one of the main lines of research pursued in this book. Was there a split or continuity between Illich's intuitions on theology and his critique of technology? Were the fundamental concepts of a Western civilization that would later become 'techno-logical'[17] somehow rooted in Scholastic theology? The sacramental theology of the thirteenth century would seem to confirm just such an assumption. Theologians

> ...found the term *instrumentum* extremely useful in ascribing to seven of these blessings such a peculiarity that a separate category for the sacraments became indispensable. The blessings and the sacraments were thus separated from one another: blessings may be imparted by anybody—the head of the family, a priest, or the Pope—who is within the Church's fold and wishes to praise God and ask Him, at any given moment, to look on something in a particularly favorable way. Sacraments are something altogether different. They are acts which require a tool, a tool that has been created by a human being and then used by God Himself as an implement to perform—inevitably—a given function (Illich, 2005, p. 79).

In the same text, Illich also distinguished sacraments from older blessings and defined them as a new 'apparatus'[18]

17 The French word *technologie*, literally 'a discourse on techniques,' has nothing to do with the way the term 'technology' is employed in American English, as the latter tends to be mixed up with 'technique.' The corresponding French adjective could therefore be written by inserting a hyphen (i.e., *techno-logique*) to stress its relationship to the discourse on techniques. It is in that sense that Jacques Ellul employed it in his *Le bluff technologique* (1988). In his view, the techno-logical deception consisted in the deft way in which the discourse on techniques managed to evoke a reassuring feeling of 'the banality of everyday life,' which appeared to make redundant any critical reflection on tech-niques and their instruments. Ellul was wont to write the word 'technique' with a capitalised initial letter. Those who (somewhat hurriedly) hailed Ellul as the 'French Heidegger' had perhaps in mind Heidegger's concept of *Gestell*, the device which absorbs into a 'system' all of the aspects associated with specific techniques, thereby deeply affecting modern Western culture, or even going as far as replacing it.

18 'Apparatus' translates the everyday French word, *dispositif*. See Agamben's booklet *What is an Apparatus?* (2006), in which the author clarified the philological

that suitably matched the addition of the *causa instrumentalis* (a kind of offshoot of the *causa efficiens*) to Aristotle's four causes (*materialis, formalis, finalis, efficiens*). That new theological concept, formulated between the end of the twelfth and the beginning of the thirteenth century, designated an apparatus of an instrumental nature. Sacraments were seven rites whose correct performance 'forces God to employ them as instrumental causes aimed at the desired purpose' (Illich, 2005, p. 79): they had been conceived as *instrumenta divina*—instruments put at the service of divine intentions. Unlike blessings, sacraments were acts performed *for* something and aimed at a well-defined purpose.

In the following centuries, the concept of *instrumentum*, or instrumental tool, was to redefine tools that could be held and wielded by hand as artifacts placed at the service of human intentions, and a new era began which Illich would later describe as *the era of the tools*.[19] That was to become the era of technological development and of the West's material supremacy.

At the other end of the spectrum—ranging from the beginning of the technological or *instrumental* era to what Illich saw as its end—there is the contemporary confusion between means and ends, which complicates a clear definition of a tool. The following question may therefore be raised: could this confusion between means and ends be a sign of a drift in our perception of technology toward an attitude of blind submission to 'tools' which, to the very extent that they become the object of religious worship, cease to be what they once were—artifacts that could be put back in their box after use? If tools stop being tools as such, what do they become?

The critique of the Pope's volunteers for Latin America already constituted, in embryonic form, a critique of the in-

link between the theological concept of dis-positio (*oikonomia* in Greek), the Latin verb *dis-ponere*, and the German verb *stellen* from which Heidegger's concept of *Gestell* derives.

19 The concept of instrumentality cannot be separated from the evolution of contingency, 'one of the few concepts with an unequivocal Christian origin' (Illich, 2005, p. 65). See 'Contingency Part 1: A world in the hands of God' and 'Contingency Part 2: The origin of technology' in Illich, 2005, pp. 64–79.

dustrial tools' boundless powers and of the equally boundless proliferation of the needs generated by the economy. Both instrumentality (the nature of Western tools) and the economy are an expression of the means-ends logic. In both cases, this logic leads to its own opposite: means become ends in themselves, while an almost quasi-religious veneration attends the unique idea of self-referentiality surrounding both the economy and the superpower of technological means which have, in fact, no other end than their own (equally self-referential) power.

II. Rethinking the Tools after Illich

The Mexican philosopher Humberto Schwarzbeck (born in Monterrey, who writes under the pseudonym Humberto Beck) has recently published an important book on Ivan Illich's thought (Beck, 2017). Since his analysis was methodologically restricted to the works Illich wrote between 1971 and 1981 (the ones he defined as *pamphlets*), Beck was able to reread *Deschooling Society* (1971), *Energy and Equity* (1973—though previously published as an article in *Le Monde*), *Medical Nemesis* (1975), *The Right to Useful Unemployment* (1978), and *Shadow Work* (1981)[20] without being led astray by the evolution of Illich's ideas on the tools and his self-critique in the 1990s. To give those approaching Illich's thought for the first time sufficient leeway to explore it at their ease, Beck provided didactic stability to actually shaky ground by allowing himself the liberty of bracketing what Illich once told Cayley in one of their radio talks:

> Now that you are sitting here with me and are subjecting me to severe questioning as regards my works, which you have read carefully, I can see that in your examination of what Illich said and meant, you would be able to plow on victoriously, and I would not even be accorded the honors of war! Whenever I look at an old book of mine, I feel both embarrassed and fascinated. With a well-sharpened pencil, I managed to say quite a few things rather well. But both the context and the

20 The dates given here are those of the books' first edition, which was usually (though not always) in English.

> way I express things have changed. I therefore close the book and put it away. That is the peculiar experience I am presently going through: you are asking me questions about a man that no longer exists (Cayley, 1992, p. 120).[21]

A quarter of a century has elapsed between the publication of those conversations and the writing of Beck's book—more years than separated Illich's first *pamphlets* from the publication of his first conversations with Cayley. If something did indeed change over those years, it was, in Illich's opinion, the degree of readability that his 'first books' had in his own eyes. When he was busy writing them, he was also engaged in several struggles in the Latin America of that bygone period. That said, Illich's self-critique should not be taken as an invitation to judge what any retrospective interpretation may find in those texts as more important than the texts themselves: to my eyes, what Illich said and wrote remains far more important than anything modern and postmodern commentators may have to say about them.

Since Illich was a born actor—even though, to my knowledge, he never played a character on stage—he put his undeniable thespian skills at the service of the causes he defended, which might explain the unease and slight irritation he felt whenever he was reminded of actions that, once the heat of the moment had dispelled, he tended to consider from a more balanced perspective. This notwithstanding, it should be borne in mind that in the 1980s, when public protests took place against the deployment in Germany of *Pershing* missiles trained on the Soviet Union, he took active part in the organization of street demonstrations and composed *pamphlets* that were subsequently handed out to passers-by.[22] He once even

21 Illich subsequently stated: 'I wrote those books as an answer to a specific situation… But they are now dead, they belong to another period' (Cayley, 1992, p. 138).

22 *Auch ich schweige hier* öffentlich ('I too have decided to keep silent,' which was translated and published in Italian in Illich, 1992, p. 32). In 1982, shortly before Christmas, a number of people took to the streets of many German cities carrying a placard around their necks with the writing '*Auch ich schweige hier* öffentlich:' without uttering a single word, they distributed to passers-by a short text which explained why discussing in any way the instruments of mass destruction that had become so powerful as to baffle their definition as mere weapons was a form of complicity.

went as far as letting himself be wrapped up stark naked in a bag that was later placed on a pavement.

I am a member of a Mexican group presently occupied with rereading the works Illich published between 1971 and 1981. What interests us is isolating the themes and subjects which Illich sketched out in those works with a 'well-sharpened pencil' that deserve to be brought to the fore once again on the political stage. Regardless of the notion that modern institutions may derive from the Church of the second Christian millennium, and may constitute a corruption of it,[23] a renewed discussion of these themes requires no profession of faith by the participants in the debate, except possibly a display of good faith on the part of all involved, as well as mutual trust. In my view, the choice of bracketing the new considerations that Illich developed from 1981 onward and the process of self-critique that he initiated after 1990 may only be justified in the perspective of highlighting those ideas of his from the 1970s that still deserve to be discussed today.[24]

Misunderstanding the relationship between autonomy and instrumentality

In his book, Beck proposed to envisage modernity as the tension between autonomy and instrumentality. He defined modernity as 'a set of operational concepts concerning objects and subjects understood as objects.' In his view, modernity produced the mirage of a self-founding of the human world strengthened by

23 By applying to the Church the Latin saying *corruptio optimi quae est pessima* or *corruptio optimi pessima*, Illich defined the invasion of consecrated places at the hands of secular powers (or, in Agamben's words, of the *anthropos tes anomias* ['the man of lawlessness']) as the corruption of what was best.

24 In the early months of 2016, I prepared a series of short texts, which I considered to be 'summaries,' in view of the congress that had been organized to mark the ninetieth anniversary of Ivan Illich's birth (4 September 1926). Each of them dealt with a situation that had progressively deteriorated since the 1970s; examples in this sense were *the outright transfer of privileges from the poor to the rich*, which in my opinion was maximized by all public transport systems across the industrialized world, or the possibility to organize public debates on the urgent need to impose a maximum level on the production of material goods and services, as well as on any expansion of the market which may drastically reduce the ability of the poor to derive 'use-values' from their own environment.

diffidence toward any form of external reality, whether that reality involves God, the sacred, the past, or tradition. In modern terms, the world is the autonomous founding of man by man.[25] However, Beck argues, this way of defining autonomy requires the opposing consolidation of the material, natural, and social world as an entity that resists the subject's will to dominate it—a balance being disrupted by an increasingly powerful instrumental manipulation. It therefore follows that the world and everything that constitutes it become redefined as the *means* to achieve the ends of the autonomous subject, whose ultimate destiny is, consequently, the assertion of autonomy through instrumental domination of the world, an assertion that becomes an end in itself.

In the pre-modern world, the will to instrumental domination was contained by culture—contained, as Jean-Pierre Dupuy would put it, in both senses of the verb: enclosed and restrained. At the dawn of modernity, nonetheless, instrumentality ceased to be contained by culture and entered a phase of exuberant expansion, which patently manifested itself in the boundless growth of the technological sphere. Besides its known disruptive effects, this expansion also led to a fundamental perversion, namely the transformation of means into ends. Once freed from all restraints and raised to the status of being its own end, technical instrumentality evolved into an imperative of an almost religious nature, and turned against mankind. Since Technique has now become separate and detached from the whole of the cultural and ethical relationships inherited from the past, in the modern world it threatens to turn into an autonomous system that, by implacably meeting the demands of efficiency, tends to progressively colonize all aspects of human life.[26]

25 The contemporary philosopher whose thought has developed this position in the most satisfactory way is unquestionably Cornelius Castoriadis (see Castoriadis, 1975).

26 See the evolution of Jacques Ellul's thought from *La Technique ou l'enjeu du siècle* (1954) to *Le Système technicien* (1977). Illich was familiar with his writing and acknowledged his debt to him in the statement he gave at Bordeaux's *Institut d'études politiques* on 13 November 1993, on the occasion of the celebration of his eightieth birthday: 'Master Ellul—though I would much rather address you as "Maestro Jacques"—I was very touched by your comparing a teacher to an ox that opens a new furrow by pulling a plow. I have endeavoured to follow your example in a spirit of filiation, with all the

It is in the context of the historical tension between means and ends, and between instrumentality and autonomy, that Beck poses the question of how to situate Illich's critique of industrial production and of the endless tools at its disposal. Illich observed that above a certain growth rate, the modern project of instrumental domination was overturned to such an extent that its spread could not help causing effects that were the opposite of the ones pursued: the educational means discouraged the desire to learn, the speed of transport created barriers between people, and hospitals gave rise to new diseases. In every domain, the tools escaped human control. To use one of Illich's turns of phrase, they became *counterproductive*. It was through the study of the industrial production of goods and services that Illich illustrated the subversion of the tools and of the institutions occasioned by their own growth.

Beck recounts Illich's argument that, beyond a certain critical threshold, every technological project to dominate the natural and social world is affected by an upheaval that transforms obviously destructive means into ends—as if it were a matter of curing one evil with evil itself, or of shielding the veneration for the techno-logical Moloch from any rational critique. Illich had the courage to preserve just that kind of critical rationality in the face of the attitude adopted by his contemporaries, who were mesmerized by the feats modern instruments could accomplish: beyond a certain size, a certain level of energy consumption, of speed, or of planning, every instrument (or indeed every institutional apparatus of an instrumental nature) *inevitably* draws most people away from the ends for which it was originally devised. Instruments of disproportionate size damage nature, demean social relationships, and establish a tyranny of the experts that denies people their autonomy.

As Beck reaffirms, following Illich, instrumentality makes no sense unless it is kept below certain critical thresholds which are traditionally defined, implicitly, through a combination of culture and modesty in the power of the instruments. Since those boundaries had been done away with, Illich pro-

faux pas which that may entail' (Illich, 2004, p. 147).

posed a fundamental two-sided reflection on the thresholds which had to be identified rationally and on the constraints which had to be defined politically. In other words, his reflection focused on the *dimensional thresholds* which needed to be identified if any action performed by means of instruments was to acquire once again a human meaning within a set of *constraints* that would enable a given community to implement those very thresholds at a political level.[27] The political possibility of reducing the technological sphere to a more equitable scale is what nourished Beck's hope for the coming of 'another modernity.'

'Social theories' and their underlying 'axioms'

In the early 1990s, Illich saw industrial society as placed at the junction between the formal structure of the institutions he had criticized and certain ways of perceiving social reality, to which he regretted not having been sufficiently sensitive. Was the degree of society's intelligibility exclusively due to the conceptual constellations that claimed to rationalize it? Or did the things taken for granted—the unquestioned certainties typical of the contemporary age—take root in an inextricable tangle of concepts and precepts, of rules, practices, and rituals? In a crude echo of Mary Douglas's thought, it may legitimately be claimed that the perception of sensible things informs a certain approach to society, the categories of which, in turn, pervade that perception (Douglas, 1970). Illich equated those combina-

27 See *Shadow Work* (Illich, 1981, the French edition of which is to be found in Œuvres *complètes*, vol. 2). On pages 95 and 96, one may find what constitutes a short essay on the three stages of the public debate on the limits to growth. The first stage dates back to the late 1960s: 'If the key objectives of industrial production are not modified, the biosphere will soon become uninhabitable.' The second followed soon afterwards: 'Together with the limits to the production of commercial goods it will also be necessary to assess the limits to be set on care services.' In the 1980s, the debate on limits reached a third stage: 'While the first stage focused on goods and the second on services, the third concentrated on *the commons*. In other words, after the first two stages (the acknowledgment of the limits to be placed on the production of goods—which required great energy consumption—and of services—which beyond a certain level destroyed people's trust in their autonomy), the debate on the need to set limits had to focus on the defense of what was left of the age-old subsistence skills of *the environment's use-values*, which had historically been closely associated with community areas such as *the commons* and their various equivalents (*Allmende, Gemeinheit, wastes, open fields, usi civici*, or, in classical Spanish, *ejidos*).'

tions of epistemological and perceptual postulates to 'axioms.' In geometry, an axiom is an unprovable and ultimately arbitrary proposition that serves as the basis for a theorem's proof. Axioms are thus the indispensable foundations on which theorems are developed and proven.

Such a mathematical metaphor enabled Illich to draw a distinction between what he defined as 'social theorems' and the 'axioms' on which they relied. For instance, the fact that the extant economic order is largely based on inequalities that can only increase constitutes a 'social theorem' whose underlying 'axiom' is that employment is the only kind of productive activity that is tolerated and legitimized (as well as, in many cases, legal). As mentioned above,[28] Barbara Duden has pointed out that Illich suggested that the spindles around which the axioms' conceptual and perceptual thread was wound were more deeply concealed from view than the looms on which social theorems were woven (Duden, 2010). Humberto Beck mentioned the following as examples of axioms underlying modern social theorems:

- Subsistence activities exist only to be replaced by the consumption of goods and services.
- Needs are determined on the basis of goods and services as defined by experts.
- The environment is a reservoir of resources for the production of industrial goods.
- The needs felt by all human beings are essentially identical.

Axioms of this kind are interwoven with conceptual and perceptual certainties that are never called into question and constitute the modern frame of mind.

In contemporary economic societies, the dominant axiom is the one concerning scarcity, the formulation of which is to be found, in one shape or another, right on the first pages of any textbook on economics. For instance: 'The economy deals with the allocation of limited goods to alternative purposes which are in competition with one another.' Scarcity, both as an

28 *Cf.* Preface, p. xxiii.

economic concept and as a typically modern experience, is not tantamount to a limited availability of resources but rather to the tension between finite availability and the endless growth of needs and desires.

The economy is constantly generating new types of scarcities, which are necessary for its functioning. In fact, a false belief pervades the general perception of the economy: the claim that modern scarcities are of the same nature as the penury of the past is an act of deception that official history performs as soon as it presents the subsistence of the past as an antecedent of the modern economy. The phrase 'subsistence economy' is the expression of just such a fallacy. For those aware that subsistence rooted in a given culture and an economy disembedded from any kind of culture constitute two heterogeneous realities, scarcity becomes essentially synonymous with *economy*. Pre-modern subsistence was not prone to scarcity but could be affected by penury, which was often not an individual experience.

> What other observers perceived as the advent of the capitalist industrial economy was described by Illich in anthropological terms as the disappearance of culture, understood as a structure that kept in check the conditions under which scarcity appeared in a given society (Beck, 2017, p. 114).

In Illich's view, the history of the modern world was inextricably linked to the history of scarcity: it was the history of the war that the State and the Market waged against the common folk's subsistence. The economy generates scarcity whenever it replaces an independent activity with the consumption of a certain good (of which there is a shortage, by definition). Every step of that substitution increases the *economic nexus*—that is to say, the loss of vernacular skills rooted in culture, as well as people's dependency on industrial goods and services.

Chapter 2: Encounters

Jean Pierre Dupuy, who knew Ivan Illich well, recounted how on one occasion they chanced to meet in a Parisian street. More than on the encounter itself, he focused on that moment of uncertainty which usually precedes such instances, when one friend spots the other and, unbeknownst to the latter, studies him for an instant, before calling his attention or entering his field of vision. Illich, Dupuy told me, gave him an impression of 'absolute freedom.'

Illich's intellectual meanderings conveyed a similar feeling to me. It was impossible to stop him, or to counter: 'But you previously said such and such.' Did he contradict himself? I do not believe so, even though he was perfectly capable of engaging somebody in a conversation for weeks, only to suddenly leave them in the lurch and turn to the pursuit of another idea.

For instance, after inviting me to deliver a speech on the 'concept of energy as a social construct,' sometime during the first three months of the seminars which were held at the University of Marburg in 1981, he abandoned me to find interlocutors ready to follow me on such an arduous endeavor, and turned his interest to a history of pilgrimages instead. He could easily start a joint research project with somebody and then do a sudden about-face, leaving one to face an audience clamoring for his presence on stage, only to pop up again at the next bend in the path with a stack of new concepts, metaphors, and interlocutors. Indeed, a suitable illustration of this is the fact that a more precise definition of the concept of energy as a social construct was ultimately reached thanks only to a conversation with a linguist.[1]

Illich could not countenance meditating on a given topic without also having a group of friends to discuss it among themselves; it was literally impossible for him to have a theoretical debate without also having a party. To name but one example, that was exactly how the research on the industrial origin of the concept of energy eventually led to the discovery of a new

1 See 'L'énergie, un objet social' (Illich, 2010). It is the French translation of the opening speech of the 'The Basic Option Within Any Future Low-Energy Society' seminar which was held at the Colegio de México in July 1983.

class of words which, in common modern parlance, are as interchangeable as Lego bricks: development, structure, services, communication, information, resource, sexuality, solution, function, resources… energy.[2]

The linguist Uwe Pörksen expanded Illich's initial intuition into a theory of 'plastic words' (or 'amoeba words'), devoid of a precise denotation but endowed with an ever-expanding abundance of connotations, which give those who employ them a veneer of exceptional knowledge: 'Our city must develop spatial structures for the health service and ensure the supply of the necessary energy resources.' With a few modifications, those same words could provide the content of a speech on the expansion of the education or urban transport services.

Up to this point, the focus has been on the trail which took the adult Ivan Illich from Rome to New York, and thence to Puerto Rico and Mexico. Those place names constitute mere points of geo-chronological reference in a thematic itinerary which they cannot possibly define exhaustively. A chronological account of Illich's thought could never fully capture its essence and his motives: his keenness on meeting people and his openness to surprise, his loyalty to his friends beyond all his about-faces, and his unquenchable curiosity.

He believed that every meeting, or even a simple conversation, could occasion the development of thought of all those involved. In this sense, a deeply original thinker such as himself was by no means an individualist. Moreover, the man who from the 1980s onward was to make a living by teaching in universities was far from ready to submit to the usual university practices: he steadfastly refused, for instance, to give marks to his students. His rebellion against university procedures nonetheless sparked one of the most perceptive studies on the origin of that institution (see Illich, 1991a).

My recollection of those now remote years (i.e., the 1970s in Cuernavaca) mingles some of the most salient moments in Ivan Illich's life with the interest I then had in material culture

2 *Cf.* Pörksen, 1995. In the early 1980s, Illich got some of his friends involved in 'an inquiry into the obvious,' which eventually developed into a systematic research on the contemporary mental topology and its hidden axioms.

and in its distortions at the hands of the Speed Imperative, and also with Illich's appeals to reposition modern tools within a set of political boundaries to be defined on the basis of rigorous dimensional parameters.

But did Illich have a house, or soil beneath his feet? He did indeed, a house made of unbaked clay in a village close to a provincial city. As for the concept of soil, it entailed the concept of footprints, as well as the notion of the past and the present intertwined together; defending one's right to leave one's footprints in the soil meant denouncing an urban civilization that strove to bury it under a thick layer of cement.

I. A Mexican Village, the Hub of the Criticism of Industrial Production

A rootless cosmopolitan?

I first met Ivan Illich in Cuernavaca in 1973, soon after I had relocated to Mexico. He had already spent twelve years in that weird and fascinating country which our frequent conversations enabled me to begin to understand. At the time, I did not imagine that the metaphors which he provided would later form the basis of a radical criticism of the development project which the rich countries had devised for the poor ones, and, on top of that, also of a criticism of the economy and its fundamental axiom, namely scarcity. Since I subsequently took part both in his research on economic development and in his formulation of a criticism of the *scarcity* generated by the economy which manifests itself in the dependency on inevitably *counterproductive* services, in the present chapter I shall endeavor to forget what I am only too familiar with.

In the early 1970s, what I knew (or had learned) about Ivan Illich portrayed him as a man with no national affiliation, a 'born' polyglot without a mother tongue who had been born in Vienna to a Jewish mother and a Catholic father from Dalmatia, and who traveled on an American passport. In 1962, the future Pope Paul VI invited him to the Second Vatican Council, which Illich later deserted because the Council refused to issue a formal complaint against states in possession of nuclear weapons, i.e., tools of genocide. He had previously acted as deputy parish priest in a Puerto Rican parish in New York, and in 1956 he had been appointed deputy rector with the office of rector at a university in Puerto Rico. In 1961, he had founded a training center for well-meaning lay and religious missionaries in Cuernavaca, where he ultimately reached the conclusion: 'To hell with good intentions,'[3] and advised his trainees to return to their homes as an act of friendship towards the Latin American people.

In 1968, he was summoned to the Vatican by the Congregation for the Doctrine of the Faith (the former Inquisition) to provide answers to about eighty questions. He later told me that once he had made his presence known, he was led up a winding staircase and into a wide room with a low ceiling, where a man sat waiting at the far end of a long table with his face hidden by a cowl. 'Who are you?' Illich asked. 'Your judge,' a cavernous voice replied. Looking back on that conversation after all this time, I now appreciate that that was Illich's way to enable my mind to comprehend a drama whose behind-the-scenes I was not yet ready to fathom. What is certain is that Illich refused to answer any questions concerning any third party involved.

Thereafter, the Center for Intercultural Formation (CIF), which Illich directed in Cuernavaca, lost (almost) every form of financial support from the Church and was converted into a center of critical studies, or one should perhaps say a 'think tank,' which did not issue diplomas and was almost exclusively supported by its students,[4] namely the Center for Intercultural Documentation (CIDOC). In the same period, Illich wrote a number of books that were of momentous importance. From

3 Translator's Note: That was the title of the conference on the Inter-American Students' Project which was held in Cuernavaca on 20 April 1968. An Italian translation of it is available at: https://pulgarias.wordpress.com/2017/05/20/al-diavolo-le-buone-intenzioni/

4 An excellent language school was opened right next to CIDOC, in which the Spanish language was taught to the volunteers bound for missions in Latin America; the dollars they paid for tuition was what financed CIDOC, also thanks to a favorable exchange rate. Students were made aware of the reality of the places they were going to visit. Illich advised them in the strongest possible terms against carrying out their mission, and many did indeed give up.

1980 he gradually began to shun the limelight and published more than he had when he was a media celebrity. Apart from what I had a chance to learn from Illich himself, all of this has been abundantly documented. I would especially recommend David Cayley's introduction in Illich and Cayley (2005), as well as the book by Thierry Paquot (2012). I got to meet Illich in person before I became familiar with his history, the details of which I learned at a time that lies outside the temporal framework I intend to impose on the present chapter. What Illich had to offer to a square architect, such as I was at the time (think Mondrian or Mies van der Rohe), was a new perspective on the world, which in my case was also a perspective on a new world.

Our conversations, which never really focused on our personal biographies, were mostly concerned with topics associated with material culture: motorized means of transport as 'the worst of all forms of exploitation,' as he would often say (an opinion which I shared wholeheartedly); refuse and waste, which he saw as the expression of the 'disvalue' which in modern times does away with use values, thereby creating a vacuum that is filled by exchange values; and the denied freedom of access to water and its sources, which is so essential to all forms of possession: 'haurire aquam,' the act of drawing water which according to Roman jurists was one of the fundamental freedoms that make the act of inhabiting a place feasible.

A pilgrim in a world gone mad

In 1982, Frau Kappert, who had let out a flat to Professor Illich during his stay at the University of Marburg in Germany, to which I had accompanied him, was astounded, and even shocked, when he described the farewell breakfast she had offered him as a *Henkersmahlzeit*, the last meal given to a condemned man. It was the end of a cycle, and Illich expressed his refusal to indulge in any kind of nostalgia by means of a somewhat brutal form of sarcasm. Both his youth and his early adulthood had been marked by painful separations with which he often coped with sadness, but without giving in to regret. The circumstances of his life forced him to change place and theater of operations, but never made him feel dejected. He might as well have echoed the words which the farmers evicted from the Russian shtetl of Anatevka utter in the musical *The Fiddler on the Roof*: 'It was a place' (a mere location we had to pass through).[5]

What lingered on after each separation were the ties of friendship. That was an expression of what is known as devotion, something quite different from loyalty. One is devoted to a friend, and loyal to an institution: devotion thus comes before loyalty, even loyalty towards one's country. Illich was devoted to 'the Church as She' more than he was loyal to the institution that was still the Church, and which Illich termed in English 'the Church as It.' He sometimes attended the forms of popular devotion which took place in the small chapel located in the *barrio* of *Los Ramos*, the Mexican village in which he resided for a long time. According to David Cayley, Illich used to translate the Vulgate's *Deus deorum* as 'the Lord of the idols,' thereby implying great respect for the ways in which people perceived and expressed the divine. In an interview with Cayley, Illich once confessed:

> Whenever I find myself in prayer in Mexico, I always bow towards Popocatépetl or Izztaccíhuatl,[6] the Landlords of the Valley in which I live. I want them to act as the idols or the spirits which one can admire on the capitals of the Romanic churches: dragons, whales and sirens. They have all been incorporated into those churches to prop up the building that symbolizes the whole universe, the cosmos in the hollow of God's hand (Cayley, 1992, p. 204).

In Illich's eyes, Romanic churches constituted a visual representation of how the Gospel's 'Good News' could be grafted onto vernacular cultures without destroying their individual sense of what was right and appropriate for *that* specific place (he was, however, to add: 'Who knows if that is actually God's will').

While he reminisced with no trace of bitterness on his Roman years and all the hassle he had to endure at the hands of

5 Translator's Note: *Cf.* http://rai.it/dl/portali/site/articolo/ContentItem-d35b77b2-7e11-4826-b601-625bfc243d9e.html?refresh_ce

6 Translator's Note: Two large volcanoes that are visible from Cuernavaca.

the Inquisition, he would later state that what had stayed with him from that period was a concert of voices. Those were the voices of the living, with whom he prayed by reading the Roman breviary out loud, *cum fratribus absentibus*, as a form of preparation for death. I once heard him outline the plot of a novel he never got round to writing: tired of the living, the dead decide to leave the earth and take with them all traces of the past. A world without the dead, without a past, in which everything is contemporary, actually reminds me of Orange County, the affluent neighborhood located between San Diego and Los Angeles that lacks any temporal depth (at any rate, that was the impression I got when I passed through it about twenty years ago): a place where everything was insufferably new.

The notion of a pilgrim that breaks through the 'original shell of gestures' and dives headlong into the unknown with full trust in his being 'in the hands of God' was for Illich a source of inspiration; the same was true of the underlying notion of contingency,[7] 'one of the few concepts of expressly Christian origin' (Illich, 2005, p. 65), as he had learned from the historian and philosopher Hans Blumenberg, whom he admired.

CIDOC: A podium, its topics, and its audience

Illich's attachment to the Church was twofold: through his faith (the concert of voices), and through his criticism of it. The first kind of attachment he expressed through his faith in a world envisaged as similar to a body of flesh and bone. The second through a criticism of the institution of the Church, which led to a historical re-examination of the modern world: all modern institutions were mere caricatures of the Church itself. The Church was striving to achieve something that was actually impossible: to do right by mankind in spite of it, to turn grace into an obligation, and to make having the freedom to choose one's friends become the norm. Modern institutions, conversely, established rituals that made freedom unthinkable, and turned a service (*servitium* in Latin, *diakonía* in Greek) into one of the

7 Translator's Note: On the concept of contingency, see p. 40 below.

driving forces behind the economy. The education service was an institution that delivered scarce goods and had to be attended by legal obligation. The compulsive use of daily transport was a ritual that destroyed the freedom of movement as well as the places and the time one could set aside to wander about. Modern medicine did not help patients to 'feel well in their skin' but forced them to wear a body that was mapped out, classified, and ultimately iatrogenic: a body built by doctors. In short, those were some of the lines of discussion that were pursued at the Center for Intercultural Documentation in Cuernavaca in the early 1970s, and which were later expanded, sometimes after a thorough revision, during the seminars which Illich gave in Germany, the US, Italy, and sometimes also in France.

All of these topics converged on a study of the counterproductivity of industrial institutions. With a hint of exaggeration, it may perhaps be claimed that the counterproductivity of any given institution consists in the fact that it delivers the opposite of what it promises: schools actively discourage autonomous learning, motorized means of transport increase the time required by compulsory daily transfers, and the medicine industry tends to turn each patient into a chronic one. This counterproductivity was defined according to the following threefold classification:

- Technical (or clinical, in the case of medicine) counterproductivity counters one product with another one, thereby occasioning a generalized congestion. During the rush hour, for instance, every vehicle is a cause of obstruction for all the other ones.
- Social counterproductivity is the conflict between an industrial product and the skills replaced by that same product. The circulation of vehicles, for instance, makes traveling dangerous, or even impossible.
- Structural counterproductivity is the paralysis of the ability to conceive other possible approaches. For example, if I say 'I need a bottle of water' rather than 'I'm thirsty,' I am excluding from the horizon of my possibilities every non-industrial way to quench my thirst.

The critical concepts discussed during the seminars held at CIDOC also included radical monopoly, the nature of the professions that provided services, and the way they brought about the elimination of the separation of powers which constitutes democracy's fundamental cornerstone, namely the distinction between use values and exchange values. I would therefore raise the following question: could the ideas of a man who developed a coherent criticism of industrial society in the 1970s—a bygone era—still be the germs for innovative ideas for the weird times in which we presently live? The topics listed above clearly show that at CIDOC, where I studied and then taught from 1973 onward, religion was hardly ever discussed. After 1970, the faith of that true believer became apophatic, 'unstated,' and unexpressed; he neither imposed it on anybody, nor did he make it a compulsory premise for the proper understanding of his investigations.

A polyglot chorus of voices in a countryside village

The disciplined conversations that took place at CIDOC were sometimes resumed in a blend of overlapping voices at Illich's house, made of unbaked clay in the village of Ocotepec, near Cuernavaca. In both of those places, I had a chance to meet, among others (it is for me impossible to list them all here): André Gorz (one of whose articles, which was published in *Le Nouvel Observateur* under the pen name of Michel Bosquet, first drew my attention to CIDOC's existence) and his wife Dorine; John McKnight, a professor from Chicago who criticized aid programs and dubbed them 'a mask for charity;' the sociologist, ecologist and theologian Wolfgang Sachs, who would later be the editor of a ground-breaking book on the criticism of development (Sachs, *Ideas in Progress* series); Jean-Marie Domenach, the former director of the *Esprit* magazine, as well as his successor, Paul Thibaut; Freimut Duve, a historian, politician, and the editor of the *Technologie und Politik* series issued by the Rowohlt publishing house; Heinz von Förster, one of the first thinkers behind cybernetics (whose contribution was also instrumental in establishing its name) and a renowned conjurer; the psychologist Michael McCoby, a close collaborator of Erich Fromm; J.

P. Naik, who was in his youth a member of India's Civil Disobedience Movement, and who later became an internationally respected reformer of what he still termed Education; Franco Basaglia, the then director of Trieste's psychiatric hospital and the founder of a movement for the liberation of all men and women declared 'insane' from institutional confinement; the children of the Italian film director Roberto Rossellini; and Valentine Borremans.

Since there will be occasion to make further reference to him, I should perhaps also mention Gutierre Tibón, a polyglot of Italo-Mexican extraction who was a scholar on Mexico's ancient cultures, as well as the inventor of the typewriting machine and a philologist in five languages. Among those who used to frequent CIDOC and Ocotepec, there were also a modest, spiritual and jocular Persian wiseman called Majid Rahnema (I was greatly surprised to learn that he had acted as minister under the Shah, and I never imagined for one minute I would later become a very close friend of his, or indeed that we would co-author a book on the 'power of the poor') and the French engineer Jean-Pierre Dupuy, with whom I shortly afterwards wrote a book full of mathematical references on the topic of counterproductivity (Rahnema and Robert, 2008; Dupuy and Robert, 1975). As an expert in mathematical economics, Dupuy had contributed with Illich to a narrower definition of that concept, which was subsequently illustrated through the example of transport. However, despite all of our commendable efforts, the criticism of that institution will necessarily have to be reformulated, lest we get bogged down in resignation to a false fate.

In hindsight, that polyphony of languages (which were usually mutually translated by Illich himself) in a countryside village takes on in my mind the appearance of a dreamlike experience.

Bygone times, recollections of youth

Nostalgia was forbidden. The hope of those years in Cuernavaca: that a renewal movement would emerge from the fringes of industrial society! A popular byword at the time: the future!

Illich aroused the enthusiasm of his young (and not-so-young) interlocutors by encouraging them to prepare for the great debates that were expected to eventually characterize the end of the twentieth century. He himself actively contributed to the endeavor by devising a prediction on the industrial mode of production's final outcome, and Valentine Borremans fully supported him by stressing that besides the criticism of compulsory education, it was also necessary to radically question the whole of contemporary society's industrial *ethos*. Dupuy and Robert believed that their criticism of the compulsory motorized transport which swallowed up large chunks of life's time was their own way to prepare for those necessary debates. The documentarists Marie-Claude Deffarge and Gordian Troeller, who spoke German while at work and conversed in French the rest of the time, shot a film about CIDOC that was later broadcast by Radio Bremen with the title *Kein Respekt vor heiligen Kühen* ('No Respect for Holy Cows'); in their private conversations they used to refer to the institute as the 'kitchen of the future.'

The 'technological imperative' that holds modern imagination captive

In 1972, Valentine Borremans and Ivan Illich published a *pamphlet* entitled *La necesidad de un techo comun (El control social de la tecnología)*.[8]

That writing was aimed at a group of Latin Americans who had gathered at CIDOC to discuss a hypothesis which the then director of the center, Valentine Borremans, first developed in 1971, and which postulated that the industrial mode of production's characteristics was such that they would successfully manage to prevent any political process from keeping it under control. That seemingly discouraging claim was nonetheless counterbalanced by a word of hope: *the society that accepts to impose a common ceiling (i.e., an upper limit) on some technical dimensions of its industrial mode of production will be able to propose political*

8 'The need for a common roof (The social control of technology),' which was added as an Appendix to the Spanish edition of *Medical Nemesis* (Illich, *Obras reunidas*, 2006, pp. 761–763).

alternatives to industrial technology. Such a society could inspire a world movement in favor of a new popular policy that allowed common people to determine 'under which upper limits a society wishes to live' (Illich, *Obras Reunidas*, 2006, p. 763).

This notion, of the imposition of upper limits on the industrial mode of production, inspired most of the works I penned in my youth, and gave substance to an intuition on which I had been meditating ever since I witnessed, during a prolonged stay in Amsterdam, the birth of a movement for the renewal of the ideas on the 'project of the cities,' which advocated the replacement of all cars with bicycles. At the time, the whole world appeared to be subservient to what Valentine Borremans called 'the technological imperative,' namely the notion that any technological advance achieved in any part of the world had to be placed at the service of a restricted privileged group in the West, with no regard whatsoever for the price that the rest of society would eventually have to pay for it. The technological imperative was the main driving force behind the huge mass of vehicles which, from the 1950s onward, threatened to obliterate everything that was still alive, spontaneous, and convivial in our city streets.

As for myself, what was I exactly doing in that jailhouse?

What was being proposed by Amsterdam's anarchists, who were flooding the city streets with the bicycles their supporters had donated, all painted in white to signal they were meant to be used by the general public, went far beyond the *bicyclisation* of the city. It concerned the radical questioning of the car imperative that was beginning to make a shambles of European cities, one after the other, by weaving through their historical fabric motorways, bypasses, and other suburban ring roads in the vain attempt to achieve the impossible, namely increasing the average speed in industrial cities.

In 1962, Amsterdam's road traffic was overwhelmingly made up of bicycles, and the time required for me to move from one place to another was far less that what was needed eight years later, when I found myself driving a car along those same routes. That is what spurred my interest in material culture, which was the object of many a conversation I had with Ivan Illich.

Indeed, the approach adopted by those city planners who colonize the future by means of regulations branded into the cities' living flesh like indelible tattoos ought to be turned on its head. A motorway running through an urban center constitutes a 'suture that separates,' as the philosopher and city planner Henri Lefebvre, who was on various occasions a guest of Mexican universities, used to put it: it links places and 'helps one to save time' lengthways (as is usually the case with those who travel on a motorway), while it also 'makes one waste time' crossways, as experienced by those (usually the more indigent ones) who have to drive through a city by resorting to a bridge that makes their daily itinerary considerably longer. It is fair to say that the urban structures dictated by the imperative to prioritize motorized traffic entail a clear-cut transfer of privileges from the poorer strata to the richer ones.

Illich, for his part, advocated the political establishment of negative design criteria that would reduce such transfers and the time required by compulsory motorized transport.[9] Given the absence of any political definition whatsoever of upper limits (as regards speed, technological sophistication, and public funds), the modern approach to transport planning appeared to him to be an endeavor that would inevitably swallow up much of life's time (*chronophage*), and which would ultimately achieve results (the increasing waste of time forced on poorer people, and subsequently also on the not-so-poor) that were diametrically opposed to their stated purpose: namely, to place at everybody's disposal tools that were mistakenly believed to help people save time.

City traffic has to be thought over again. Priority ought to be given to autonomous forms of locomotion over heteronomous mobility, i.e., to transfers on foot or by bicycle as opposed

9 Lower or 'minimum' limits: every inmate held in our penitentiaries should receive a minimum daily ration of four pounds of bread. Upper or 'maximum' limits: no motorist driving on the roads of our city should be allowed to travel faster than 18 mph. Since the average daily speed in the megalopolises equipped with an underground system is about 9 mph, the establishment of a higher upper speed limit could paradoxically increase the traffic's average speed. However, that argument has never been deemed worthy of a serious discussion.

to the dependency on motorized vehicles. Jean-Pierre Dupuy, who was endowed with the gift of being able to explain concepts simply and clearly, once told us that, in his view, autonomy and heteronomy should be managed according to their lexicographic order: in a dictionary, 'rhythm' takes alphabetical precedence over 'Saturday,' which in turn comes before 'tobacco.' Autonomy is a fundamental part of ethics. Illich maintained that from a political point of view, it was necessary to strive for what he called the positive synergy between autonomy and heteronomy, that is to say, between what could be achieved independently and what required external help. A feat of nineteenth-century mechanical engineering such as the bicycle, with its tubular structures ensuring lightness, its wheel spokes working under tension, its ball bearings and inner tube tires (all of which are components that very few city dwellers could manage to produce on their own), greatly expands the freedom of movement and the range of action of those who avail themselves of it. It is for that reason that what was once called 'the little queen' constituted the prototype of the positive synergy between autonomy and heteronomy. The addition of the internal combustion engine to the ingenuity of those initial technical advances later enabled the motorcar to oust the little queen, and in the process it imposed and subsequently generalized the negative synergy which prioritizes heteronomy at all levels and presses autonomy into its service, in a scenario that has its most emblematic expression in the compulsive quest for a means of transport in the corridors of Paris' Montparnasse–Bienvenüe underground station.

Since my narrative is based on a reconstruction, it must inevitably appear to be somewhat romanticized. Neither Illich nor myself were native to that village. Yet, we both pinned our hopes on it: we prayed that its way of life would not wane and disappear. We both lived in a village and we did not own a car. Cars spoil everything. Nonetheless, neither of us considered 'living without a car in a village' to be a solution to the ongoing environmental and urban catastrophe. If ever, that was a selective sacrifice that expressed our personal sense of what was good and proper and what was not. Living without a car in a world that had the presumption of making its use compulsory thus became a matter of *hexis* (habitual disposition), or attitude, rather than the political attempt to 'act better that others do.'

II. The Lifeblood of a Territory

In 1970, Cuernavaca, a provincial town located about 50 miles south of Mexico's capital city, had fewer than 100,000 inhabitants. By 2010, the process of urbanization, among other factors, had made their numbers soar to around 500,000.

North of that town, there was a large rural village called Ocotepec, which, at the time I am going to attempt to recall in these pages, still grew maize in the surrounding fields; it was an indigenous village, in which 'customs and traditions' of yore still held sway. Although that village is nowadays surrounded by the city and threatened by speculators, it still lives by its rural traditions, the *usos y costumbres* that enable Mexico's indigenous communities to retain a degree of juridical autonomy even though the great majority of their members no longer takes up farming.

From 1970, various economic forces and political powers have been actively undermining the conditions of existence of its traditional agriculture based on the *milpa*, the thousand-year-old practice of jointly cultivating three different plants (maize, black beans, and pumpkins) that grow well together, watered as they are by seasonal rainfall. One of the prerequisites for the *milpa* to be successful is that the farmland must not be subjected to speculation. The latter initially attributes 'floating values'[10] to the land in question, and subsequently imposes a modification of its intended use in order to maximize profits. Floating values are essentially offers for the alternative use of the farmland that are made to its owner, and as such they constitute a clear sign of growing instability: who knows if in a year's time my neighbor's *milpa* will still yield a field full of maize? At the present juncture, floating values are gathering like black clouds in the sky over Ocotepec.

10 Harvey, 2009, p.187. The expectation for a given plot of land to fetch a higher price in the future usually encourages its owner to disregard the conditions of its present use. When that expectation becomes generalized, it causes waves of destabilization in the use of the soil.

In the late 1960s, an odd-looking resident of Ocotepec, who was as lanky as a teenager and as in control of his movements as a dancer, began to attract the attention of some of the world's critical minds, including mine.

There was no need to hear his slightly foreign accent to guess that he was not native to the place, for his aquiline profile and his slender figure made it readily apparent. Yet, nobody in the village called him 'stranger,' never mind '*gringo*.' His name was 'don Iván.' In the *barrio* of *Los Ramos*, all his neighbors also knew him as *el escritor*, 'the writer.' He was acquainted with each and every one of them, and was not averse to attending the feast day and religious celebrations that were held at the small local chapel.

That writer was also a historian. He was as familiar with twelfth-century philosophers as if they had been personal friends of his, and could read with ease their flexible and malleable medieval Latin, a language which, if only he had suitable interlocutors at his disposal, he would have also been able to speak fluently. In the company of his friends, this historian displayed an extraordinary gift as a storyteller: he could weave together, with no trace of pedantry whatsoever, an account of the village's recent events with a way of looking at things that elsewhere belonged to bygone eras, but which still lingered on there, such as the perception of the difference between women's and men's tools. Any young man who did not fully comprehend the import of his observations on the tools' gender would be asked to indulge in a little mental experiment. He would be told to imagine that he was entering the kitchen of one of the village's houses while *mole* (a brown-colored sauce made with ground chili peppers and a bit of chocolate) was being prepared, and that he was approaching the big *marmite* with a spoon in his hand. If he belonged to the village, the young man could not help knowing that ten women would likely swoop in on him to snatch from his grip a tool which, especially on a feast day, was only meant to be wielded by a woman's hand. Further similar examples could be provided just as easily: there were tools that had such a masculine connotation, and others that had such a feminine one, that in the now remote 1970s, the locals avoided 'exchanging' them: any woman walking down the street with a machete in her hand would have made it known to one and all that no man lived under her roof, while a man carrying a basket under his arm would have signaled that there were no women in his house. Whenever somebody doubted that those distinctions were not just notions held by the villagers' minds, but rather actual perceptions deeply ingrained in their flesh, the writer would point out the degree of self-assuredness with which the villagers were still able to tell whether the nature of any kind of food, drink, potion, or remedy, as well as of any physical or moral ailment, was actually warm or cold. As a woman from Los Ramos would say, 'Here cold and warmth have nothing to do with temperatures: there is nothing warmer than ice.' That pair of opposites (just like other forms of 'duality' that belong to the natives' cosmovision, such as the earth and the sky, life and death, day and night, men and women) expressed a deep-seated sense of complementarity.

Many years later, in the company of a different set of friends and under a different sky, that writer was to look back on Ocotepec as he began to develop new ideas on appropriate measures, on what is adequate for, and in compliance with, common sense, and on the complementarity of apparent opposites. He intended to discuss *proportionality*, which was being crushed by the lead weight of the systemic, unnuanced and dictatorial *pensée unique* associated with a late modernity that could not, and cannot, be described as capitalist any longer, since nothing exists beyond it. It no longer possesses an external space from which it may be observed; it is, in fact, crisscrossed with cracks. It is through those very cracks that poets and those whom Subcommander Marcos used to call 'rain prospectors' catch a glimpse of another possible world.

Spiritus loci

Ivan Illich settled down in the city of Cuernavaca in 1961, and a few years later he had a house built for himself in Ocotepec. Allow me to begin by introducing, without any bias or prejudice, the 'spirit of the place.' My personal belief in it relies on the same approach which also informs my belief in indigenous medicine:

I consider it to be a frontier of the dominant episteme. That frontier is a sort of no man's land where modern individuals lose their bearings, as they find themselves entering a territory that does not match either their convictions or the knowledge that was forced down their throats while the bottom of their trousers was being worn out on school benches. That territory is in sharp contrast to the certainties they acquired in the cozy environment of their familiar, 'normal' knowledge, even though those same certainties, when observed from the other side, from the perspective of the insubordinates, the poor in spirit and a handful of clear-headed men, appear to be nothing but madness. Illich was indeed one of those who considered the familiar certainties on which industrial society had been built to be alien, if not worse.

Illich's initial approach to any new location was to see it as a heterogeneous (and at first glance unfamiliar) place that was in sharp contrast with the outer shell of habitual gestures that was part of his nest of origin. (That having been said, it should also be added that the historical circumstances surrounding his life never allowed that man, who was born from a Jewish woman in Vienna in 1926, to have a 'nest of origin' which could afford him any degree of safety).[11]

The contingency of being 'in God's hands' seems to me to be the very opposite of the modern sentiment of having been 'thrown' (*geworfen*) somewhere in the wide interstellar spaces, what Heidegger termed *Geworfenheit*. Unlike the fixed outer shell of sedentary peoples, the pilgrims' horizon became relative: it turned into a circle that moved along with them, and it no longer provided a mediation between what was 'ours' and what was 'other,' but merely between what was already visible and what was yet to be so. In the Middle Ages, contingency was envisaged in such a way as to soothe the fear of the unknown, as well as of what was *still invisible*.

Illich put down roots in a concrete place and accepted its horizon. While he sometimes stated that living in Mexico

11 See the two chapters devoted to contingency in Illich, 2005: 'Contingency 1. A world in the hands of God,' and 'Contingency 2. The origin of technology' (pp. 50–82 of the Italian translation).

(where he settled down at the age of thirty-five) was for him tantamount to living on the moon, he was in fact the exact opposite of an astronaut breathing canned air from a plastic umbilical cord. He knew what he was doing, and he did take lungfuls of that 'moon's air.

'Where the moon's navel lies'

According to the etymology of the Aztec (or Nahuatl) language, *Mexico* means 'the place where the moon's navel lies:' had the Aztecs spoken English instead of Nahuatl, their capital city would have been known as *Moon-navel-ton*, as I was once told by Gutierre Tibón, an old friend of Ivan's and a philologist who had been living in Cuernavaca since 1940, and who had discovered the deeper meaning of Mexico's name. *Me* (*metztli*) is the moon, *xi* (*xictli*) the navel, and *co* a locative postposition meaning 'the place where' (while prepositions are placed before a word, postpositions come after it; thus, our expression 'in the water' would be rendered by Nahuatl speakers as *a-pan—a*: water; *pan*: in).

At first glance, it was an odd country, a world (that of the Aztecs and of Nahuatl speakers) which the vacant gaze of its stone gods made rather disquieting to newcomers; a world first subjugated by Spanish culture and later by an overbearing modernity, buried for five centuries under multiple layers of external contributions. Yet, according to the anthropologist Guillermo Bonfil, that same world—the *profound Mexico*—still constitutes the country's cultural underbelly (Bonfil, 1987).

As a country, Mexico is hospitable and hieratic at the same time, and just like the Athens of the past. it keeps within itself the 'metic' (or *met-oikos*, as the ancient Greeks were wont to say), the intruder who 'shares our home.' Around 1970, Cuernavaca, a city whose size was still fairly modest, was located in the midst of luxuriant forests. *Cuernavaca* is the result of the Spanish distortion of its original Aztec name *Cuauhnahuac*, which designated (assuming that place names have any real meaning at all) a place in close proximity to trees, or at any rate surrounded by trees (from *cuauhuitl*, a tree, and *nahuac*, a postposition expressing proximity).

Recollections from a long-bygone era

The years between 1961 and 1976 encompassed two separate phases in Ivan Illich's life: the first one (1961–1968) witnessed his initial prudent contribution to, and his later criticism of, the 'aid programs' that the rich countries (including the Vatican) launched against the poor ones. The second one (1968–1976) entailed the radical criticism of the certainties and the guiding ideas which underlie industrial society's practices, or, as he used to say whenever he had a conversation with mathematicians, 'the axioms on which industrial society's theorems rely.' A more precise temporal context for the expression 'industrial society' should perhaps be added here. What is being referred to, of course, is the industrial society of the early 1970s.

Providing a date for the object of Illich's criticism does not entail, however, that the latter is dated. While his criticism was well grounded in that period, it also tended to look beyond it, just as a flying fish does when it occasionally leaps out of its natural environment, water. The *water* of Illich's criticism was the modern way of life, imported from the rich countries that implemented what he used to call the industrial mode of production. Strictly speaking, the conditions of feasibility for such a mode of production have nowadays ceased to exist. It took Illich at least a decade to come to the realization that those conditions were on the wane. In his view, that mode of production had previously been restrained by the limitations that were inherent to the materiality of industrial tools, regardless of the magnitude of their size. From the years between 1970 and 1980, nonetheless, those limitations and that materiality began to be compromised by the emergence of artifacts that matched less and less the characteristics which had defined tools from the twelfth and thirteenth centuries onward. It was for that reason that Illich later claimed that the writings he produced in the 1960s and the 1970s actually belonged to a different time. This statement, however, should not be too hastily understood as self-criticism. Those 'writings from another time' provided an overview of a landscape in which, to some extent, we still spend many hours on a daily basis, enduring the loss of time while driving on often congested roads.

The landscapes of history and underground forces

Illich belonged to those historians who are capable of intuitively guessing the great tectonic movements beneath the landscapes of history (the *long-term movements*, as the members of the *École des Annales* used to say),[12] which bestows on them a clairvoyance that is too easily mistaken for powers of prediction. In his criticism of professions,[13] for instance, Illich sought to conjure up the era beyond professions which those movements (which are indeed presently underway) could eventually usher in.

Throughout his life, he never relented from his meditation on the evolution of the sequence of odd sociological formations that have emerged from the 1950s onward, or indeed from his attempts to devise a suitable name for their most emblematic expressions: the age of the liberal professions followed by the age of the dominant professions, in the context of which he developed his criticism and concomitantly voiced his hope in the future deliverance from the professions' yoke, but also evoked the looming threat of a new Iron Age. Every social structure that had a beginning is also bound to have an end: professions will not last forever. But what if, as Jacques Ellul feared, all the expressions of what used to be the industrial society were to coordinate their activities in such a way as to leave no room for the unexpected, thereby depriving all the parties involved of any leeway, and to ultimately merge into a single system? Ellul's book on the technical system (1977) was an attempt to provide an answer to just such a question. In such a system, as Illich began to point out in the late 1980s, consultants, facilitators and post-professional experts would become the interfaces that turn their clients into

12 Translator's Note: A group of French historians who in the first half of the twentieth century started a new school of thought (the '*Nouvelle Histoire*') which included in the study of history disciplines such as sociology and geography. The group took its name from the *Annales d'histoire économique et sociale* magazine which Marc Bloch and Lucien Febvre founded in 1929, and which is still being published as *Annales. Histoire. Sciences sociales.*

13 See the criticism of what Illich called *disabling professions* (Illich, 1978). See also Paquot, 2012, p. 68; Illich, 1977.

subsystems. Medical examinations, for instance, would become sessions for the dissemination of the perceptions which patients require to function as a subsystem of the wider bio-medical system. Once the kind 'medical consultant' had turned into an interface between the bio-medical system and the subsystem of his patients, he would show a pregnant woman an ultrasound image and say: 'That is going to be your baby.' Thereafter, he would give her plenty of advice, urging her to act on that image and take an 'informed decision' by selecting an option from a menu of pre-determined choices.[14]

The critical nature of the last phase was the expression of a knowledge that Illich had not possessed before 1980. What was clear to him at the time was the fact that the professions which dominated the institutions and exercised a strict monopoly over services in the early 1970s would not last forever, and that the same was true for our dependency on the services under their control. That awareness seeded the revolutionary nature of his historical studies and his genealogies, which showed the temporal dimension underlying even the most deeply rooted certainties.

Back to the soil of the village

There are two ways to protect the *possibility* of village life. The first consists in the adoption of its horizon, its own sense of measure, and of the primordial matter which its mud represents. Mud is what gets stuck to one's feet or to the soles of one's shoes, and it is what covers the soil. The soil is what one finds under one's feet (hard when it is dry, as soft as mud when it is wet), unless it has been buried under layers of cement, tarmac and bitumen. That is where everything begins and is also brought to completion, that is what marks the beginning and the end of each of life's cy-

14 See Silja Samerski's German-language book entitled *Die Entscheidungsfalle. Wie genetische Aufklärung die Gesellschaft entmündigt* ('The Decision Trap: Genetic Education and its Social Consequences,' Samerski, 2015). (In Italian language, see the conference 'The myth of informed decisions and/or autonomy. How free and personal decisions become an illusion in a world dominated by risk,' the transcripts of which were published as part of the proceedings of the conference 'Ivan Illich. "The peaces of the peoples". A revisitation of the great intellectual's thought,' Lucca, 13–14 June 2003, pp. 20–22: https://www.provincia.lucca.it/retescolastica-scuolapace/pubblicazioni/ivan-le-paci-dei-popoli-una-rivisitazione-del-pensiero-del-grande-intellettuale).

cles. The soil is a much more primitive and concrete matrix than earth (or Planet Earth), which is the subject of speculations and the object of astronomical abstractions. Illich was much more interested in focusing on the soil than on the earth. With his philosopher friends, he strove to 'humbly look down at the soil.' The vibrant appeal for the establishment of a philosophy of the soil (please note, of the soil, not of the earth), which he made in 1990 as part of the 'Declaration on Soil,' known as *The Hebenshausen Manifesto*[15] (Illich et al., 1990), read as follows: 'Soil—its cultivation and our bondage to it—is remarkably absent from those things clarified by philosophy in our western tradition;' 'Philosophy has not brought forth the concepts that would allow us to relate virtue to common soil;' 'As philosophers, we emphasize the duty to speak about soil.'

By evoking the memory of Ocotepec, a village whose demise I will sorely bemoan if the urban sprawl currently underway succeeds one day in swallowing it up, I also intended to mention the soil on which the writer-philosopher used to tread as he made his way 'home,' that same soil which, in 1970, still retained the Nahuatl character that Illich saw as a matrix of virtue.

The second way to protect the 'matrix of virtue' which village soil can potentially represent is to identify its enemies, the excesses that are incompatible with its sense of what is right and appropriate, the illusion of something 'better' to be gained from a future with no definite collocation that justifies the annihilation of the present's blessings. Around 1970, Illich identified in the professions the mirage-inducing structures that could one day justify, in the name of progress, the cloak of cement and certainties cast over every inch of the soil. The mirage in question was that of a better future, which justified the destruction of everything that was actually good there and then. Illich, who could speak perfect French even though he was no Frenchman, had indeed internalized the old French saying: *lemieux est l'ennemi du bien* ('the best is the enemy of the good').

15 A small rural village not far from Göttingen, where Sigmar Gröneveld used to put up Illich in the house he owned there.

Chapter 3: Wanderings and New Visions

Illich's stay at the 'Berlin Institute for Advanced Study'

Illich spent the 1981–1982 academic year at the *Wissenschafts-kolleg* in Berlin,[1] a university center for advanced studies that had been inaugurated only recently. His fellow students included Uwe Pörksen, a German linguist, essayist, and novelist, to whom Illich presented the first drafts of a research project that marked a clean break with the line of his previous works in the 1970s; the same project was also discussed with the historian Barbara Duden, who was then teaching at the *Technische Universität* in Berlin. The focus of his critique was no longer meant to be his previous publications, but rather a number of beliefs specifically held by the modern world, such as the delusion that women could ever achieve equality with men *in the context of a growing economy*.

Furthermore, Illich dared to suggest that the tools available in every pre-industrial society possessed a gender, as was clearly demonstrated by the situation in Ocotepec, where the underlying nuance associated with every tool was still palpably either predominantly feminine or masculine. That consideration was to constitute the core part of Ivan Illich's most controversial book, *Gender* (1982), which marked a dramatic turning point in his evolution as a thinker engaged in clarifying concepts. Indeed, many of the ideas he expressed in that book clashed head-on with the certainties that used to be jointly shared by progressive spirits in the early 1980s. If the claim that gender equality was an empty dream within the context of a growing economy was met with shock, its corollary led many of his former readers to turn their backs on him: *equity* between the genders (Illich never used the term *equality*) required a thorough reassessment of the premise on which the economy relied, namely scarcity—

1 For a lively account of what took place in the months he spent at the *Wissenschaftskolleg*, see Pörksen, 2014. For a list of Illich's fellow students (who also included Gerschom Scholem) between 1981 and 1982, *cf.* pp. 226–227.

an explanation which, at the time, raised a number of questions. Contrary to the belief that scarcity could only be reduced by increasing the production of goods and services considered to be in short supply, Illich maintained that *the limiting scarcity was only compatible with a reduction of all economic productions, whether material or otherwise*. Moreover, the notion that the tools themselves had a gender, i.e., that they could be associated either with the male or female world, appeared to disregard a fundamental postulate of modern industrial society, namely that the egalitarian access to gender-neutral tools and institutions was the inalienable right of every human being.

It did indeed look as if Illich intended to project onto a progressive modernity, which was ideally *unisex*, the knowledge he acquired in the kitchens of an obscure Mexican village.

Teaching in the US and in Germany

In the autumn of 1982, Illich gave eight lectures at the University of California in Berkeley, which he delivered on a weekly basis, on the subject of vernacular gender. The two months he spent there clearly marked the change of course that he had finally entered and which had been in the works since 1976. I would first like to discuss the bibliographic volume that collected his writings and then to address the above-mentioned change of direction.

In 2005, a group of his friends and students from the University of Bremen in Germany published a bibliography[2] of Illich's work that was deemed to be complete. The list began with the dissertation he wrote for his PhD in history which he was awarded in 1951: *Die philosophische Grundlagen der Geschichtsschreibung bei Arnold Joseph Toynbee* ('The Philosophical Foundations of Toynbee's Historiography'). The works he wrote between 1971 and 1976 (the period in which he became a media sensation and published what he later described as 'his *pamphlets*')[3] were displayed on the first four pages, while the works

2 Collectif des amis de Brème, 2005. Thierry Paquot has developed an excellent summary of that list (2012, pp. 114–121).

3 See especially *Deschooling Society* (1971), *Energy and Equity* (1973), *Tools for*

completed after 1976 were inventoried from page 5 to 26.

From a quantitative point of view, the works included in the second group were three or four times more numerous than those in the first. There was another quantitative difference, however. While many of his books dating to the 1970s were printed in hundreds of thousands of copies, his later work enjoyed a much more limited circulation: although the sales of some of his books reached tens of thousands of copies, most only sold a few thousand, and his articles appeared either in smaller magazines or as self-published dossiers (which were mainly issued by groups of students from the Pennsylvania State University and the University of Bremen).[4]

In 1982, Illich was invited, with all the honors, to hold an autumn seminar of seven weekly sessions at the University of California in Berkeley, which was then at the forefront of academic critical thought. As the weeks went by, tension mounted between the teaching staff that attended the seminar and the speaker, for reasons that were not immediately apparent but which came to light many years later, as I am going to elucidate in Chapter 5.[5] There are two considerations that must be made here in connection with Illich's change of attitude:

1. Illich had no desire to be bound by the sense of 'responsibility' towards his regular readers, which some expected him to feel. Indeed, he had come to realize that the alternative would have forced him to acquiesce in perpetuating two of the mirages they nurtured. The first was the belief that the citizens of the rich countries had the responsibility to improve the condition of the poor ones, while the second was the illusion that industrial society could actually achieve the equality between men and

Conviviality (1973a), *Medical Nemesis: The Expropriation of Health* (1975).

4 Besides the series that was edited by his students at Penn State and at the University of Bremen, see also the *Oakland Tables* publications issued at the time when Illich's friend Jerry Brown was the mayor of Oakland.

5 The most thorough account of that incident may possibly be found in the book which Martina Kaller-Dietrich devoted to Ivan Illich's life and thought (2007, pp. 165–168 and 177–181).

women it had promised to deliver.

2. Illich was tired of repeating the same arguments of his *pamphlets* repeatedly in his seminars, and at the same time somehow sensed that most of his regular readers were not going to approve of his new ideas. He therefore decided to dissociate himself from any putative role as 'cultural idol' or 'guru' with which they might have wished to invest him.[6]

After CIDOC was closed down in 1976, Illich rejected two different kinds of offer. He first refused to join the hired teaching staff of any university regardless of its reputation, as Professor Nathan Glazer from Harvard University had asked him to do. He subsequently considered the opportunity he was given to move the center of his activities to Paris, but he ended up turning the offer down, fearing as he did, with a good measure of anxiety, that he would eventually be swallowed up by the world of 'those cousins of his,' as he once commented sarcastically. In the early 1980s, conversely, he signed a contract with the Department of Condensed Matter Physics within the Faculty of Physics of the Pennsylvania State University (Penn State), in which the Bengali physicist Rustum Roy had opened a small STS center (meant to address the study of the relation between Science, Technology and Society). Illich committed himself to delivering an evening seminar once a week. I was invited to some of the first sessions, and I remember that in its initial phase that initiative only managed to attract about half a dozen students. I also recall that one of them once asked him whether he was related to a gentleman of the same name who had made quite a stir ten years before. Was he perhaps an uncle or a cousin of his? In a fairly short time, nonetheless, Illich succeeded in drawing a large audience once again.

While he continued to teach at Penn State, in the five-year period between 1990 and 1995, Illich also gave weekly seminars

6 Barbara Duden (2010, p. 137) inquired into the causes behind 'the changed attitude of the public's reception of Ivan Illich,' and quoted David Cayley (1992): 'Illich was a man who managed to escape his own glory because he refused to remain shackled to the positions he was the first to explore, and which he later presented once again.'

to Professor Rykwert's students at the University of Pennsylvania in Philadelphia (Penn). The topics he addressed included: proportionality in the history of architecture, the orders in Italian architecture,[7] the rituals associated with the founding of cities in Antiquity, and the art of dwelling in a place. Between 1989 and 2002, Illich also taught for three months a year at the University of Bremen.

A very pleasant subversive plan

Illich harbored a subversive plan: shifting the universities' center of gravity from the classrooms to rooms endowed with a good supply of wine and a kitchen in which to cook spaghetti, and located close to a well-stocked library. Indeed, Illich saw friendship as the only ground from which *scientia*, or science in its noblest sense, could successfully blossom. Besides his weekly seminar, he offered the academic community something that no other university could provide with the same degree of intensity, or indeed the same atmosphere: his *living-room conversations*. By capitalizing on his boundless convening powers, he invited the best thinkers and writers to those meetings in order to get them to engage with the topics that were meant to be addressed during that week's conversation: the architectural historian and philosopher Joseph Rykwert on the subjects of the house, the threshold[8] and the city; the historian of the body Barbara Duden on the weakening of the somatic perceptions of a body created by means of anatomical and physiological descriptions; the German Egyptologist Jan Assmann on *ma'at* and the perception of truth, justice and cosmic harmony in Egypt at the time of the Pharaohs; the Norwegian criminologist Nils Christie, who saw crime prevention by means of detention in jail merely as a growing industry, especially in the USSR and the US; the psy-

7 Translator's Note: 'In general terms, architecture defines an *order* as a series of similar elements which are aligned horizontally, such as windows, arches, niches, shelves, etc.'

8 Translator's Note: Illich stressed the importance of 'thresholds' as the element that made for the distinction between the street and the house, and between the external space and the internal one into which one is invited in order to enjoy friendship and sharing. See Illich, 2005, pp. 146–152.

chologist and philosopher Bob Kugelman; the phenomenologist Robert Romanyshyn; the German medievalist Ludolf Kuchenbuch, who studied textual history and the relation between writing and orality; Aleida Assmann, a historian of literature and an ethnographer of popular cultural memory; the Mexican activist Gustavo Esteva;[9] and Teodor Shanin, a great expert on rural cultures and the founder of the Moscow School of Social and Economic Sciences, who told us at length about the extensive transformations that were underway in the USSR at the time of *glasnost* and *perestroika*.

Those conversations usually took place on weekends in a house that Illich jointly rented with the historian Barbara Duden on Foster Avenue at Penn State. Credit must be given to Josh Mailman from New York who, for a while, volunteered to supply wine, which was excellent. In this regard, it may perhaps be appropriate to dispel here a lingering prejudice against US oenology. I remember with special fondness a first-rate white wine from New York, whose vineyard of origin was obviously not situated at the foot of skyscrapers but rather in upstate New York. After his weekly evening seminar, Illich opened his house (which was only a few steps away from the Pattee Library), his kitchen, his cellar, and his private library to whoever was willing to delve further into the topics that had just been discussed.

In parallel to the three-month course that he held every year at the Pennsylvania State University, he embarked on a similar experience at a number of German universities: the one in Kassel (where the rector of the *Gesamthochschule*, Ernst-Ulrich von Weizsäcker, had already invited him to give a cycle of twelve conferences during the 1979–1980 winter semester), in Marburg, in Oldenburg, and finally in Bremen, where he gave various seminars and welcomed to his table all those who wished to prolong their meditation on the topics at hand, and where he was equally active for a three-month period every year. It was in that Hanseatic city that that migratory bird established his last nest. For more than ten years, he held his weekly seminars on

9 During the 1980s and 1990s, Esteva published a great number of Illich's texts in the two weekly magazines he directed consecutively, *El Gallo Ilustrado* and *Opciones*, with the present author's technical help and support as translator and editor.

Friday evenings to allow the conversations which had started in the classroom to continue in the living room of Barbara Duden's place in Kreftingstrasse; these lasted well into Saturday, and sometimes even into the following Sunday, fully in keeping with the tradition of his living-room conversations at Penn State. His table witnessed the emergence of a circle of intellectuals who, after discarding their professional blinkers, had engaged in reflections on the meaning of appropriate measure and proportionality, on the history of the body or 'historical somatics,' on the history of the senses (sight, hearing, and touch), and, in contrast to the carnal burdens of the past, also on the experience of scarcity in a disincarnated world.

Illich's innovative university practices were particularly well received in Bremen, the city that awarded him its annual Culture and Peace Prize (*Kultur und Friedenspreis der Stadt Bremen*) in 1998. Illich felt that that prize somehow brought him much closer to a poet he was very fond of, Paul Celan (who was born in Chernovitz in Bukovina, an area on the Carpathian Mountains that used to belong to Romania before the Second World War, but which is now in Ukraine), who in 1985 had been awarded the city's literary prize (*Literaturpreis der Stadt Bremen*). The city of Bremen symbolically presented Illich with the keys of the city, thereby making him an honorary citizen just as it had done with Paul Celan, quite a few of whose poems Illich knew by heart.

I somehow wish I could enable my readers to relive the situation that Illich's audience experienced at Penn State and later in Bremen, when the thought he developed after 1980 could stand on its own two feet without being propped up by his works dating to the period of his mediatic visibility. Indeed, his students found themselves tackling the later part of Illich's work *in statu nascendi*, assimilating the 'second Illich' directly without having previously got to know the 'first one.' Indeed, Thierry Paquot believes there is no point in splitting up work that displays great internal unity, at least for those who know how to read it.[10]

10 In his foreword to Illich's complete works issued in French (*Œuvres complètes*, 2005, pp. 7–22), Thierry Paquot wrote: '...Illich was not two or three different people, but rather one single person, who by means of his obstinacy, daring, and originality carried

This notwithstanding, Illich's work also included a few instances of thought disruption, which ought to be identified. One of them, which Illich acknowledged himself, was the shift of his focus from what tools *did* to what they *said*, as well as the realization that institutions could not, or no longer could, be seen as tools.[11]

Schools claim that man is a lifelong consumer of educational services: 'from sperm to worm,' as Illich stated in English; in Latin, he expressed it as *homo est homo educandus*, with a clear reference to the Latin saying *nutrix educat, magister docet*. Literally, 'a lifelong infant.' Motorized transport services maintain that man is an invalid incapable of moving on his own legs towards a destination that may have some meaning for him: *homo est homo transportandus*. Health systems argue that man is nothing other than an actual or potential patient whose perceptions are managed by doctors: *homo est homo iatrogenicus*.

Finally, I would also like to add that if there is anything that marks out Illich's post-1980 work against that of his years as a media celebrity, it is the fact that it has not yet been read as properly as it deserves to be.

Continuity and discontinuity

As a rule, the authors and the editors of recent publications on Ivan Illich have adequately presented the years between 1970 and 1980, and have mentioned that he kept on writing even after 1980, but have in fact mostly confined themselves to listing those of his works that were issued by commercial publishing houses.

on his uncompromising analysis of modern society' (p. 13). One of the theses advanced in the present book is that there is remarkable continuity between seemingly distinct domains, namely Illich's reflections on missions in the 1960s and his later criticism of development. As I see it, in an unexpected yet increasingly convincing fashion those two research lines subsequently converged into the historical philosophy of tools, the development of which Illich kept working on for about three decades.

11 'I did not notice that demarcation point at the time of my first books, and I am sorry to say I wrongly convinced some people, including some of the best ones, that it was possible to describe the education system as one of society's "tools," or the health system as an "apparatus"' (Illich and Cayley, 2005, p. 120).

> The second half of Ivan Illich's life is thus a sort of *terra incognita*—especially as far as his French 'papers' are concerned—from which two islands suddenly emerge: *Gender* [1982] and *In the Vineyard of the Text* [1991]. The first was generally deemed a blunder, and a politically incorrect one at that, while the second was seen as an unjustifiable change of course in favor of an obscure subject matter, namely the monastic way of reading and its transformation in consequence of a change in the books' typesetting procedures in the twelfth century (Duden, 2010, p. 137).

In the 1970s, Illich's work was first and foremost a matter of analyzing the counterproductivity of the industrial mode of production and the destructive consequences it had for nature, as well as the unrestrained growth of the services sector and the damage that services wrought on culture. For instance, although schools were seen as tools of education, they did in fact *turn* their customers into beings with a thwarted curiosity and a repressed autonomy.

After the turning point of the 1976–1980 period, Illich became convinced that the underlying root of the modern ecologic catastrophe was the destruction of the symbolic world, a *de-gen(d)eration* (with the implied sense of a 'loss of gender' which he attributed to that word), a *de-materialization*, a *dis-incarnation*, or a 'loss of the senses' (Illich, 2004). Furthermore, he saw a kind of symbolic reversal of the relation between the inside and the outside and the progressive elimination of every boundary or limitation. In German, he employed the word *Umstülpung*, which means 'eversion' (as when one turns a glove inside out). In the French and English languages, embryology has popularized a roughly equivalent term, *invagination*, which some philosophers have then borrowed in the figurative, 'heraldic' sense of *mise-en-abyme*.

Polanyi's influence

The symbolic eversion to which Illich referred was a historical event in the same sense that the appearance of the newly-autonomous social 'spheres' mentioned by Karl Polanyi (1944) could be said to constitute one. What the historian Illich observed, as he moved along the path that led him from the past to the present, was an uninterrupted movement of eversion, or, more literally, of *per-version* (a word I would recommend as the most suitable translation of the German *Umstülpung*), which should in no way be interpreted in a moralistic or sentimental fashion. To illustrate the great eversion represented by modernization, Illich sometimes resorted to another metaphor. Let us imagine, he would say, the pre-modern world as a multicolored Persian rug. That rug could well be a map of the world's past cultures. Each of its portions could symbolize a specific culture, quite distinct from its neighboring ones. All cultures are *different*, yet all find their place on that map. The one exception is modern culture: it is not merely different from historical cultures; it is radically *other*. To accommodate it, one would have to turn the rug over and place it on the rug's reverse side, where only a uniform gray weft is to be seen. Claiming that the world has undergone, and is still undergoing, a process of modernization is tantamount to saying that the rug of historical cultures has been turned over in such a way that whole portions of it have been upended. Cultural differences disappear, and nothing remains but the gray uniformity of their reverse side. Instead of talking of a process of modernization, one could also say that the world is becoming *Westernized*.

In his book *The Great Transformation* (1944), Polanyi described the path towards modernity as a progressive 'disembedding' process, which had led to the emergence of modernity's autonomous spheres (Education, Politics, Religion, Technique, the State, Military Arts… and especially Economy, the 'sphere' whose progressive emergence Polanyi reconstructed). For his part, what the historian Illich strove to highlight were certain critical stages of this process, the 'key moments'[12] of the world's modernization—Westernization.

12 See 'Kuchenbuch's crab' in Illich, 1992, p. 194.

The world's modernization or Westernization

With just two metaphors, Illich managed to express what modern languages still cannot formulate. First of all, he maintained that the real cosmological revolution had not been achieved by Copernicus, who placed the sun at the center of the spheres' revolution, but rather by Kepler, who managed to smash the spheres by replacing the perfect circles on which planets moved with ellipses (just as Canguilhem and Bachelard had already suggested). Thereafter, it was as if the fragments of the smashed celestial spheres had reassembled themselves as social spheres: for instance, those of Politics, Science, Medicine, Law, Religion, and especially that of Economy. Illich would then encourage me to ideally travel back in time by taking leaps from one century to the next. The first leap, he would say, will land you at the start of the twentieth century. There, you will come to the realization that the social spheres are constantly present: Education, with its hallowed places and its rituals; Medicine, with its hospitals; Science, with its universities and its institutions, Law… One leap after the other, you will reach the beginning of the nineteenth century, and then of the eighteenth, and of the seventeenth. With each leap, the landscape will change considerably, but you will still be able to identify some antecedents of the spheres you are familiar with. Yet, at the turn between the sixteenth and the fifteenth centuries, those specialized social spheres will burst like soap bubbles. Or, to be more precise, at that juncture those specialized domains will not yet have been carved out from their common cultural weft.

In his second metaphor, Illich spoke of threads, rather than of spheres. Let us imagine, he would say, that at the beginning of the twentieth century you pulled on the thread called Economy. What would eventually unravel towards you would be economy and yet more economy: prices, the law of supply and demand, inflation. The same would be equally true of the early nineteenth, eighteenth and seventeenth centuries. And the same thing would happen if you pulled on the Political thread; everything that ensues would have a political hue to it: the balance of power, the concentration of the latter into one or more pairs of hands, and issues of legitimacy. Then you come to the end of the fifteenth century, which in a broad sense marked the beginning of the modern age. You think you have finally spotted the Religion thread, you pull on it, and what is unreeled towards you has a political coloring; you pull some more, and the coloring becomes jurisprudential, or military, or scientific—an inextricable interweaving of various elements that still prevailed at the time of the discovery-conquest-invasion of America, which ushered in a reassessment of the West's geographical, economic and political ideas (*cf.* O'Gorman, 1958).

Before 1500, there were practically no separate spheres or threads in the warp that constituted European culture. Everything was encrusted, wedged, and entwined with the rest.[13]

Reclaiming modernity for history

Any discussion on a historical understanding of modernity must necessarily mention, at the other end of the spectrum, the contribution of German historiography. After the end of the Second World War, German historians found themselves in a unique position, as they were forced to assimilate a past that the German language enabled them to define as *bodenlos*: without soil, without its own place in history, abominable. Their answer to it was what they termed *Zeitgeschichte*, the 'history of the present;'[14] it was the historical recounting of a period of unprecedented horrors, a historiography that desperately struggled to contextualize the Third Reich's abominations while at the same time moving beyond that perspective. It was a historiography that did away with the separation between history and the present time and thus expanded its scope until it came to include today's history. Illich realized that in the mirror of that 'history of the present time,' the Nazi period was a grotesque prefiguration of what could eventually coagulate into being under our very eyes and what we still refused to see. In the seminars he

13 See Louis Dumont's foreword to the French edition of Karl Polanyi's book (1944).

14 Although they called it 'contemporary history' or 'new history,' some French historians, including Pierre Nora, have made a similar attempt (*cf.* Nora, 2011).

held in German, his intuition led him to draw a distinction between two historiographic approaches and two kinds of history: the 'histories of developments' (*Entwicklungsgeschichten*) on the one hand, and the 'histories of the losses' (*Verlustgeschichten*) on the other. It was not a matter of drawing a balance between gains and losses, much less of indulging in an analysis of 'costs and benefits.' It was actually a matter of having a clear view of what had been lost, without harboring any delusions about its possible restoration. I shall now compare those two approaches to writing history.

The histories of developments

Examples of what may be subsumed under the 'histories of developments' include the history of transport across the centuries, dental care, health facilities, education institutions, as well as the history of all kinds of progress, ranging from the domain of military arts to that of news broadcasting.

Official history is the epic retelling of the victories achieved over the *obstacles* posed by traditions, the delays of the past, and the underdevelopment of the traditional forms of self-organization. It is first and foremost an account of the triumphs of the State, the Market, and Technique. Official history is a history of developments. It retroactively explores the origin of the present circumstances as regards science, technology, logic, politics, or philosophy. In its rear-view mirror, the present time appears to be a point on which all of the past's movements converge. That same mirror, nonetheless, tends to record only the contributions from the past for which the present circumstances seem to constitute the inevitable point of arrival.[15]

The historiographic piecing together of those developments tends to minimize or even obliterate losses, and whenever it does acknowledge them, it offsets them against the profits.[16]

15 An attitude which Alain Caillé termed *retrodictive*, and which he attributed to Fernand Braudel (*cf.* Caillé, 1988).

16 See the analysis developed by Jean-Pierre Dupuy and Jean Robert as regards the irreparable, utter, and impossible-to-fix damage wrought in this sense; a damage which is not merely 'the destruction of a specific component of humanity's inheritance,

The history of developments is essentially the all-embracing history of anything that can be reduced to a value: Education, Health, Progress, Communications, the World Market, Development, Technology.

The histories of the losses

For those who draw their conclusions from 'sailing towards the past,' the very concept of development crumbles to pieces, because it entails the notion of 'what will come to pass' even though the future is unpredictable. Conversely, the historians of the losses are a bit like Walter Benjamin's 'Angel of History,' and observe the disappearance of whole worlds of materials, perceptions and ideas.[17]

The 'histories of the losses' include, for instance, the loss of intensity of man's smell perception, the loss of man's self-perception of his body, and the progressive elimination of traditional, *vernacular* modes of production of use values. The history of developments is basically blind to the losses which populations had to endure at the time of the great discoveries and the subsequent invasions. Even if I were to confine myself to the weakening of the intensity of perceptions during that period, I could still name quite a few studies that document the depletion of the vocabulary relating to taste, smell, and touch. The Old High German language possessed three times as many words designating pleasant smells as does its modern descendant. According to Illich, the Cartesian dimensionality's growing monopoly subsequently weakened perceptions and stifled the ability to sense auras.[18]

The worst losses over the past five centuries have concerned the forms of subsistence that are rooted in society's material cultures. The disappearance of the very words that could provide the means for a discussion of those losses is part of a

but rather the destruction of the ties that link man to the environment and the others, a destruction that leaves him folded on himself and alienated from the world...' (Dupuy and Robert, 1975, p. 24).

17 See 'Kuchenbuch's crab' in Illich, 1992, pp. 182–201.

18 See Illich, *H_2O and the Waters of Forgetfulness*, 1985, pp. 47–64.

sequence of events that the hegemony of the history of developments makes it impossible to document. Once some of the terms that used to enable distinctions between tastes and smells have vanished, it becomes quite difficult to document the weakening of their relevant perceptions. By the same token, it has now become quite difficult to speak of subsistence as something that is radically distinct from the formal economy, because the economists' language has banished to the fringes of underdevelopment the words that could have ensured such an approach. If I may now turn once more to Polanyi, I would like to stress the fact that, in his view, the centuries of modernization after the fifteenth were marked by a progressive *disembedding*, a severance, or a 'de-cosmization' of historical tissues that could, by that stage, be reconceptualized as separate spheres (*cf.* Polanyi, 1944). The history of developments also includes the history of the emergence of those separate spheres, whereas the history of the losses cannot be separated from the progressive shredding of the cosmic warp that linked together all human activities.

Those two forms of historical narration are intertwined, and, to be able to tell them apart within history's warp, it is necessary to keep a philosophical distance from them. It is not a question of denying the developments, but rather of finally understanding that they do not make up for the losses. First of all, the economic imprint on modern thought should be eliminated: the millions of Native Americans and Africans who died in the wake of the European invasion of the Americas were by no means the 'price' to be paid for the establishment of New Spain's flourishing culture, just as the slave trade and the extermination of the 'Red Skins' were not the price for North American democracy. One can simply not speak of 'prices' or 'costs' when the ensuing losses go beyond any possible form of reparation.

Chapter 4: Systems... in People's Heads

In Cuernavaca, there was a group of friends (including me) who used to meet on a regular basis to develop their reflections together with Ivan Illich, and who now still keep meeting to develop their reflections after Illich. Javier Sicilia, who is a poet, novelist, journalist, and man of action, gave us the chance to write for two magazines, which he later got to direct, *Ixtus* and *Conspiratio*. In 2003, after Illich's death, we set up a read-aloud group, in accordance with Illich's encouragement, to preserve a diversified approach to our reading. We started by meeting once a week, and we kept doing so for the following ten years. On four separate occasions, that same group of friends also convened an international conference on the meaning of Ivan Illich's thought at the dawn of the third millennium.

In March 2011, Javier Sicilia was cut to the quick when hired killers murdered his son Juan Francisco, along with six of his friends, for reporting several abuses carried out by the police. Within a few days, Javier Sicilia summoned a gathering of Mexico's 'Movement for Peace with Justice and Dignity,' which set up numerous convoys meant to travel the length and breadth of the country and urge the victims of violence, or alternatively their parents and friends, to speak up and publicly denounce the assassins. The movement also organized a convoy in the US in order to raise the awareness of that country's citizens as to the close link that existed between the legal ban on various substances classified as 'narcotics' and the extreme level of dominance over the country that Mexico's 'drug cartels' had achieved by benefiting from that same ban.

Since 2003, Javier Sicilia has been steadily assisting Valentine Borremans, who holds the copyright of Illich's work. The present chapter was shaped by a series of conversations with the above-mentioned group of readers. In our capacity as the 'Friends of Ivan Illich' in Cuernavaca, we read his writings from his 'years in Cuernavaca' and sought an answer to the following question: which of the theories he developed in those writings might deserve to be revived in our day and age, which is so different from the 1970s? Lurking right underneath that question, however, there was a second one, one that went even deeper: what kind of epistemological cataclysm underlies such a momentous change? The attempt at an answer, provided below, could perhaps be summarized as follows: what differentiates the present age from the now remote 1970s is a change in the perception of those artifacts that are still called tools, even though they have now lost most of the characteristics that marked them as such for centuries. This chapter shall therefore endeavor to identify the actual epistemological landslide that characterizes the present time.

I. The Heyday and Decline of the Age of the Tools

Ivan Illich's thought also explored the world of tools, or, as it is more commonly known, of technology. His meditation on the tools began with his encounter with Latin America at the beginning of the 1950s (and especially after he became acquainted with the concept of 'appropriate measure' formulated by Leopold Kohr, whom he met in Puerto Rico); it was advanced by his criticism of a development plan masquerading as a mission in the 1960s, as well as by his comprehension of the tools' historical nature in the 1980s until the early 1990s, when it began to be influenced by the intuition that the age of the tools might actually come to an end.

For more than seven centuries, the West was instrumental—that is to say, it revolved around the *instrumentum*.

After the end of the Middle Ages, what defined tools was the intention of those who employed them, which was usually expressed by the word 'for.' However, at the beginning of the 1990s, Illich formulated the hypothesis that once Western culture and Westernized cultures had deserted the tools with which they were familiar, and had been invaded by artifacts with very ambiguous purposes, they had tentatively set a course towards a 'farewell to the tools' that had shaken their very foundations. He also came to the realization that the concept of tool, which had guided his historical studies and his analysis of contemporary society, was about to fall apart. To be more precise, he realized that the category of instrumentality itself had turned into a purpose, because it had come to coincide with society, thereby removing the 'for' that supported it from the outside.

It was at that stage that artifacts began to proliferate, which:

- could not be defined as means pursuing clearly defined ends;
- were no longer (or were no longer exclusively) at the service of personal intentions;
- no longer possessed a direct relation with their users' body.

Since those artifacts had lost every restraint, they were no longer tools in the strictest sense of the word. Indeed, Illich defined them as 'systems.'

1. Starting from the 1970s and through 1980s, the Western world began to experience one of its greatest historical transformations, which Illich described as a 'collapse' or 'landslide.'
2. Illich launched the idea that this landslide, which could not be contained, was a symptom of the end of one of Western culture's most fundamental concepts, namely that of the tool. Traditional Western tools remained external to their users' body, or, to use a term favored by Illich, they had a relation of 'distality' to the body, understood as the distance that underlay the relation between users and tools, and which enabled the former to take or leave the latter. Since the 1970s, that relation underwent a reversal that was the prelude to its final demise; new artifacts began to multiply that were still described as tools, but which were no longer endowed with distality. He believed the loss of that feature and the emergence of artifacts that incorporated and took over their users' bodies to be the deeper reason behind the series of collapses that took place with increasing frequency from the 1970s and 1980s.

When Illich was planning to write an epilogue to the industrial age

In his 1973 introduction to *Tools for Conviviality*, Illich wrote:[1]

> Over the next several years I intend to work on an epilogue to the industrial age. I want to trace the changes in language, myth, ritual and law which took place in the current epoch of packaging and of schooling. I want to describe the fading monopoly of the industrial mode of production and the vanishing of the industrially generated professions this mode of production serves (Illich, 1973a, p.ix).

As the French and Mexican editions of Illich's complete works show, after *Tools for Conviviality* he published many books and articles that represented a clear step in that direction. This notwithstanding, he never got round to writing the epilogue he had announced. In my view, that was due to the fact that the sun went down on the industrial mode of production well before he could act, or, to be more precise, that the scope of that sunset (which Illich was the first to discern) has been so wide as to go beyond the two centuries which can reasonably be ascribed to the industrial age. Illich suddenly understood, or believed to have understood, that the years between 1970 and 1980 were witnessing the beginning of the decline of what the historians from the *École des Annales*[2] had described as a *temporal movement of Longue Durée*, i.e., in the present case, the age of the tools, the last incarnation of which was the industrial age.

Illich never wrote the epilogue he had promised. Nonetheless, in his short essays and in his conversations, he outlined a compelling picture of the epilogue to an age that had lasted for

1 The foreword Illich wrote for the Italian edition of his book read as follows: 'I first developed the idea of a multidimensional analysis of industrial overdevelopment in 1971, in a working paper which I prepared together with Valentina Borremans as a starting text for a Latin-American conference to be held at the *Centro intercultural de documentación* (CIDOC) in January 1972… After nine months I then wrote two versions of it that were intended for publication: one in English, the other in French. The present text in Italian does not constitute yet another version of the same, but neither is it a mere translation of the French text: indeed, it includes my answers to the punctilious, respectful, and fitting observations made by my Italian editor, Donato Barbone' (Illich, 1973a, Italian translation, pp. 7–8).

2 Translator's Note: See footnote 12 on p. 43.

about eight centuries: the age of the tools.

A hypothesis that has to be handled with care

I am fully aware that what I have just written above will not necessarily meet with the favor of my readers. A new idea has much to gain from being presented as a hypothesis open for debate. The idea that the late industrial age may be characterized as an epilogue is countered by the extant clear signs of intensified industrial production: the frenzied building of factories, dams, thermal and nuclear power plants, urban elevated highways, the growing distances covered in the commuters' daily migrations, the concentration of housing areas in places that are increasingly removed from the industrial ones, *fracking*, plans to link Asia and America by rail... Could I myself refrain from defining those works and those concentrations as 'industrial?' Indeed, I could not. Therefore, how is it possible to say that the industrial age has ceased to be instrumental, and that industry has become 'post-instrumental?' For my part, I take this notion seriously and consequently wonder: in what way could one speak of a 'non-instrumental' prolongation of the industrial age, i.e., of a prolongation that is not based on tools understood in a classical sense? If I were asked by my readers to expand on this point, I could possibly suggest a concept of Greek origin, the *hysteresis* ('delay'), which may be defined as the persistence of an effect long after the disappearance of its initial cause. I could also add that the characteristics of a given age may become magnified at the time of the latter's decline.

Illich, however, tackled those questions from the perspective of a historian. Everything that has an end must necessarily also have had a beginning. If something began to enter its decline around the 1970s or the 1980s, what was it exactly? And when did it have its inception? To that double question, Illich provided a precise answer. With regard to the 'what,' Illich replied: the new concept of tool; with regard to its beginning, he pointed out twelfth-century scholastic texts such as *De variis artibus* by Theophilus Presbyter (*cf.* Dodwell, 1961) and *Didascalicon* by Hugo of Saint Victor (*cf.* Lemoine, 1991), both of which have been dated by most historians to the year 1128. The new concept of tools was believed to have subsequently paved the way for a new, long-lasting historical age: the age of the tools. That was Illich's hypothesis.

The historicity of the tools

The industrial age was chock-full of machinery, equipment, and technical devices that concomitantly supplied both services and jobs. The 'solution' to every 'problem' that might have arisen in the course of that cycle consisted in the acquisition of an even greater quantity of equipment. The most generic term employed to designate the 'problem-solving' elements that populate the landscape of the industrial age is 'tool,' a word which describes a kind of artifact that in the twelfth century began to be called in Latin *instrumentum*. Illich confessed to David Cayley that when he had written *Tools for Conviviality*, he had seen tools as just tools, or, to put it differently, that he had believed tools to be coextensive with human history and to have always existed. Medieval, Greek, Egyptian, Neolithic or Paleolithic craftsmen devised and used tools regardless of whether they were primitive or refined, simple or complex, made of stone or metal. To Illich's mind at the time of writing *Tools for Conviviality*, tools were, despite all of their patent differences, one of history's constant features.

Illich also told Cayley that his intuition on the historicity of the tools had begun to take shape in the course of his conversations with the philosopher of engineering and technology, Carl Mitcham, who was one of his colleagues within the Science, Technology, and Society Program at Pennsylvania State University (Illich, 2004, p. 261, footnote 1). Historicity did not concern what tools were in terms of their shape or material composition, but rather the *ideas* and the *concepts* that underlay them. Classical Greeks, for instance, envisaged a hammer (which was no less of a hammer than the modern tool bearing the same name) as an extension of the hand that wielded it. The Greek word *organon* was what designated the tool. A hammer was thus an organ just like the hand that held it, while hands were described as 'the organ above all organs.' *Organon* qualified 'anything that could help human beings fulfill their essence.'[3] Every artifact that matched that definition was therefore termed an *organic tool*. Each organic tool was *suited* for a specific hand at the time, the axe for the farmer's hand, and the sword for a free man of noble birth (*kaloskagathos*).

In the twelfth century, a number of scholastic writings began to index a new concept of tool under the name *instrumentum*. This *non-organic* tool, which was actually instrumental (a concept that was originally more theological than technological), was defined by its reference to the hand's conceptual independence and could consequently be called an *instrumentum separatum*. The notion of the tool's conceptual disconnection from the hand made the tool available to everybody, which, a few centuries later, led to the emergence of huge armies of farmers equipped with swords and daggers. In rough terms, that was the line of discussion pursued by the conversations between Ivan Illich and Carl Mitcham on the *historicity of the concept of tools*.[4]

The concept of instrumentality in its philosophical context

In the twelfth century, the idea arose that angels, or beings made of pure fire and immaterial, were in charge of ruling celestial bod-

3 *Cf.* Grönemeyer, 2012, pp. 102–111 (the title of her book's Italian translation is: *Chi lavora pecca. Un appello per la difesa del buon lavoro*). Marianne Grönemeyer wrote that, according to Aristotle, 'an *organon* is anything that helps living beings live and contributes to their health.' In her works, the author claimed that the soul 'must fulfill the essence of what it is meant to become.' For that reason, a soul 'needs a new body... made in such a way as to be able to support it in the accomplishment of its tasks.' Every living being has to perform all the acts which are required for it to 'become what it is.' From the twelfth century onward, there obtained the dissolution of the 'inseparable interplay between soul and body, which had previously enabled the latter to become what it could and had to be... and tools, which had assisted the body—in its interplay with the soul—could subsequently be isolated.' The separation of the tools from the hand and the demise of the notion that tools were at the service of the soul's becoming turned tools into 'means' in a new way: they were no longer an intermediary 'between two,' as Plato's proportion (*analogía*) had been, but rather *instrumental means* with arbitrary purposes.

4 Mitcham sent me his version of the conversations he had with Ivan Illich, which I have translated into Spanish but which still awaits publication. For the English publication, see Mitcham, 2018.

ies.[5] Since they were pure spirits, they needed intermediaries to influence matter. Thus, according to Illich, planets were employed as tools to move celestial spheres. The teachings of St. Thomas Aquinas concerning this topic, which relied on six or seven hundred years' worth of ideas, images and Neoplatonic concepts, 'represented the universe as a hierarchy ruled by a sovereign that was even greater than Charlemagne' (Illich, 2005, p. 74).

According to that view of the cosmos, the *instrumentum* was first and foremost at the service of *divine intentions*. In their capacity as tools in the hands of God, priests may administer sacraments regardless of their personal qualities. In the same way that a lead pipe could convey water just as efficiently as a silver pipe, St. Thomas Aquinas suggested that a mediocre priest could channel divine grace just as well as a good one.[6]

In the twelfth century, the intentions behind the use of tools became more humanized, and European culture became progressively instrumental: it did so tentatively at first and in a more aggressive fashion after the fourteenth century. It developed (or endeavored to develop, sometimes centuries before it became materially possible to do so) tools and instruments suited for all possible *intentions*, including that of flying like birds. Later, in the shadow of colonialism and in the wake of Development, Europe (i.e., the West) offered those tools to the whole world.[7] The refusal to accept that offer was branded as a sign of barbarism. The lack of Western tools was defined as underdevelopment. As Illich noted, by the end of the twentieth century,

5 In reference to this point, Illich quoted the work of a forgotten historian, Thomas Litt, who wrote a book on celestial bodies (Litt, 1963). *Cf.* Illich, 2005, p. 73.

6 *...sicut dictum est, ministri Ecclesiae instrumentaliter operantur in sacramentis, eo quod quodammodo eadem ratio est ministri et instrumenti. Sicut autem supra dictum est, instrumentum non agit secundum propriam formam, sed secundum virtutem ejus a quo movetur. Et ideo accidit instrumentum, inquantum est instrumentum, qualemcumque formam vel virtutem habeat, praeter id quod exigitur ad rationem instrumenti; sicut quod corpus medici, quod est instrumentum animae habeantis artem, sit sanum vel infirmum; et sicut quod fistula, per quam transit aqua, sit argentea vel plumbea. Unde ministri Ecclesiae possunt sacramenta conferre, etiamsi sint mali* (III., q. 64, a. 5, c).

7 'Science, State, and market are based on a system of knowledge about man, society and nature that claims to be valid for everybody and everywhere. Since it is knowledge that has successfully discarded the last vestiges of its peculiar origin, place and context, it does not belong to any specific place, and can consequently spread everywhere' (Sachs, 1992, p. 435).

many of those that were still called 'tools' no longer answered merely human intentions: they had become 'a-human,' a word which in my opinion has the same meaning as 'systemic.'

That cultural crisis was for Illich also a profound crisis of the instrumental certainties, a crisis whose scope was like the one in the twelfth century, when the concept of *organon* was replaced. However, contrary to the meaning of the Greek word *krisis*, which entails taking a decision and overcoming the obstacle, the crisis of the instrumental paradigm, which was being experienced in the modern age, left no leeway for real decisions nor afforded enough critical distance to examine it from the outside. It therefore seemed that our society was experiencing an insoluble crisis of instrumental, economic, and colonialist ideas or concepts, those very ideas which were implicit in the concept of Development and of Western culture's superiority. As Illich suggested, at the epicenter of that cultural earthquake was the crumbling certainties concerning the tools' nature, which had never been questioned before. In other words, the contemporary crisis seemed to reveal the demise of the instrumental categories that had for a long time characterized the West. In Illich's view, that progressive demise constituted the actual telling sign that the *instrumental age*, or *age of the tools*, had reached its end:

> If it is true that 'tool' is a concept that can be situated within a specific age or era and is distinctive of a given period, a period in which the concept of tool, or technology, as one more often says, becomes perhaps the most unquestionable of everyday certainties, then the possibility is opened of doing what I have been trying to do during the last fifteen or twenty years: to claim, or at least establish the hypothesis, that sometime during the 1980s the technological society which began in the fourteenth century came to an end (Illich, 2005, p. 77).

The genius of Illich's historical research consisted in the concomitant exploration of the age of the tools in light of its beginning and with a keen eye trained on its end, an end which took on the appearance of a crisis that could not be solved and was consequently irreversible.

A 'long-lasting crisis' is an oxymoron

A crisis with no end, no solution, no critical moment, a crisis that goes on indefinitely, would entail an endless decision-making process, and that would be an oxymoron. Being forced to take decisions forever would be tantamount to 'a paralysis of any real power of decision,' as the geneticist Silja Samerski wrote in her doctoral dissertation that documented the counseling meetings for pregnant women in which 'kind consultants' actively prepared them to take 'informed decisions.' In those sessions, women were informed of their coming child in terms of risk profiles developed in laboratories and population estimates.[8]

The decision-making aspect of a crisis entails a distance and a lapse of time, a spatial and temporal boundary of sorts, the freedom to say, 'I would need a moment to think about it,' and a chance to breathe. In his conversations with Illich, David Cayley once asked him a question about time, and was given the following reply:

> If I rightly understand you, you are fishing for my reflections, or even feelings, about the mood in what is called postmodern poetry, novels, and philosophy, about what has happened to the temporal dimension, to temporality in the course of our lifetime. How has that passage, that mountain we came across in the 1970s, affected our sense of—I use the word for lack of anything better—timeliness and spatiality and frontier—the three inevitably go together. Now, in order to speak of this transition, this transformation, the transmogrification to which you allude—we both know what you are alluding to even though we are not quite certain of precisely what we are speaking about, and that's one of the

8 Her dissertation has been published in English (Samerski. 2015). On the same topic, see also the speech she gave in Lucca as part of the conference *Ivan Illich. Le paci dei popoli* ('Ivan Illich. The peaces of the peoples') under the title 'Il mito della scelta informata e dell'autonomia. Come le decisioni personali e libere divengono illusione in un mondo dominato dal rischio' ('The myth of autonomous and informed decision making. How free and personal decisions become an illusion in a risk-dominated world,' Samerski, 2005). The conference proceedings are also available online at: https://www.provincia.lucca.it/sites/default/files/16_maggio_2005.pdf

> difficulties in this particular conversation—in order to understand this transmogrification, I at least have to look at it historically (Illich, 2005, pp. 180–181).

Our fundamental certainties, those which are usually taken for granted and which for decades, or even centuries, were the basis for Western philosophical, social, economic, and political ideas and concepts, have all become weaker over the past thirty or forty years. Or, to put it more precisely: the axioms on which our social theorems rested have become shaky. In his last conversations with David Cayley, Illich ascribed the crisis of civilization that affects the modern age to a far-reaching metamorphosis of the ideas and perceptions that for many centuries had shaped the West with a relative degree of coherence. At the present stage, one may be tempted to suggest that a potential way out of that 'crisis' could consist in the re-establishment of the instrumental categories. The thinkers and artists who have infringed upon those categories in the fields of logic, mathematics, geometry, or music ought to be banned in the name of common sense! Nonetheless, Illich's research during the 1980s and the 1990s did not move in that direction. By no means did Illich wish to see the instrumental categories restored.

The blessings that still gratify us

In the conversations which I mentioned above, Ivan Illich presented David Cayley with two arguments. The first of them ran as follows:

> In this world I couldn't find a better situation in which to live with those I love, and those are exactly people who are overwhelmingly aware of the fact that they have passed beyond a threshold. And because they are no longer so deeply imbued by the spirit of instrumentality, or of futility, they can understand what I mean by gratuity. I do believe that there is a way of being understood today when you speak about gratuity, and gratuity in its most beautiful flowering, is praise, mutual enjoyment, and what some people, such as those who propose a new orthodoxy, discover, is that the message of Christianity is

> that we live together praising the fact that we are where we are and who we are, and that contrition and forgiveness are part of that which we celebrate, doxologically (Illich, 2005, p. 229).

Illich's second argument stated:

> The age in which instrumentality was a key that increasingly opened all doors lasted from the twelfth century to sometime during the lifetime of my audience. There's nobody in my audience without one foot in the age of instrumentality. And they are barely aware of the fact that they have passed over into the age of systems,… in which you can't speak about the instrument anymore (Illich, 2005, p. 204).

Illich's first argument celebrated the end of an age in which everything had its usefulness, and an ever-decreasing number of things were supplied gratuitously. The second suggested that many of our contemporaries might have unconsciously slipped into a new age that is even more ruthless than the previous one: the era or the age of the systems. It is necessary to keep those two moments in Illich's thought distinct: he first celebrated the demise of the instrumental categories as an opportunity for renewed freedom; he then proceeded to mention the threat posed by a far bleaker order. The hope he pinned on the new possibilities opened up by the demise of instrumentality converged with the hope Jacques Ellul placed in a 'sudden burst of freedom.'[9]

The second quotation conveyed Illich's fear that a new 'history of the developments' was about to begin, a history in which every invention and development could contribute to strengthening the integration of all apparatuses (whether material, institutional, or intellectual) into a well-oiled system,[10] a

9 Moreover, a communication from Daniel Cérézuelle dating to May 2007 stated: 'Throughout his work Ellul specified that against the "power of things" (of Technology, of the State) a sudden burst can always take place, albeit with great difficulty. For instance, in *À contre-courant* he wrote: "I am still convinced that man remains free to begin something different from what seems to be inevitable." And in *La Technique ou l'enjeu du siècle* he added: "Is there really no other way to accomplish such work? I believe there is."'

10 See Ellul, 1977, Italian translation, pp. 15–16: 'Technology is not satisfied with

windowless prison, deprived of any external space, otherness, or beyond.

It is necessary to remind those who believe that this threshold has already been crossed that the future does not exist as a *time that was once the present*, and that, inasmuch as the future is a form of present still in the making, the present time will necessarily have to become the object of criticism: 'We do not wish to live in the shadow of the future!' Illich's contribution to that criticism consisted mainly in his essays on: the post-industrial transformation of the concepts of boundary, spatiality, and temporality; the vestiges of vernacular genre in the late industrial age; the never-irredeemable loss of the senses; what survives of the right sense of proportion; and the blessings which we still can enjoy.

On 23 March 1996, Illich gave a conference to the members of the *Catholic Philosophical Association* in Los Angeles.[11] The topic he had chosen was the historical emergence of what has just been discussed above: a new concept of tools, the instrumental means that in the twelfth century consigned organic tools to history's dustbin. The latter were not mentally disconnected from the hand and expressed a correspondence between the body and the cosmos. The new notion of tools, conversely, shattered that cosmic correspondence. The main argument of Illich's speech was that the perception of the extant difference between organs and tools '[had] become a necessary prerequisite for ascetic practice, i.e., of the quest for a good life in the world of technology.' Drawing such a distinction avoids confusion between the useful production of a given service with the love of neighbor: 'The instrumentalization of tools has blinded,

being and, in our world, with being the *main factor* or determinant: it has become a System… I would like to emphasize that industrialization is characterized by a proliferation of machinery and by a certain organization of production: two technical factors. Today's industrialization, which is still considerable, has very little in common with that of the nineteenth century, and even more importantly, it is plunged in a set of equally important phenomena which it partially determined, but which have become detached from it, and by gaining volume have acquired a power of transformation that escapes the control of industry proper. Contemporary society is still industrialized, but that is no longer its most essential characteristic.'

11 'Ascesis in the Age of Systems: Philosophical Propaedeutics to the Christian Use of Instruments,' in Illich, 2004, pp. 261–267.

numbed and deafened the sense of gratuitous love, it has led to confusion between love and service, and has drowned out the Good News' (Illich, 2004, p. 262).

The notion of a special intention resting within tools is a specifically Western one, just like sex or speed measured in miles per hour (two non-comparable dimensions that cannot be mutually proportional). Hence, the danger that the Churches may justify the growth of state-run service agencies aimed at an ever-expanding customer base. What Illich feared the most, however, was in fact the symbolic value of such growth: namely, that instrumental values could overshadow people's vocation to mercy. Ancient Greeks envisaged an ax as an *organon*, an organ on a par with their skin, their knife, or their hand, 'the organ of all organs.' Over the second Christian millennium, nonetheless, an ax was redefined as an *instrumentum*. Illich saw that conceptual shift as a decisive step towards the modern world. Illich believed that if the notion of an 'instrumentalization' of the tools during the High Middle Ages were taken up by the philosophy of technology, the essential difference between organic tools and instrumental means could eventually become its cornerstone. That was not to be, however. Most philosophers of technology have never really become aware of the difference between organic instruments and instrumental means, and their understanding of tools and 'technology' is consequently completely ahistorical. Furthermore, the modern man no longer defines himself as a builder of tools, but rather as their user. Each of the tools he now employs represents an intention that was defined by a planner, an educationalist, or an engineer. Tools and technology are nowadays placed within a heteronomous sphere that discourages all forms of fundamental philosophical reflection.

The same period in which the transition from organic tools to instrumental means took place also witnessed another change: to Aristotle's four causes (*causa materialis*, *causa formalis*, *causa efficiens*, and *causa finalis*), a fifth one was added, the *causa instrumentalis*. In a way, this cause enabled the substitution of the tools with those who perform a given action. The eleventh and the twelfth centuries, for instance, saw the spread of a new kind of plow (the moldboard plow) that required less strength and ability on the part of its users. That new tool was therefore capable of mentally replacing people as the *instrumental cause* of plowing.

A few personal considerations on the epilogue to the instrumental age

I shall now list some of the characteristics of the concept of tool which emerged since the twelfth century and which, according to Illich, began to disappear in the 1970s and the 1980s.[12]

1. In the twelfth century, it became possible to conceive tools or instruments as means aimed at a well-defined purpose; every means that had a predefined end or objective could thus be described as a tool. In consideration of the fact that they too had a predefined objective, from the nineteenth century onward, service institutions such as schools, transport and hospitals also began to be seen as tools.
2. Tools were at the service of *personal* intentions that had somehow become incorporated into the tools themselves and had become 'instrumentalized.'
3. This notwithstanding, since it was a *causa instrumentalis*, a tool or an instrument was a cause that lacked intention.
4. Tools were kept distinct from the hand that held them; they were in fact in a *distal* relation to it: their *distality*[13] constituted a critical distance that afforded the decision to take or leave the tools.

12 The sources from which this fairly succinct summary of the *instrumental tools'* characteristics has been drawn are essentially Chapters 4, 13 and 18 in Illich, 2005, pp. 64–79; pp. 157–168; pp. 201–204, and a few chapters in Illich, 2004 (Italian translation, pp. 147–215 and 261–267).

13 'Distality' designates the distance between one part and the whole, in relation to what is considered to be the central point of reference. There is a well-defined distance between the hand and the center of the body. The tools' distality defines their distance, or rather their separation, from the body. Artifacts that integrate their users as if the latter were a part of themselves lose what has been a defining characteristic of the new concept of tools since the twlelfth century: distality. Systems turn those 'who use them' into sub-systems. The medical check-ups performed by kind facilitators who are also medical experts turn into implantation sessions of the 'perceptions' which patients require to function as a sub-system of the bio-medical system.

5. Anything that was endowed with usefulness could be seen as a tool: *usefulness* was a characteristic associated with *instrumentality*.
6. Bodies were physically placed *face to face* with tools.

The association of tools with well-defined intentions and their *face-to-face* relation with their users' bodies clearly indicated that each tool was by its very nature limited and was used opposite or outside something that was not the tool itself. After 1980, Illich began to become aware of the sudden appearance of devices that were coextensive with the social space and were devoid of distality, which he described as systems. I believe that to be the point in time when the beginning of the epilogue to the age of the tools should be situated.

II. The Epilogue to the Age of the Tools: Tools Which No Longer Deserve Their Name, and Institutions Which are No Longer Tools

The systems' loss of any external space destabilized the ground on which Illich had built his criticism of the tools in the 1970s. Before 1976, he had taken a special interest in what tools did and in their material consequences. At a later stage, towards the end of the 1970s, he had paid great attention to what they said, and to their symbolic repercussions. However, in a world in which tools (which were still external to the body) were expelled from the systems (which lacked a space that was external to them), it became quite difficult to draw a distinction between what they did and what they said. Systems dictated their imperatives without differentiating between what was real and what was symbolic, and imposed on their users what they were and what they were meant to be. Systems 'swallowed up' their users and turned them into a part of themselves by integrating them as sub-systems.
Waiting for Godot

The industrial age designated the whole of its tools with the word 'technology,' and it was the technological imperative that led poor countries to import their tools and needs from the rich ones. In the 'technical system' which threatens to supplant the industrial age, that same word technology identifies the systems in their entirety, thereby making the distinction between tools and systems rather difficult. Consequently, the *systemic commandment* stealthily takes the place of the technological imperative. In my opinion, that was Illich's main intuition as regards the analogy between waiting for Godot in Beckett's renowned play, and waiting for the end of the industrial age: the impossibility of parting ways with the tools, as well as the near-impossibility of perceiving the scope of the age of the systems and of appreciating its specificity, namely its lack of any external space whatsoever.

Before the industrial age, being a tool, or, to put it in another way, what defined a tool as such, i.e., its instrumentality, was situated in a dimensional container underneath a set of thresholds that were hard to cross: Napoleon I's armies could not march faster than Caesar's. The new powers of the industrial age enabled the crossing of those thresholds and allowed for any 'natural' limitations to be disregarded. Napoleon III took pride in having covered 56 miles in an hour. The industrial man, nonetheless, does not appear to be able to understand that beyond those thresholds and limitations, tools may in fact lose their instrumental nature, their being tools. When that happens, they do not merely become counterproductive, but they also end up turning into something different from a tool even though they are still described as such.[14] Illich managed to outline that transformation of the tools into something different from the tools by bringing into the picture the loss of their being distinct from the body: a system is different from a tool because it swallows up its user's body and turns it into a part of itself.

Firstly, the industrial tools' counterproductivity referred to the fact that they produced the opposite of what they promised, in ever-growing quantities and with ever-increasing frequency. For instance, whenever transport tools (i.e., vehicles) get their users stuck in traffic, they deserve to be deemed coun-

14 For the hypothesis that the Western and Westernized worlds are emerging from the age of the tools only to descend into the age of the systems, see Chapters 13 ('The age of the systems') and 18 ('From the tools to the systems') in Illich, 2005, pp. 157–168 and 198–202.

terproductive. Secondly, that means that if they keep preserving their size and power beyond a certain level, they will inevitably end up losing the characteristics that qualify them as tools. By that stage, however, it will become impossible to describe them as counterproductive, because their purpose will have ceased to be human. For instance, if one of transport's hidden purposes was to wear out citizens to such an extent as to discourage every form of rebellion, then the imposition of three or four hours' worth of compulsory 'daily migrations' from their homes to the factories and back could be described as politically productive. By the same token, the computer now sitting on my table is not a tool in the same way as a hammer would be, because the fact that it is part of an anonymous control system entails that, strictly speaking, it does not obey my intentions. In a way, my computer is spying on me, and allowing it to do so is not part of my intentions. If a personal computer is redefined as an artifact of social control, the vague sense of unease that ensues could, in certain contexts that are removed from people's daily lives, be seen as 'productive.' In a similar fashion, as Sajay Samuel has pointed out, 'the production of danger becomes a resource for risk management' (Samuel, 2010, p. 190).

At the time when Illich was analyzing counterproductivity in the 1970s, he was faced with a world in which tools and institutions matched human intentions that were easy to understand, and whose definition could provide underlying support for his criticism: under the aegis of the 1970s' education industry, the incentive to the desire to learn constituted the benchmark against which schools were evaluated, and to the extent that they did not stimulate autonomous learning they could with reason be deemed to be 'counterproductive.' In the context of this analysis, the tools' actual impact (what they do) could be seen as a departure from what they promise. For instance, beyond a given threshold of permissible speed, motorized transport takes up an increasingly greater amount of its users' lifetime, especially as far as poorer workers are concerned, even though they promise to save time for poor and rich workers alike. What Martin Fortier (2016) termed 'peirastic criticism'[15] is, in my view, legitimate as long as tools and service institutions can be assessed on the basis of the premise adopted by those who planned them and submitted them to the citizens' vote. For instance: 'Dear transport planners, you have stated that your goal is the reduction of compulsive transport time which has been imposed on citizens-workers-tax payers. You claim you can achieve that by increasing the permissible speed with the ultimate goal of "saving time". The studies on transport, nonetheless, show that in those cities where a subway system is available, the traffic's average speed is about 9 mph (therefore even less than in those without a subway system), and that it is impossible to increase it without the adoption of special measures, which, as is the case of tolls, violate the principle of free circulation by excluding those users who cannot afford them. Without other exclusionary measures, such as the tariffs imposed for the use of the urban road network, the average daily speed in any given city would generally tend to decrease.[16] The only way to achieve the goal you have set yourself would be to establish an urban upper speed limit that is twice the speed that can be comfortably reached on a bike. The only way to reduce transport's chronophagy is therefore to reduce the range of permissible speed.'

The method known as 'peirastic' (a Socratic word) is effective as long as the goal envisaged by the promoters of service

15 Translator's Note: From the Greek *peiraō*, 'I strive to persuade by deriving my argument from the interlocutor's own premise.'

16 The English statistician Reuben J. Smeed (1909–1976) believed traffic jams to be a limit condition that revealed its essence. Said idea was prompted by the experience he accrued during the war as an RAF consultant. Smeed used to advise pilots on bombing missions to Germany to fly back in as close a formation as possible; while that strategy admittedly increased the risk of collisions within the squadron, it reduced that of being fatally hit by German anti-aircraft artillery. After the war, Smeed applied his statistical knowledge to car traffic and became one of England's foremost precursors of congestion pricing in downtown London. He advanced the hypothesis that the transport industry's customers would not be ready to put up with an average speed that was less than 9 mph (which is actually the *current* average speed in cities such as Paris, New York or Mexico City, and which is far less than the average speed in downtown London around 1970). His proposal in favor of 'urban tolls' was not implemented in his lifetime, but was taken into consideration once again in 2003, when the average speed in downtown London dropped to 8.6 mph. After the introduction of the tolls, the average speed soared to 10.5 mph but subsequently dropped rapidly because the cars' circulation space was also allocated for other uses, such as accommodating bicycle and bus traffic (*cf.* Smeed, 1964).

infrastructures suits common-sense arguments, such as curtailing the waste of time occasioned by transport. When that context is no longer referable, the service industry becomes a factor promoting the hegemony of the economy and the increased perception of scarcity, which is the engine of economic growth. Every notion of the limitations that give meaning to action vanishes, and the boundless growth of the services may end up appearing to be the indispensable prerequisite for all rights, which is nonsense.

When scarcity is perceived to be chronic, it may be defined as the inability of industrial society's products to appease people's senses: regardless of their quantity, 'they will never be enough.' Beyond a given threshold, for instance, the quantity of petrol that is made available to the transport industry, as large as it may be, will never manage to quell the sense of urgency that leads car drivers to compete with one another to gain access to the fastest thoroughfares. This competition encourages engineers to multiply the number of urban expressways, bypasses, and elevated highways, and it forces their users to take long detours that diminish the real displacement value (as reckoned against the actual distance between the start and end points) of every mile they travel. In other words, the larger the number of expressways and elevated highways that are available, the more vehicles run in circles.

There comes a time when the dialogue between citizens and technocrats loses all meaning; that usually happens when the latter no longer see their actions as a contribution to the services they have defined in agreement with the citizens, but rather as serving systemic purposes that are expressed by means of generic terms, such as Employment, Growth, Education, Accessibility, or Health. To the extent that citizens-customers-tax payers introject them as their 'need for services,' those abstractions deserve to be defined as 'dislocated practicalities.'[17] For example, whenever employment turns into a political slogan that

17 *Cf.* Illich, 2004, p. 215: 'Abstract concepts are given a "shape" by means of images and diagrams that rape the eye and deceive it into believing in dislocated practicalities. People are used to being horrified, distressed or encouraged by the graphic representation of quantitative data for which there is no counterpart the eye may perceive.'

pervades all election campaigns, workers-tax payers-voters are led to consider it as a necessary precondition to having bread on their tables and an emergency fund in their bank accounts. The abstraction underlying that slogan simultaneously conceals and confirms the reality to which it is bound: the growth of the road networks that link the places where economic activities are carried out to the inhabitants, the pillaging of nature that supplies the raw materials needed by the industry, and the demise of street activities, the hub of urban culture.

The intrinsic limitation of the criticism that Fortier termed 'peirastic' is none other than the limitation on the ability to assess the products of a set of tools based on the human purposes they are meant to serve. At present, the growth of the school services, the transport infrastructures, and the health industry no longer suits their users' personal or community purposes, but rather obeys a kind of 'systemic commandment' that cannot be identified with human intentions.

III. The Descent into an 'Age of the Systems' Is Not Inevitable

In the context presently under examination, the word 'system' becomes closely associated with the demise of the age of the tools as the West has known it since the twelfth century. Tools used to be in a direct, face-to-face relation with their users' bodies. Systems do not have anything with which they may interact face-to-face and do not possess an external space. They absorb their users within themselves and know no boundaries: they are coextensive with social space.

The age of instrumentality, during which the concept of tool was indeed the 'key that opened all doors,' lasted more than seven centuries. The historians of the tools who study that period from the moment instrumental tools could be perceived to be distinct from organic tools have the advantage of a unique overview of the history of the second Christian millennium, which could constitute the starting point for a new philosophy of technology.

The age of the tools, of instrumentality or 'technology' may be contextualized within the history of the Western and Westernized world as a long-lasting movement whose last avatar was the industrial age.[18] Since 'the ages that follow one another always overlap,' contemporary history may still be able to conduct a direct investigation by carrying out phenomenological studies on the industrial age, which in Illich's view was on the wane. Illich himself may be one of the most significant witnesses of the age for which he planned to write an epilogue. Recall that in the 1990s, he explained convincingly that the epilogue to the industrial society he had in mind might be nothing other than an epilogue to the instrumental age, or the age of the tools.

The end of the instrumental age, the greatest 'collapse' experienced in the second millennium, is a one-of-a-kind 'crisis' because, unlike what could be done about every other previous crisis, there is no conceivable decision that may overcome and end it (the Greek word *krisis* means 'decision'). This crisis 'with no chance to decide,' which traps us 'over here with no over there' (Hüben ohne Drüben), cannot be overcome, just as it did not once seem possible to overcome instrumentality, the horizon of Western culture.

Moving beyond the mental topology of instrumentality?

Instead of experiencing a crisis for which a solution is being sought, we are now living at a time of growing developments that conceal the *possibility* offered by the present moment (Fortier and Paquot, 2016). In a few short essays which Illich wrote for, and often with, his students in Bremen and at Penn State, he stressed the new possibilities opened up by the end of the 'spirit of instrumentality and usefulness.'[19] Those possibilities have nowadays become available, but in order to be seized they require acts of courage that call to mind the 'great sudden burst' Jacques Ellul hoped for, a burst which some of Illich's students had the daring to self-induce.

18 Translator's Note: The Sanskrit term *avatar* means 'incarnation.' In modern languages, it is employed with the meaning of 'a return,' 'a further expression,' 'a new manifestation,' or else to designate a representation that only exists in virtual reality.

19 These meditations are to be found in several notebooks which Illich's students published under the general title *Schriften Bremen* ('Writings from Bremen'). See, for instance, the essay devoted to the history of the gaze ('Zur Geschichte des Blickens,' in *Schriften Bremen*, vol. I, 1994–1997).

At the same time, Illich voiced (I am almost tempted to add: too soon) his fear of a possible descent into a new age, an age that was going to be even more ruthless than the preceding one, and for which it is not possible at present to outline any phenomenology whatsoever, since the concepts that would afford a proper understanding of it do not yet exist; indeed, any attempt in that sense would at best deliver a phenomenology of the late industrial age.

Was it really too soon? Illich did admittedly write several essays in which he drew a comparison between an 'age of the tools' and an 'age of the systems,'[20] even though one has to disregard the fact that in those two expressions the word 'age' neither carried the same weight nor implied the same kind of meaning. In the first instance, that word carried the weight of what had been experienced by those who are now reckoned among the dead and possessed the meaning it had accrued over many centuries. In the second, that word was devoid of any weight or meaning whatsoever; it evoked that 'shadow' of the future in which Illich repeatedly stated he did not wish to live. A descent into the age of the systems could therefore imply a descent into the shadow of a future that will presumably be systemic.

During a meeting in Cuernavaca on 4 September 2016, to celebrate the ninetieth anniversary of Illich's birth,[21] William Arney reminded us, among other things, that 'the systems are present in people's heads. ...Systems force those who submit to them to behave as if they were part of the systems themselves. They have to become *incorporated* into the systems' (Arney, 2016).

William Arney was one of the first writers to employ the word 'system' with a meaning akin to the one proposed by Illich. In his book *Experts in the Age of Systems* (Arney, 1991), he mentioned the condition of inner death (real, but dead) experienced by the physicists who had taken part in the Manhattan project.

20 See, for instance, 'From the tools to the systems,' in Illich, 2005, pp. 201–204.

21 The seminar, which was organized by the *Programa Universitario de Estudios de la Complejidad y Ciudadanía* (PUECC) of the Autonomous University of the State of Morelos (UAEM), was entitled *Iván Illich, 90 años. Lo político en tiempos apocalípticos* ('Ivan Illich, 90 years. Politics in apocalyptic times').

The 'system' was in charge, and they were conscious of being nothing other than mere cogs in the machinery that was building the bomb. This notwithstanding,

> ...the good news is that the system is a non-thing... it is just a vision, a way of thinking. To acquire a 'systemic view of the world' one must be trained to do so. Instead of being sensitive to simplicity and autonomy, one must learn to see the complexities and their undefined interconnections. One must face the fact that systems are 'black boxes,' and it is therefore impossible to get to know them. One must accept that systems are not entirely predictable. One must put the freedom of autonomous action on hold, and favor heteronomy instead... However, when one is offered a new way of seeing things, a new way of thinking, it is still possible to answer 'No, thank you,' even though it is often difficult to do so (Arney, 2016).

Arney also added that Illich seemed to believe that in the age of the systems, politics had changed, and that political criticism itself had been absorbed by the political system. In the last years of his life, Illich focused his meditation especially on friendship, as the only possible foundation on which to base the 'accomplishment of one's existence' and the possibility of a new kind of politics. In a conversation with Jerry Brown and Carl Mitcham, he stated: 'I do not believe that friendship can actually blossom in today's political life. In fact, I believe that if there is still a chance left to have a political life in the world of "technologies," it will only be able to blossom through friendship.'

> That is why I am convinced it is my duty to cultivate disciplined, detached, respectful and tasteful friendships. These friendships must always be mutual, you and I, and I am always waiting for somebody else to appear on the scene who might lend new life to communal living. Perhaps it will then be possible to find out what good actually is (Arney, 2016).

As far as I am concerned, I steadfastly refuse to move out of a celebration of gratuitousness that marks the end of instrumentality and usefulness into the fateful dawning of the age of the systems without taking a pause for consideration. I feel the need to take a moment for myself to breathe, and to reassess a number of the late instrumental age's fundamental categories: spatiality and temporality, and along with them the concept of boundary, the world's habitability and the questions it raises, the reformulation of natural forces on the basis of an approach that takes into account their scarcity, energy, scarcity itself, which is economy's fundamental postulate, and the mix-up between information and knowledge. It is impossible to examine the 'axioms on which the modern mental topology rests' without also tackling those aggregates of concepts and perceptions. Questioning those categories could in fact amount to the expression of a new kind of freedom which finally removes the blinkers that ensure our psychological comfort and reassurance, for instance, of the kind that is still provided by the notion of the West's superiority. Another painful issue is represented by the West's fundamental paradox: a culture that was born from the faith in the incarnation of the Word has become the most disincarnated one in the whole of history. Hence, the origin of the age-old adage to which Illich made reference: *corruption optimi quae est pessima*, which I promised myself I would not quote more than twice throughout the present book.

In the last years of his life, together with his friends in Bremen and at Penn State, Illich discussed several issues that questioned modern thought's fundamental categories:

- a somatic history, or a history of the self-perception of the body, together with Barbara Duden;
- a history of the 'instrumentalization' of the gaze, which was thus deprived of its moral dimension;
- a history of the 'instrumentalization' of the alphabet, which began in the twelfth century and which led to a genealogy of the dematerialization of the text;
- the demise of the great tradition of proportionality ushered in by the mathematical formulation of the tempered chromatic music scale in the seventeenth century.

From the kitchen-forge of the future to the alchemy of possible scenarios

Unlike what obtained in Cuernavaca in 1975, today's task no longer concerns 'preparing the great debates of the end of the twentieth century,' which sadly never took place, but rather addressing, in a humbler yet more in-depth fashion, what has been and will be no more, as well as coming to terms with what may come. It is also about sensing what is *possible*. While it is true that Illich addressed the *age of the systems* just as he had previously discussed the *age of the tools*, the word 'age' did not have the same meaning when applied to the 'weight' of the past as opposed to the *emptiness* of a future that, by its very nature, *is not yet there*. Of course, something could well materialize suddenly and befall humanity when least expected. And indeed, a sudden burst can always occur, even if it is only expressed by three humble words: *no, thank you*.

The instrumental premise underlying industrial society (as well as Western culture over the past five or six centuries) is about to crumble to pieces under the blows of one of the farthest-reaching transformations ever witnessed by the second Christian millennium. However, we do not yet possess the concepts to define 'what is about to come,' which is already visible in the new artifacts that are presently proliferating everywhere. The only thing that can be stated with any certainty is that the latter no longer suit the classical notion of tools. They may be called 'systems,' and it may be observed that their users are in turn no longer professionals in the classical sense but rather 'helpful facilitators' acting as interfaces,[22] who turn their customers into sub-systems and supply them with the semblance of perfection required by such a transformation. It is no longer possible to disregard the fact that the incorporation of the users into the system precludes the possibility of envisaging the latter as a tool facing the body.

There is also another consideration that must necessarily occasion further meditation on the use of the word 'technology' in the age of the systems. That term has not ceased to evoke the

22 On the history of the word *interface*, see 'Guarding the Eye in the Age of the Show,' in Illich, 2004, p. 178.

smells, oil and rhythms of industrial tools, and its application to the silences punctuated by a 'click-clack' sound of systems sets 'technologies' up as the antecedents of the systems themselves, thereby creating a false sense of continuity. It is consequently the duty of the philosophy of technology to denounce that deception: presenting the systems as a form of technology is tantamount to taking a tranquilizer or casting a veil on a historic change that after the 1980s has led to the emergence of a new world for which there is still no name.

That change also constitutes the frontier beyond which it is impossible to preserve the distinction between what artifacts do and what they say, since they are no longer tools. Systems issue orders: 'See, this smudge on your ultrasound scan is your future baby.' The systems' a-human statements are irrefutable, and they leave no room for any dispute, objection, or conversation. Since they are virtual, the 'facts' they present as evidence are neither real nor symbolic. Rather than modifying perceptions, the systems synthesize an altogether new class of perceptions. The actual introjection of those semblances of reality would be a huge anthropological catastrophe. There are, of course, those who have rebelled against that numbing of the senses, as, for instance, the Zapatist communities on the mountain ranges in southern Mexico (where I now live), who are presently carrying on an anti-systemic struggle.

Under the systems' implacable light, new 'needs' arise, and once they manage to take hold, it becomes impossible to conceive the world without also taking them into account. Since we are now faced with these new needs without borders, are we to hold an *auto-da-fé* for the so-called 'apps?' Or should we perhaps shift the light under which we examine them, in the hope of gaining a clearer view of what they leave in the shade? Should we abandon the virtual dimension to re-establish some of the distinctions between material and symbolic effects? Should we re-establish some of the distinctions between our bodies and the systems that strive to reduce them to one of their sub-systems? Or is it about time that we tackle the issue of the discrepancy between my computer's seemingly instrumental nature and the boundless networks with which it forces me to interact?

Chapter 5: Vernacular Gender

Milestones: An interpretation informed by personal reminiscences

The period Illich spent at Berlin's Wissenschaftskolleg in the 1981–1982 academic year was of capital importance for the birth of the book he devoted to gender (1982). Whenever he was preparing a new book, Illich, who was a meticulous 'man of letters,' would draw up a short draft of his new project and send it to a fairly large number of his friends, whom he would encourage to share their comments with him. 'An author's words are no longer his as soon as they begin to circulate…,' stated the first paragraph of Thierry Paquot's Introduction to Ivan Illich (2012, p. 3). That aphorism is more pertinent than ever when applied to Ivan Illich as an author. After its initial distribution, the text in progress became a fabric whose threads often bore the traces of a multitude of voices. It is in that sense that the comparison he drew between his writing style and that of his friend Paul Goodman is to be understood: 'He claims he has never written a line without having first pronounced it out loud. I, on the other hand, have never pronounced a sentence I could not have also written down in exactly the same words.' Be that as it may, Illich was by no means one of those authors who toiled on a text on his own. I would prefer to compare him to one of those scribes of yore who were able to transcribe their friends' oral improvisations.

What I have just written above is, of course, not supposed to be taken literally: Illich was a 'scribe' in the modern sense of the word; he was an author. What I mean to say is that his sophisticated art of writing drew on reminiscences of ancient writing practices, which most of the writers who work on their texts in complete solitude have now all but forgotten. Illich was no solitary writer. Gender is an instance of a work whose earlier versions revealed an echo of the voices belonging to some of Illich's fellow 'classmates' at the *Wissenschaftskolleg*'s first session.

A sharp eye cannot fail to notice that Illich's book tackled the issue of equity between the genders from a very peculiar perspective, which was altogether different from the one that began to be developed after 1982 under the heading of 'gender studies.' With only a little exaggeration, it may be claimed that those studies have generally recast the issue of the lack of equity between men and women in the context of the inequality between races, classes, sexual identities, and, in more recent times, in accordance with the approach adopted by decolonial studies.

Some of my friends expected me to praise the surplus of works that have appeared in connection to that topic since 1982, a topic that can now legitimately be seen as a new field of study. While I am aware that I am going to let them down, all I can do at present is to explain as clearly as possible the reasons that have induced me to decide otherwise.

Firstly, in 1982, that field of study was just beginning to be dug into. Although I have no intention to start a debate on 'precedence,' I believe it may be stated categorically that Ivan Illich was the first writer to come up with the idea that the concept of duality derived from the grammar of Romance languages could be employed to designate a reality that had become inaccessible to modern human beings. Illich held that the masculine-feminine duality (which usually defines grammatical gender) lent itself to the successful retrieval of some aspects of a relationship that had existed in the past and forgotten in the modern age. A concept that contributes to (re) discovering a perception that has become inaccessible may be defined as heuristic.[1] Instead of being a concept that portrayed what had been, 'vernacular gender' was, in fact, a heuristic that lent coherence to the historical archive referring to the relationship between men and women. Illich the historian and his friends in Berlin sought to discern that now-forgotten relationship in what still survived of it.

However, retrieving that concept to essentially turn it into the equivalent of sex or, even worse, into its historical origin, is tantamount to flattening it and destroying its heuristic hue. Conversely, accepting the heterogeneity of gender and sex

1 Translator's Note: This word, which derives from the Greek *eurīskō* (to find, to discover), designates a hypothesis that is adopted to develop research in a new, original direction.

would lead to the adoption of different concepts to describe modern situations dominated by sex on the one hand, and a past pervaded by gender on the other.

In summary: Ivan Illich availed himself of the notion of gender as a masculine-feminine duality, which he derived from grammar, and turned it into a heuristic concept that could convey something of the atmosphere of bygone ages in which the various moments of the day, places, idioms, songs and dances, tools, and body attitudes were patently characterized as either feminine and masculine.

Before the introduction of the word 'gender,' the difference between men and women was expressed by the word 'sex,' which conveys the idea of separating or dissecting something. Shortly after the Berkeley events briefly described in this chapter, feminists adopted the concept of gender but deprived it of the heuristic meaning that Illich had ascribed to it. According to their redefinition of it, gender did not exactly coincide with sex (the former was reputedly cultural in nature, whereas the latter was believed to be biological), but it was sufficiently close to it to be presented as its historical antecedent. Vernacular gender, on the other hand, saw sex as an anthropological reality that had no roots in the past and was consequently rather disquieting. The adoption of a gender that was not heuristic in nature as a category almost akin to sex was an operation meant to assuage that very sense of unease.

David Cayley has drawn my attention to the possibility that besides the opposition of some Berkeley's professors to Illich's theory on mutually constitutive dissymmetric complementarity (as he was to define proportionality many years later, the gender of which was represented by the historical paradigm), there might have been in the Berkeley of 1982 a generalized reluctance to take into consideration his critical view of modernity, the development of which had been encouraged by his reading of writers such as Karl Polanyi and Louis Dumont. In June 2019, I wrote to Cayley: 'In a manuscript you sent me a few months ago you seemed to suggest that one of the reasons behind the rejection of Illich's reflections on vernacular gender was his criticism of modernity. Modernity's progress would wipe out all the motivations that could have possibly justified the patriarchal order.'

Cayley replied as follows: 'I believe the writer you are implicitly referring to is Clair Brown, who in her contribution to the criticism of Illich in the Feminist Issues magazine of the spring of 1983 wrote:[2] 'The mass production and distribution of material goods ensures that most people living in the developed countries have access to a nourishing and well-balanced diet, a warm and comfortable home, and functional and elegant clothing.'

Regardless of whether the patriarchal order is intrinsic to human history, or exclusively pertained to the culture of the Aryan hordes that invaded 'Old Europe' three or four millennia ago, modern comforts have deprived patriarchy of any raison d'être. If that is the argument then it has lost its premise, given the extent to which the criticism of economic growth and development have now become the norm.

Around 1980, Illich was convinced that the women's movement (and especially its German branch) was developing several intuitions that could potentially have led to a radical revision of the then-current economic theories. He suspected the existence of a close link between scarcity and the erosion of gender perception, and he expressed that idea by insisting that equity between the genders required negative economic growth, whereas economic growth favored the emergence of new kinds of inequality in addition to all the other inequalities inherent to the known forms of patriarchy.[3]

2 Brown, Clair, 'Separate and Unequal,' in *Feminist Issues*, 1983, p. 21.

3 See Barbara Duden, '"Le genre neutre" et la nouvelle précarité de la condition féminine. Féminisme et crise des structures de 'pouvoir par la satisfaction des besoins' ('"The neuter gender" and the new precariousness of the female condition. Feminism and the crisis of the centers of power for the satisfaction of needs'), in Jean Robert's French translation of an unpublished German original. In the early 2000s, the European Union encouraged member states to pass laws aimed at the implementation of the ideal of complete equality between the genders, thereby eliminating any lingering traces of the patriarchy of the past. However, the ensuing leveling of the male and female condition has entailed the advent of a labor market generally aimed at women that offers them underpaid, often degrading, and stressful jobs. A growing number of feminist voices have openly stated that the costs of the formal equalization of the male and female condition are in fact borne by women, who are forced to accept jobs that impose on them new forms of discomfort and difficulty.

****+****

One morning in the early 1970s, I happened to find myself in Illich's kitchen in Ocotepec. While frying some eggs in an old copper pan, Illich told me about Karl Polanyi, the author of *The Great Transformation* (1944).[4] Although his tone was sarcastic, I immediately understood that he was not really upset with that economic historian, but rather with himself: 'I cannot overcome his position.' It was as if a wall of sorts prevented him from moving further.

As early as 1944, Polanyi described the path to modernity from the fifteenth century onward as a process that had disembedded distinct spheres (Politics, Religion, Education, Pure Science, and especially Economy, whose empowerment Polanyi described at a later stage) from a shared polyvalent fabric. If the original meaning of the Greek word *kosmos* is borne in mind, one may even speak of a 'cosmic' fabric, given that everything contained within it derived its very being from something opposite, in the same way that a river's right bank may be seen as such only thanks to the existence of the left one.[5] Polanyi managed to describe the shredding of that polyvalent fabric made up of mutual correspondences without being able to outline what had preceded it, namely a world of activities, perceptions, and ideas that were incorporated into each other, in the same way that the concept of threshold cannot be separated from that of a mutually constitutive correspondence between the inside and the outside.

In his struggle to knock down the wall that barred his path, Illich managed to achieve much more than Polanyi. Illich shed a new light on the past that did not only alter the shape that the 'histories of developments' had imposed on it but also called for a radical revision of contemporary history. Seen in that light, the path to modernity turned out to be in fact a path to 'mo-

4 In Polanyi's view, the 'Great Transformation' was not the one undergone by traditional societies, which he described as disembedding, but rather the hope that the horrors of World War II could lead to the celebration of the demise of the 'satanic mill' which destroyed ordinary people's subsistence in the name of progress.

5 For the Ancient Greeks, the word *kosmos* designated order well before it was even applied to the world as such; the verb *kosmein* meant lining up things opposite one another, just as two armies would do before engaging in combat.

nism,' and to a world in which things were no longer themselves by virtue of their mutual correspondences, just as a mother was a mother by virtue of her child, but actually led an existence that was separate and cut off from any cosmic fabric.

About ten years after that morning breakfast, Illich was able to specify the nature of the fabric that had existed before the progressive disembedding which Polanyi identified as the essence of the path to modernity. He described it as a network of dissymmetrically complementary correspondences and gave it a first tentative name: *vernacular gender*, a concept he was to take up many years later under the name of *proportionality*.[6]

Illich borrowed from grammar the word 'gender,' which in Romance languages designates the 'masculine-feminine' duality. In the early 1980s, the word 'sex' was employed to draw a distinction between men and women for the simple reason that, in biology, it identified the difference between male and female. By expanding on that biological classification, anthropologists were still able to speak of the allocation of labor *by sex* in so-called primitive societies.

The concept of vernacular gender was a heuristic[7] because it allowed for the discovery of what was usually overshadowed by the projection of modern concepts onto the past. Rather than the object of empirical studies, it was in fact a light under which the past could be examined. Claiming that gender was vernacular implied that it was local, oral, and rooted in a well-defined territory, unlike sex, which Illich qualified as 'economic' because it was just as universal as scarcity (the cornerstone of economy).[8]

Illich began to develop the concept of gender after CIDOC, the thinkery he had set up in Cuernavaca, was shut down in 1976.

In the early 1980s, several US feminists also began to employ the word 'gender,' but they did so without preserving the

6 See for instance 'Proportionality,' in Illich, 2005, pp. 132–138, or the notebook edited by Illich's students and friends in Bremen, 'Über Proportionalität' ('On Proportionality'), in *Schriften Bremen* 1994–1997 (Duden et al., 1997).

7 Translator's Note: See footnote 1 on p. 89.

8 On the economic concept of scarcity, see pp. 21–22 above.

heuristic dynamism which Illich had associated with it. If observed in light of vernacular gender, the past becomes so different from the present that the latter does not even seem to have a past. When gender studies (which are now so fashionable in academia) envisage gender as an antecedent of *sex*, they appear to be fulfilling a need for conceptual tranquilizers in the face of the sense of anguish caused by a present without a past.

The first written drafts of Illich's new theory were published in 1981 and 1982.[9] After 30 September 1982, Illich commented on his texts in the course of seven meetings with Berkeley's students and professors. In my view, those meetings revealed a conceptual breakthrough that had been in the making for some years. In fact, *Gender*[10] was a double watershed in Ivan Illich's work. First, at a conceptual level, right from the first draft, Illich began to question some of the concepts that had informed his previous writings. Thanks to long conversations with friends and colleagues (notably the linguist Uwe Pörksen and the historian Barbara Duden), Illich became convinced that the analytic tools that he had employed in his previous works were contaminated by the keywords that industrial parlance had popularized. He therefore proceeded to carefully sift through the linguistic structure of his earliest writings: 'I noticed that they contained the *a priori* assumptions current at the time of writing, which did not just pervade the thought expressed therein but also, and to a far greater extent, our sensory perceptions and our inner perception of social reality.'[11] Second, this caution would also account for the fact that, during the trimesters he taught at various US and German universities, Illich introduced his students to the study of the history of sensory perceptions, gave a number of lectures on the history of the gaze and on musical proportions, and wrote a few draft texts on olfactory at-

9 The first commercial edition of *Gender* (Illich, 1982) was issued by Berkeley's Heyday Books.

10 In the following pages, all quotations have been taken from the Italian edition, which Neri Pozza re-issued in 2013 in an expanded and revised version (*Genere. Per una critica storica della disuguaglianza*); it has now also become available as eBook.

11 La construction institutionelle d'un nouveau fétiche: la vie humaine,' in Illich, 1992 , pp. 218–231

mospheres, and the senses of touch and taste.[12] Incidentally, the writing of *Gender* also represented the turning point after which Illich withdrew from the limelight, and continued to carry out his research mainly among various groups of his friends.

A mutually constitutive dissymmetry between 'two'

Illich did not introduce the expression *vernacular gender* to describe the 'usual' relationship between men and women, but rather to designate *a radical historical transformation of that relationship*. He was the first to apply a grammatical term to a relationship between men and women that was far older and more widespread than what was described as a relationship based on *sex*, which was a recent addition to history's archives.

Nonetheless, unlike gender research centers, which began to proliferate in the 1980s, Illich employed the notion of gender heuristically as a conceptual counterpoint to sex. If it is understood in the sense in which Illich used the word, gender no longer exists, other than as a relic.[13] Illich resorted to it expressly for the purpose of addressing the past without colonizing it with modern concepts. Illich the historian was thus able to describe as the transition from *vernacular gender* to *economic sex* what Polanyi had earlier defined as the progressive disembedding of well-defined spheres from a shared fabric, a disembedding process which, from the fifteenth century onward, became the essence of the 'path to modernity.' Gender was thus distinct from sex, which was characterized by the *male/female* dichotomy.

Defining gender as *vernacular* entails acknowledging its being rooted in specific territories, as well as identifying the plurality of its local expressions. Conversely, describing sex as *economic* implies the admission that its defining trait is its being

12 The English transcripts of those lectures on the physical senses may be found in the notebooks published by the STS center at the Pennsylvania State University, which was then directed by Carl Mitcham, who possesses their complete collection, while the German ones were included in the various notebooks issued by the University of Bremen, such as for instance *Schriften Bremen* (Duden et al., 1997; 1999).

13 Illich often attempted to understand a given social condition by tackling it from its opposite, be it the dominant sex from what was left of vernacular gender, or economy's modern hegemony from the pre-modern populations' subsistence activities.

'everywhere and nowhere,' in accordance with the kind of universality that it shares with scarcity itself, i.e., modern economy's fundamental postulate.[14]

The mutually constitutive dissymmetric complementarity that Illich defined by using the word gender gives new impulse both to the history of the past and of the present. Gender is the usual, traditional, vernacular way in which the extant difference between bodies, their relevant domains, the various ways of speaking, and the tools employed by men and women are perceived. It is specific to every region and even every village, and the dividing line between male and female clothing draws in every valley a pattern that is as original as the motifs on local textiles. Sex, for its part, is universal, and since the economy has nowadays become the universal overriding concern, it is apt to define the duality that characterizes modernity as economic sex. While gender relations are 'cosmic' in the sense that the domains of men and women are dissymmetric yet mutually constitutive, sex-based relations are monistic, given that male and female are manifestations of the ontologically same human being, though differentiated by secondary sex characteristics (namely a bulge in the blouse or the trousers). Their differences are secondary because human beings are essentially one: they ideally speak the same language, are aware of the same reality, can use the same tools, are placed in the service of the same machinery, and can also be envious of one another.

It is worth stressing this point once again: according to Illich, the path to modernity, which started in the fifteenth century, described by Polanyi as a 'disembedding' process and by Marx as the rise of capitalism, could historically be defined as the shift from vernacular gender to economic sex. Vernacular life gives a gendered nuance to every part of the village and to every moment of the day. Economic life presumes an undiffer-

14 Although Paul Dumouchel proposed to define scarcity simply as the relationship established by a set of goods and resources that was not sufficient to satisfy everybody's needs and desires, he actually went further than such an ahistorical and universalizing definition in his analysis based on a reading of the liberal tradition's 'pioneers' in light of René Girard's mimetic theory (see footnote 129 below). Dumouchel saw scarcity as a prototypical mimetic relationship (see 'L'ambivalence de la rareté,' in Dumouchel and Dupuy, 1979).

entiated time and space that is suitable for human beings. This space-time universality defines modernity and makes local, practical perceptions of reality obsolete. The universality of industrial society could not continue to exist without the dominance of economic sex.

The endless 'crisis' from which no way out can possibly be found, namely the nightmare of being locked up in a world of artifacts that have lost their instrumental character, is also a crisis of the relationship between men and women. When pushed to its limits, economic sex becomes utterly impossible to live with and leaves no chance to revert to vernacular gender. Conversely, pre-industrial societies, for all their diversity, were unthinkable without vernacular gender.

Sex is a biological concept, whereas gender may be seen as a cultural perception. By exploiting that distinction politically, some writers have undertaken research on the 'social construction of gender,' which denies the heuristic essence of Illich's work. In the egalitarian utopia developed by feminists in the 1980s, gender appeared to be inseparable from patriarchy. The social construction of gender was reputed to be the construction of a form of inequality that had repeatedly been recreated since the dawn of time, or else was the consequence of the imposition, after the violent conquest of Old Europe, of unbalanced relationships that favored men. Those who support the second hypothesis advocate a reassessment of the history of the conquest of Old Europe, which occurred in the third millennium BC at the hands of hordes known as Kurgan or Aryan that spoke Indo-European languages.[15]

This notwithstanding, what is relevant to the present discussion is that if patriarchal relationships are not natural but,

15 See Gross, 2009. For a reconstruction of the Kurgan invasions of 'Old Europe,' see the writings by the Lithuanian archaeologist Marija Gimbutas (1956). There is, however, no evidence that the period before those invasions was marked by a condition of genderless equality (or for that matter by a sort of 'female patriarchy' in which the *arché*, understood as predominance, belonged to women). Several significant archaeological finds afford the hypothesis of so-called matriarchy on the basis of the primary meaning of the word *arché* (origin, beginning, foundation): 'in the beginning were Mothers.' There was therefore no undifferentiated equality, but rather an era of 'unequalled social balance and polarity' in which men and women were 'not yet in opposition, but in a harmonious relationship' (Percovich, 2012).

based on available evidence, a historically recent phenomenon (less than five millennia), then feminists of the 1980s could rightfully harbor the hope of seeing their end. Nonetheless, in industrial societies dominated by the concept and perception of scarcity, economic growth cannot help being followed by the unequal treatment of women, which is concealed under the growing access to the labor market and 'equality laws' that generate unprecedented forms of inequality.[16]

But if patriarchy is a historical and not a natural phenomenon, then gender is not necessarily patriarchal. Conversely, whenever feminists did choose to consider patriarchal relationships as inherent to the human condition, it became hard for them not to interpret them as being synonymous with what Illich called gender. That was the avenue that many feminists pursued in the 1980s. Since they did use gender as a heuristic concept to envision how people from the past could have lived without an economic or legal sphere and without the women's submission to patriarchal power, they heroically took up the challenge of devising something that was as new as the exploration of the moon: a truly egalitarian world that was finally free from the hindrance of 'gender,' that is, from what they conceived as patriarchy. For many feminists, the study of the social construction of 'gender' was therefore meant to entail a liberating deconstruction.[17]

At Berkeley, Illich presented as a *loss* what his academic antagonists believed was a *battle that could finally be won*. They had previously asked him to be their male traveling companion, but once they realized that what he was attempting to define was the exact opposite of what they strove to create, they turned the last session of his seminar into a trial of sorts.[18]

16 See Barbara Duden's writing quoted above (footnote 3, p. 91).

17 The physicist Evelyn Fox-Keller maintains that the private sphere (female) and the public sphere (male) structure biological thought in two areas, namely the one pertaining to population genetics and the one relating to mathematical ecology, in a split that a science free from the hindrance of gender ought to see as its duty to overcome (see Fox-Keller 1985).

18 The 'trial' was held in November 1982 in a large auditorium at the University of California in Berkeley. Martina Kaller-Dietrich has carefully researched that event, of which she provided an account in her book (2007, especially pp. 165–168 and 177–181).

Illich considered the demise of vernacular gender to be the progressive obliteration of the mutually constitutive dissymmetric complementarity between the spaces and times of men and those of women, which had led, from the dawn of humanity, to the flourishing of the cultures that invented languages, community relations, conflicts and their resolution, songs, and dances. It is the same kind of complementarity that some anthropologists are still able to recognize outside alphabetized, economic, and sexed modernity,[19] and which they can still *perceive* underneath its monistic coating. If Illich was right, vernacular, oral, and common gender was indeed the primeval crucible from which all cultures have sprung into existence, and the fact that it is now concealed by economic sex has caused the annihilation of the latter's generative power.

In hindsight, the dream which some feminists harbored in the 1980s, namely placing the male and female condition on an equal footing, in fact hid a reality made up of unprecedented inequalities. Put differently, their rational dream of abstract equality seems to have triggered unheard-of forms of injustice:

> To my knowledge, there is no industrial society in which women are economically equal to men. Of whatever economy can measure, women are consistently awarded a smaller share (Illich, 1982, p. 4).

In Illich's view, vernacular gender designated a kind of complementarity between two dissimilar elements for which

The following year, Dr. Hochschild (the event's main organizer) expressed her views on it in an article entitled 'Illich: The Ideologue in Scientist's Clothing,' which was published in *Feminist Issues* as part of a special issue devoted to a critique of Illich's theory of gender (Hochschild 1983). The same issue also included, among others, Gloria Bowles's article 'Beyond the Backlash: A Feminist Critique of Ivan Illich's Theory of Gender' (1983), as well as the anthropologist Nancy Scheper-Hughes's article 'Vernacular sexism: An anthropological Response to Ivan Illich' (1983), which stood out for its moderation, and often also for its pertinence. The writer stated her opinion that Illich had exaggerated the differences between male and female spaces, times, and activities, and she consequently called for the revision of several of his historical and anthropological arguments. In her 2007 book, Martina Kaller-Dietrich contextualized the shocked response which Illich's insistence on the difference between gender and patriarchy occasioned at the time.

19 As demonstrated, for instance, by Lorna Marshall (1898–2002) in her book *The !Kung of Nyae Nyae* (1976).

mutual attraction was an actual possibility. He argued that at the end of the day gender was just another way of addressing 'twofoldness,' or duality. 'Twofoldness' could either designate the coexistence and the desire to be reunited of two beings that were ontologically different, or else define the outcome of the splitting of something that was originally a whole. During a seminar at Penn State, I saw him illustrate that 'duality of dualities' by means of a few simple gestures. First, he placed two heterogeneous objects on the table (say, an egg and a feather) and said: 'These two objects exemplify the duality that I call gender.' He then picked up a sheet of typing paper and tore it into two roughly similar halves. 'This split of an original unity into two equal halves represents sex.' Vernacular gender falls within the first approach to duality, whereas sex (a word whose etymology conveys the notion of a subdivision and a split) derives from the second approach to 'twofoldness.' For more than five centuries, the West's history has been affected by the latter's progressive dominance. In other words, Illich believed that the part of history which Polanyi envisaged as a disembedding process was in fact marked by the progressive shift from vernacular gender's reign to economic sex's dominance. He wrote:

> An industrial society cannot exist unless it manages to impose a number of unisex premises: namely, the premise that both sexes are made for the same kind of work, perceive the same reality and, apart from a few negligible external differences, have the same needs. Also, the premise of scarcity, which is essential to economy, must logically rest on that unisex premise. It would be impossible for men and women to compete for 'work' if a new definition of it had not emerged according to which it is an activity suitable for all human beings regardless of sex. The subject on which economic theory is based is just such a genderless *human*. Then, with scarcity accepted, the unisex postulate is free to spread (Illich, 1982, pp. 9–10).

Scarcity may be understood as the lack of things. Economists consider it the fundamental axiom of their science, defined as the tension between limited means and a plurality of alternative ends competing for the allocation of those means. According to Paul Dumouchel and Jean-Pierre Dupuy, scarcity may be seen as one of mimetic desire's many faces,[20] on a par with envy, narcissism or (in more recent times, according to Dupuy) jealousy (Dumouchel and Dupuy, 1979). Vernacular gender, which prevented competition and envy between the men and women belonging to a given community, as well as between members of different cultural configurations, constituted a form of protection against the havoc wrought by mimetic desire. In 1989, the German historian Beate Wagner-Hasel succeeded in understanding what had escaped Berkeley's feminists:

> ['Vernacular gender' is] the development of a view of society that is envisaged as not being organized *a priori* around juridical, economic, or political categories, or indeed around the separation of culture from society and of the private sphere from the public one, which predetermine the institutional forms of separation typical of our societies deeply pervaded by law (Wagner-Hasel, 1989, in Jean Robert's French translation).[21]

If we, as modern people, have become capable of understanding a society organized by such categories as, for instance, law, economy and politics, it is only because we have lost the notion of gender as an organizing category of space and time. According to Illich, 'gender was destroyed by schooling,' and could thus be denied and forgotten almost completely.

> Gender is vernacular. It is as tough and adaptable, as precarious and vulnerable, as vernacular speech is. And as happens with the latter, gender is obliterated by education, and its ex-

20 According to the theory developed by René Girard, human 'desires' are 'mimetic,' i.e., imitative. They are not like a mere arrow that, once it has been shot by a subject, points towards an object. Nobody desires one thing more than another autonomously. At the root of any desire there is always a mediation: the subject reads in the gaze of a third party, the mediator, the direction which his own desire will take. Desires are always triangular (*cf.* Robert, 2009, Italian translation, p. 87).

21 The passage quoted above is to be found in the volume edited by Becher U. and Rüsen J., *Weiblichkeit in geschichtlicher Perspektive* ('Femininity in a historical perspective'), and was taken from Beate Wagner-Hasel's writing 'Das Private wird politisch. Die Perspektive 'Geschlecht' in der Altertumswissenschaft' (The private becomes political. The 'gender' perspective in ancient history), in Becher and Rüsen, 1989, pp. 11–50.

> istence is soon forgotten or even denied. Thus, many people today have lost the ability to remember or even imagine either gender or vernacular speech. For the high school graduate, his parents' vernacular has become a substandard dialect of the mother tongue he has been taught. For the daughter who returns to rural Mexico, equipped with her university degree, the gender of her old mother can easily appear as a bondage that *she* has escaped (Illich, 1982, p.105).

It is nonetheless important to stress the fact that, despite vernacular gender's fragmentation, disarticulation, and the oblivion to which it had almost been consigned, Illich believed that it did not merely continue to underlie social reality, but that, in fact, it kept being as indispensable as air was, and to such an extent that it was impossible for any society to exist by doing altogether away with it. Although he never aspired to recreate the past, which would have been utterly impossible, Illich confined himself to an intellectual 'double ghetto:' on the one hand, the infeasibility of bringing the past back to life, and therefore his refusal of any kind of nostalgia and sentimentalism on the matter, and on the other, his refusal to reach an uncritical compromise with modernity's categories or 'spheres,' such as economy, politics, law, science, etc. This 'double ghetto' was the painful outcome of his twofold rejection of any sentimentalism associated with the past, as well as of any display of intellectual submissiveness to modernity's fundamental categories, 'axioms,' or 'spheres.' Illich pinned his hopes on a 're-generation,' which in this case meant the emergence of renewed sensitivity to that repressed, yet still covertly active reality that was vernacular gender. Renewed sensitivity, however, did not mean restoration. It was not about politics, but rather about possessing intuition and antennae that could discern what survived of a relationship that had once been 'mutually constitutive.'

> In gendered society, neither time nor space are neuter. What Einstein called 'spacetime' is, in vernacular society, a function of two ambiguous movements, each of which is in itself unique. Each gender moves along its path in accordance with its own rhythm, and the vernacular domain somehow acts as

counterpoint to that subtle dance. That is why part of the vernacular domain will always remain hidden in the blind spot of men's vision. Whatever they manage to learn about that concealed part, they can only learn indirectly. *Here*, it is the men who have no right of speech, *there*, it is the women. Being a man means being aware that women know things which men do not, that they possess words to designate them, and that they have power over them (Illich, 1982, in *Œuvres complètes*, vol. 2, p. 309).[22]

I shall now reconsider Beate Wagner-Hasel's comments. Foucault claimed that if one wanted to go on thinking, it was necessary to start thinking the unthinkable. Wagner-Hasel advocated 'keeping one's distance from the world of one's experiences,' and having the courage, as Illich did, to 'think the unthinkable.' Since most historians of Western culture do not possess that courage, they basically do nothing other than supply histories of economy before economy (and of capitalism before capitalism), of the State before the State, of private life before it actually came into being, or of sex in the time of gender.

The Berkeley professors who appointed themselves as Illich's judges used a brand of feminist politics that reclaimed equality between men and women. They tended to turn every debate on the female condition, whether in the past or the present, into an argument in favor of women's equality. They were hampered by the lack of imagination denounced by Wagner-Hasel: since they were unable to contemplate the possibility of societies existing on categories other than the ones underlying their own might, they condemned Illich's lack of commitment to 'sex equality' and his concept of dissymmetric complementarity be-

22 This paragraph, which was not included in the Italian edition, was the beginning of Chapter 5 in the French edition. As a polyglot, Illich used to review the subsequent translations of his books and add a few changes in accordance with his latest lectures, his students' questions, his latest meetings, and readings. His attitude was consistent with his conviction that no vernacular language was a container into which the 'content' of a text in a written language could be poured. He was interested in ascertaining which elements of vernacular speech could survive in the written language, or even underneath it; he also paid great attention to the disciplines of reading and writing, which could safeguard what was left of orality and which he held to be the repository of a sensitivity that was both vernacular and gendered, whereas the Western tradition saw written languages as essentially alphabetic and monistic.

tween historical genders as if a patriarch had attacked women's right to job and wage equality. Illich, for his part, believed gender equality to be infeasible in any scenario of unrestrained economic growth.[23]

What was at stake in that debate was the sacrosanct principle of equality, which was stamped on the flags of the great Revolution. Although the adjective 'equal' ought to mean having the same rights and duties under the rule of law, in common parlance it has now acquired the meaning of 'issued from the same mold' and 'subject to the same rule,' which in industrialized society subjugates women to the laws of *homo oeconomicus*. The German subtitle of *Gender* read as 'towards a critique of Equality' (the same subtitle was also present in the book's Italian edition).

What the whole clash really amounted to was a frontal attack on the very concept of equality. Did Illich really propose to reinstate the inequalities of the past? That is how his position was interpreted by those committed to rid society once and for all of what were, in their eyes, the vestiges of the patriarchal order of yore. Illich, however, did not cooperate with them for an obvious reason. He held that their goal was infeasible: arithmetic equality between men and women under the overarching umbrella of an expanding industrial economy.

At this stage, it is perhaps worthwhile to illustrate Illich's economic theory: in an expanding economy, achieving equity between men and women is impossible. The European Community has passed laws that impose gender equality. The outcome has often been the emergence of new inequalities, as confirmed by Barbara Duden's analysis in the article quoted above. Illich seemed to believe that patriarchy was a form of inequality linked to gender, especially as far as the stage of its 'dislocation' was concerned. Modernity imposes sexism.

23 'Relentlessly, economic institutions transform the two culturally embedded genders into something new, into economic neuters distinguished by nothing more than their disembedded sex... Economic discrimination against women cannot exist without the abolition of gender and the social construction of sex... If that is true—namely, that economic development intrinsically and irremediably gender-destructive, that is, sexist—then sexism can only be achieved at the "cost" of a economic shrinkage' (Illich, 1982, pp. 12–14).

By the time Illich was welcomed to Berkeley as a respected professor in the autumn of 1982, he had already spent more time walking the roads of Latin America, dispelling the confusion between missions and development in which the Churches had gotten bogged down, conversing with his farmer neighbors, and giving seminars at CIDOC, than he had teaching *ex cathedra*. The observations he made while living in his Mexican village, which were enlightened by his reading of writers such as Karl Polanyi and Louis Dumont, as well as René Girard, were such that he became convinced there was something in that world, still partly in a pre-industrial condition, that restrained mimetic desires, and which prevented them from turning into the tornado that drove industrial society's members to flee ahead towards an even more unimaginable catastrophe. Around 1970, it was quite difficult for Ocotepec's men and women to feel envy for one another, and the same was equally true for all the pre-industrial societies that had been documented by historians and anthropologists. Illich's strongest argument was that gender non-equality did not imply, *per se*, one gender's superiority and domination over the other. His opponents, for their part, had no difficulty in countering that, in a historical perspective, all Western societies were patriarchal. This notwithstanding, not all of their voices rang out in agreement.

The bone of contention

Illich had explored, with friends, the topic of vernacular gender during his stay at Berlin's *Wissenschaftskolleg*. The first draft of his book in progress, which Valentine Borremans published in *Tecnopolítica*, a Spanish language magazine that she edited, closely mirrored the stage that the debate had reached in Berlin in 1981. The following year, at the start of his stay in Berkeley, Illich believed he could go on expanding the weft of his Berlin conversations (and with a good measure of naivety, I would venture to say). In that perspective, however, it would be far too easy to highlight the grotesque dissonance between the historian's encouragement to examine history in a new light, and the feminist professors' political agenda. Whereas *gender studies* marked the arena of an academic arena with tenure possibilities, vernacular gender for Illich was not precisely an object of study, but rather a light under which (*lumen sub quo*) the whole of the history of the 'path to modernity' since the fifteenth century could be revised.

Parallel to the conversations he hoped to entertain within the university, Illich had daily conversations with a group of friends he convened in the house of Professor Nishi, a Japanese theologian teaching at Berkeley who was away in Japan on a sabbatical. Illich maintained that it was far easier for a new thought to take shape in non-academic conversations than in classrooms. The small group that used to meet at his place included Susan Hunt, who baked the bread; Lee Swenson, the former head of Berkeley's *Farallones* Institute; Thea Cremer, a Dutch feminist; Wolfgang Sachs, a German theologian and pedagogue; Franco La Cecla, a professor from the University of Bologna; and me. I often heard Illich doing the dishes we had left on the table the previous evening at two o'clock in the morning. Guests who sometimes dropped in for lunch at Nishi's place included Steve, Leonard and Wade (they were former psychiatric patients who spoke at length of the need to shut down the so-called mental hospitals), Everett Reimer, an old friend of Ivan's from his days in Puerto Rico and a forerunner of the criticism of compulsory education, Gianna Pomata, an Italian historian, and her partner Tom Dewar.

On 30 September 1982, Illich gave the first of the eight weekly lectures to which he had committed himself. Some of the teachers who put him on trial at the end of November did sometimes have breakfast at Nishi's. How is the rift that later occurred halfway through that cycle of lectures to be accounted for?

In this regard, I believe that David Cayley's most recent book has managed to get to the core of the controversies generated by both Illich and his writings on gender. This core concerned Illich's vision of modernity in light of the heuristic concept of vernacular gender, a vision which, in 1982, was rejected by the majority of his university audience. In Cayley's own words:

> A careful reading reveals first of all that he did not advocate the reinstatement of gender, even though the description of its loss is in places elegiac in tone; secondly, that he drew a clear distinction between gender and patriarchy; lastly, that he dealt with gender as if it were an 'ideal type' and a window on the unisex world, to which he applied his usual approach of understanding things through their opposites.
>
> None of this was understood, either by the Berkeley women who protested him or by his critics. He was accused of sexism (which was exactly what he was trying to denounce), and he was held up as a reactionary ideologist who endeavored to add a nostalgic shine to women's oppression. Of course, that interpretation could be seen as an unfortunate bump in the road (possibly caused by Illich's authoritarian, enthusiastic and confrontational tone, which may have misled both his audience and his readers), but I am convinced that the whole issue was in fact overwhelmingly affected by the patent differences which existed between him and those who opposed his book. Illich was striving to think something which was essentially unthinkable (namely questioning and dismantling the myth of equality), whereas his opposition on the other side was attempting to implement it. Illich was seeking contemporary forms of subsistence that could draw on modern industrial and scientific technologies while effectively restraining them at the same time; his opponents, conversely, demanded more jobs and services to facilitate women's access to the labor market. It may thus be said that Illich was endeavoring to derail the victors' train, while his opponents were hoping to finally secure a good seat for themselves on it. For all intents and purposes, it was a dialogue of the deaf (Cayley, 2021, pp. 209–210).

Is there any chance for that dialogue to be resumed? As Giorgio Agamben wrote in his introduction to the Italian edition of Illich's book, the answer might be in the positive. That is why I deem it opportune to revisit *Gender*.

A dual book on a fundamental duality

Illich defined vernacular gender as a cultural and social duality that varied depending on place, time, and age. In the same way that quantum physics sees light as conceptually dual, i.e., concomitantly particle and wave, every pre-modern society rested on the tension between domains, spaces, times, ways of speaking, and male and female tools. What is generally called culture is, in fact, that same generating tension. If pushed to its limits, the voluntary implementation of gender equality destroys that generating tension, as the hecatomb of ways of acting, speaking, creating, and employing tools which has obtained over the past three or four decades would seem to confirm. Illich's book *Gender* itself also had a dual structure: it was made up of two parts of a hundred pages each, which in terms of both style and approach were widely different yet complementary, 'dissymmetric and mutually constitutive.' Even the book's formal structure underscored its topic: each of its parts displayed different sources of light.

Many years ago, the Mexican editor of *El género vernáculo* asked me to proofread the work's second part, which was simply entitled *Notas,* and which included 119 footnotes in small print, a typographical layout that did not quite manage to bring the work's dual nature to the fore. In the book's French version, conversely, the argument (the first book) took up 105 pages, while the references (125 footnotes) required 102 (*Œuvres complètes*, vol. 2, pp. 249–459).

They were two books of essentially equal length, which at first sight could be read independently of one another; however, the light they shed on the almost imperceptible, yet constantly present tension that coursed through their pages could only be appreciated after a second reading. In order to illustrate the generating tension that characterized that mutually constitutive dissymmetry between different elements, I shall confine myself to examining a few issues: what Illich termed 'probity,' the difference between patriarchal relationships and sexism, industrial society's two underlying myths, and the *gender of the tools.*

Probity

> Yves Castan has investigated what Languedoc's inhabitants meant by *honnêteté* between 1715 and 1780. I shall translate the term as 'probity.'... Part of the study demonstrated how probity kept people acting according to their gender, down to the minutest details. For example,... it was [the woman's] task to shield the house from the tax collector, who was unable to enter if she claimed to be alone. She also had to take the part of her children in an argument, even if they were inexcusably wrong. Probity demanded that she go for the face of the enemy with nails and teeth, if that were necessary. From the *man*, probity required the opposite: in any incident in which the woman was expected to defend the offspring, he was supposed to correct or punish the child, sometimes rudely (Illich, 1982, p. 112–113).

The second book amply demonstrated the extent to which men's and women's opinions diverged as to what was appropriate for each gender in a specific place and at a specific time, thereby fully defying those laws that required them to behave exactly in the same fashion.

The difference between patriarchal relationships and sexism

> Patriarchy I take to mean a power imbalance under the assumption of gender. Sexism is clearly not the continuation of patriarchal power relations into modern societies. Rather, it is a hitherto unthinkable individual degradation of one half of humanity on socio-biological grounds... The lower prestige assigned by patriarchal societies (of the Mediterranean or of any other type) must therefore be carefully distinguished from the personal degradation of each individual woman who, under the regime of sex, is forced to compete with men (Illich, 1982, p. 34).

A false genealogy: Industrial society's two founding myths

Industrial society is based on two myths. One concerns its sexed origin (sex, if seen as ahistorical and timeless, splits humanity into two kinds of neuter beings, i.e., beings devoid of gender). The other is the myth of progress towards ever-spreading equality. Those two myths are lies, as the second sex's personal experience as neuter clearly demonstrates.

> For one hundred years, history has fabricated a continuity between the genderless present and the gendered past, legitimating the descent of sex from gender. With an increasingly refined methodology, the new science has interpreted the story in sexist categories to give a past to our economic world. Without such economic reconstruction of a gendered past, the contemporary world of sexist economics could not have been made attractive, especially to those against whom it has consistently discriminated... I have tried to expose the counterfeit genealogy of sex that underlies economic history (Illich, 1982, p. 177).

The answer to the issue raised by Cayley seems to me to be quite simple: Illich's heuristics opened a yawning chasm beneath the feet of modern intellectuals who were quite determined to exploit economic sex in the context of an economy whose growth in 1982 could still let them glimpse the mirage of a world where a booming sector of hitherto unknown services would eventually free women from the duties patriarchy had assigned them. In fact, neither those intellectuals nor women heeded the premise that sexism must necessarily grow in parallel with the economy.

More than a generation later, their epigones still appear to be blind to the precarious female condition that arises from policies aimed at placing men and women on an equal footing, which also do not set any boundaries.[24]

24 See Barbara Duden's writing quoted in footnote 3 on p. 91.

Gender and tools

> Tools are intrinsic to social relationships. Each person relates to society through actions and the tools effectively mastered to carry out those actions. To the degree that one actively masters one's tools, their shape determines his/her self-image. In all pre-industrial societies, a set of gender-specific tasks is reflected in a set of gender-specific tools. Even tools that are there for *common* use can be touched by only half the people. By grasping and using a tool, one relates primarily to the appropriate gender. As a result, intercourse between genders is primarily social. Separate tool kits determine the material complementarity of life (Illich, 1982, p.90).

Indeed, there is no need to travel to exotic lands or back in time in order to find traces of the mark which gender has left on tools, some of which, such as bicycles, have preserved it to this day. Most local museums house tools whose names have all but been forgotten, and which can no longer be recognized as either male or female. Modernization has erased the tools' gender, which only survives in a few areas. The present world of genderless artifacts, which often no longer deserve to be called tools, is without precedent in the past.

> Here, men use the scythe and women the sickle. There, both use a sickle, but there are two sickles, each of a different design; the handle and blade betray the gender. In Styria, for example, men's sickles are clean-edged for cutting, and women's are indented, curved, made for the gathering of stalks... In one valley in the Alps, both genders use the scythe, but she only to cut the fodder, and he for the rye. Here, only she touches the knives in the kitchen; there, both cut the bread, but one cuts down and away, and the other draws the blade toward the chest (Illich, 1982, p. 91–92).

In Europe, the extant links between gender and tools managed to survive both wars and the destruction of the cities for a long time, until economic growth modified the countryside's lifestyle. An elderly Serbian farmer was once watching a young woman, who could have been his granddaughter, as she drove the village's only tractor during the harvesting season. 'The gender that disappears on a tractor had adapted to ever-new conditions over millennia' (Illich, 1982, p. 93). With a mixture of sadness and pride, the old man told Illich how haying had been done in his youth. 'He described gathering, loading, and storing the hay as if the work had been a ballet in which men and women each danced their appropriate parts' (*ibid.*). Thanks to tractors and unisex tools, haying has become an activity performed by male and female workers who are gender neutral.

Rather than the disappearance of lingering traces, 'the immediate material object of gender studies is the correspondence between two sets of places, tools, tasks, gestures, and symbols on the one hand, and between what in any given society are called men and women' (Illich, 1982, p. 99). In this sense, 'the association of gender with simple tools has a privileged position in research on gender: The association is directly observable… Tools are concrete entities, and the observer can directly record whether they are handled by men or by women' (Illich, 1982, p. 92).

Chapter 6: The Transformation of the Gaze into a Tool, and Beyond

In quest of the history of the body in past ages

In the early 1990s, Ivan Illich and Barbara Duden undertook a lengthy study on the history of the self-perception of the body in past ages (*cf.* Duden, 2002). In the second half of the eighteenth century, physicians imposed on society the image of an 'entitative' body, i.e., a body that had been converted into an entity built on the basis of descriptions: descriptions of illnesses, as well as of the internal organs and limbs they affected. Seen in that perspective, illnesses became conceptually autonomous entities that were 'separate' from physical bodies, and which could potentially strike all bodies beyond any ethnic, epistemic, and conceptual boundary.

Physicians shifted the focus of their attention from the patients to their illnesses. The entitative body deprived physical bodies of any historicity or cultural affiliation. To build it, physicians began to draw precise maps of the human body. At the same time, they also began to describe the organs' functions. Those graphic representations and textual descriptions eventually gave birth to anatomy and physiology, the cornerstones of modern medicine until the dawn of the age of the systems.

Those overlapping layers of anatomical and physiological descriptions buried and muted the perceived body, which was alive and felt from the inside. To be able to discuss that process, Illich and Duden preferred the Greek word *sōma* to the Latin *corpus*, which was too contaminated by imperial connotations that imposed the perspective of a mass seen from the outside, such as the emperor's army corps. The Greek word *sōma*, which may designate the trunk, the belly, the internal humors, and everything Barbara Duden defined as 'the history under the skin,'[1]

1 In German: *Geschichte unter der Haut*, the title of a book by Barbara Duden (1987). See also *Der Frauenleib als Öffentlicher Ort. Vom Missbrauch des Begriffs 'Leben'* ('The woman's body as public place. On the abuse of the concept of "life"') by the same author (Duden, 1991; translated into Italian as *Il corpo della donna come luogo pubblico. Sull'abuso del concetto di vita*, 1994). Jean Robert has translated a dozen articles by Barba-

is more suitable than the Latin *corpus* and its derivatives when it comes to discussing something for which sight is not an adequate mode of perception. The modern presumption of visualizing the flesh within by 'illuminating' it with ultrasound waves occasions a kind of dissection which reduces bodies to the condition of 'corpses that are still alive.'

The human eye is not the most appropriate organ to perceive what throbs under the skin, within the maelstrom of internal feelings and the flow of humors that constitute our felt bodies, or rather, that are us. What Barbara Duden called 'the somatics of past ages' was an attempt at understanding how those who are now dead felt their flesh vibrate under their skin. Barbara Duden believed the carnal, inner presence of that *sōma* to be the most concrete experience of all, the *concretissimum*.

Illich held that what had happened from the 1980s onward was a paradox. Medicine lost most of its power to define bodies and paved the way for a self that conformed to the systems and high technology to such an extent that patients began to see themselves as subsystems of those systems.

Until 1970–1980, medicine propagated the image of bodies in constant need of treatment. After the 1980s, that image evolved into one of 'human beings' capable of self-generation thanks to their being part of a complex cybernetic program.

Once he became aware of this evolution, Illich strove to free his and his friends' perception from the subtle trap represented by cybernetic concepts disguised as common sense. Medicine had acquired the alarming power to induce patients to commit self-betrayal by coaxing them into seeing themselves as iatrogenic constructs, only to subsequently force them to take responsibility for decisions that were to turn them into subsystems of the biomedical system.

In the early 1990s, Ivan Illich and Barbara Duden came to the realization that the evolution of medicine described above was closely associated with the evolution of visualization techniques and, besides that, of the interfaces that turned patients into subsystems of the biomedical system.

ra Duden into French.

A historical study that looks at the present while keeping distance from it

Since he had decided to concentrate on the history of the senses, Illich soon placed the *act of seeing* at the center of his research. As was his custom, his investigation addressed a number of issues simultaneously, in quest of a foothold that would enable him to subdivide the history of the visual ray, of sight, of the gaze, and of perspective into distinct periods.

His analysis was motivated by an issue that was crucial for contemporary history: how could one account for the disincarnation of the modern gaze and for the disappearance of synaesthesia between the senses and of common sense in late modernity? How was the stage reached whereby most people passively put up with the visual din to which they were constantly being exposed? As pointed out by Barbara Duden, Illich's historical research focused on the present right from the outset, even though it bowed to the need to keep its distance from it, and to allow oneself to be surprised by what glimmered in the mirror of the past. Barbara Duden has remarked that what Illich was seeking in the past was the meaning of life's deeper layers, which are now altogether forgotten. In her own words:

> At the end of the 1980s, Illich and I undertook a research project that we called *pupilla*. My background was the study of the history of the body. Illich, for his part, had carried out an investigation of the innovations introduced by scholastic scribes in the twelfth century, namely the emergence of texts that were read only with the eyes, rather than through a synesthesia between the eyes that lent voice to the lines and the ears of the reader who understood them by listening to his own voice (Illich, 1991). We endeavored to identify an access point to a proper understanding of the ethical orientation that informed a human *act*, the act of seeing, ...since late modernity's denial of its eminently active nature, caused us great concern. That project was not occasioned by academic interest but was rather the echo of a conversation between friends on the attitude that

> was most appropriate to an age 'after virtue,'[2] and on the sense of 'duty' in late modernity (Duden, 2007, p. 482).[3]

The history of the body and of the senses in late modernity

In the last interviews which Illich gave to David Cayley, he confessed that, around 1990, he had decided to concentrate his seminars and his conversations with friends, colleagues, and students on the five physical senses and their perceptions.

> Why did I want to understand hearing, seeing, smelling, touching, walking, and feeling by looking at them from the perspective of the past? (Illich, 2005, p. 104).

During the 1980s, Illich tried to understand what characterized the undisputed certainties and 'axioms' that shaped the modern mental topology, and he ended up blaming himself for having proposed an exceedingly conceptual interpretation of them. Indeed, he had come to understand that those certainties were inseparable aggregates of conceptions and perceptions. As Mary Douglas wrote,

> ...the social body determines the way the physical body is perceived. The physical experience of the body, which is always conditioned by the social categories through which it takes place, upholds a specific view of society (Douglas, 1970, p. 72).[4]

Illich wished to understand, in his capacity as a historian, how hearing, sight, smell, touch and taste could substantiate, in their synesthesia, what every age considered to be self-evident, and how they were consequently inseparable from the 'stuff of

2 Translator's Note: This is a veiled reference to the writing penned in 1981 by the Scottish philosopher Alasdair MacIntyre, concerning the need to rebuild ethics after it had fallen under the blows of prevailing liberalism.

3 This passage was taken from the (German) text entitled '"De oculo morali:" Ivan Illich zur Blickgeschichte und zum bedrohten Blicken heute' ('"De oculo morali:" Ivan Illich on the history of the gaze and on the threatened gaze today'), which was published in a collective work on 'the range of ocular perception in early modernity.'

4 That sentence was the opening line of the chapter which Mary Douglas devoted to 'the two bodies' in her book *Natural Symbols* (1970).

things,'[5] which was in turn also inseparable from the sense of the body peculiar to every age. He suspected that the endemic feeling of scarcity which characterized the modern world did not merely translate the unbalanced relationship between desires and the quantity of available goods, but it also expressed, at a deeper level, the loss of density and palpable reality suffered by the historical stuff of the things and the body that was typical of every age.

> I somehow had to explain how the senses could be fulfilled in subsistence cultures in which there is essentially no currency circulation and tradeable goods are extremely limited. I wished to understand how the physicians who operated in accordance with the Galenic tradition managed to make people feel well again without treating their illnesses (Illich, 2005, p. 104).

Thanks to his conversations with his friends, Illich understood that in order to appreciate the reality of the past, he had to take an interest in the history of sensorial perceptions. The modern man monitors his body on the basis of indicators that derive from medical constructs. This notwithstanding, although it is buried under countless layers of anatomical and physiological descriptions and therefore muted, that most intimate of perceptions, namely of one's flesh, still fights to be heard. 'Thus, in order to gain a clearer view of that "something" which people experienced as a sensual and carnal aspect of their daily lives, I concentrated on the history of the gaze' (Illich, 2005, p. 105).

Seeing and being seen take on different meanings depending on the era. In the same fashion that the primeval stuff of things has been conceived in different ways throughout all historical periods, what our eyes do (what happens when people look at each other or at the world) has also been understood in very different ways. For instance, we have 'known' from the early seventeenth century that a natural lens, the lens of the eye, focuses what we see onto the retina, the canvas that is spread out at the back of the eyeball. Because of that postulate, which was demonstrated

5 The reference here is to the English subheading (*A History of Stuff*) of *H2O and the Waters of Forgetfulness* (Illich, 1985).

experimentally by Johannes Kepler, the concept of image cannot be separated from an understanding of how the eye 'sees.'

Before the marriage between the gaze and the image

Images have not always been considered to be an integral part of the visual process. Euclid and other 'opticians' of Antiquity held that a visual ray spread from the pupil, reached the objects, absorbed their colors that were brightened by sunlight, and carried them back to the eye, where no image could enter. For an image to be transported into the eye and thus become fundamental in the explanation of the visual process, the ray's direction had first of all to be inverted: the ray of light proceeding from the sun replaced the old visual ray, the pupil's carnal emanation that linked the observer's eye to the object in his view. That inversion, which took place around the year AD 1000 and was attributed to a wise man from Alexandria, constituted the starting point of every reflection ever made in the field of modern optics. It ushered in the gradual establishment of an instrumental conception of the gaze, which progressively developed the consequences entailed by that inversion. As a tribute to the science of modern optics, given that I am a modern man, I shall no longer place the term optics between quotation marks when dealing with the period that followed that conceptual revolution.

Illich accustomed his students to identifying the history of the losses that underlay the history of developments, and thus managed to ascertain, for instance, the loss of autonomous subsistence abilities which ensued from the economy's development. The gradual transformation of the eye into a basically passive receptor of light rays, which projected onto the retina the objects' image, forced the gaze to partially lose its ancestral nature as an act that was intentional, and therefore ethical. As long as it could be considered as the pupil's erectile member, the visual ray was the *organon* associated with the act of seeing, in the same way that the hand was the organ for daily and figurative art works, and the foot the one suited to every form of ambulation. Antique opticians defined the gaze as psychopodia, i.e., as the soul's hands and feet, which were reckoned to be perhaps the foremost of the *organa* that helped human beings to fulfill their essence. Antique optics did not strive to determine the laws that governed visual rays. but were more concerned with the proper use of the eyes, with 'good vision,' and with the ethics of the gaze.

Before light rays replaced visual rays, the notion of a duplicate of reality projected onto a receptive canvas through the eye's humors was inconceivable. The *act of seeing* had nothing to do with that input of images into the eye and their capture at the hands of a natural net. Antique optics was concerned with an intentional act, namely seeing, and had nothing to do with the passive reception of light rays that formed an image beyond the eye's humors. The Greek *Ta optikà* (a neuter plural noun, and the title of Euclid's work) means 'things pertaining to the gaze' (from the noun *opsis*, the gaze). Ancient Greeks studied sight, not light; they observed the deflections of the carnal visual ray brought about by a mirror or the water surface, rather than the path covered by the fleshless light rays that enabled some of the world's messages to penetrate the eye. They believed the gaze to be a deliberate activity that answered a moral decision, and which could be trained just as effectively as speaking or listening.

A revolution that paved the way for modern optics

The concepts developed by Antique optics, in which Ivan Illich and Barbara Duden immersed themselves for many years, appear to be weird and implausible to minds imbued with modern optics' scientific certainties. Conversely, if our contemporaries had the hypothetical chance to expound their convictions to Antique opticians such as Euclid or Ptolemy, they would be faced with an even more impenetrable wall of incomprehension. Indeed, the latter held the gaze to be a carnal entity, on a par with hands and feet. Disincarnating the ray that carried the colors brightened up by the sunlight (*lux*) would have constituted a moral fault.[6]

6 Ivan Illich and Barbara Duden's research owed much to the Greek scholar Gérard Simon (1988), who was determined to understand Antique optics in its own terms, thereby preventing it from being colonized by the concepts of modern optics. Before him, many scholars of Greek Antiquity had dealt with the optics of the time without relinquishing their scientific certainties, such as the one dictating that vision forms at

At the beginning of the second millennium, the West gradually accepted the new doctrine that envisaged vision as a consequence of the light ray's penetration into the eye, and, little by little, the notion of the active gaze, the pupil's organ that stretched out towards the object deserving to be seen, was discarded. The new doctrine was developed by an Arab mathematician, physician and astronomer, Al-Haytham (965–1039), around the year 1000. Just as Euclid and Ptolemy had done before him, Al-Haytham wrote his work in Alexandria. His full name, Ibn al-Haytham Abu Ali al Hasan, was later Latinized as Alhazen or Avenetan.

> Having been entrusted with the building of a dam on the Nile, he became convinced that his task was infeasible, he 'vanished' for fear of the sultan, and began to earn his living as a scribe. He left a rather unusual treatise on the cotangent, as well as one on astronomy that influenced Averroes (Illich, 2004, p. 201, footnote 53).

While in his haven in Southern Egypt, he observed the specular image caused by a solar eclipse, which he had predicted, as it was being projected through a minuscule crack onto the inner wall of a Pharaonic tomb. Both the ensuing myth and history associated the inversion of the ray start with that anecdote.

The new theory on vision was translated into Latin and written down in the thirteenth century by a Polish monk, Vitello, who was later erroneously quoted as its author (*cf.* Duden, 2007). It was therefore Al-Haytham whom Kepler's treatise on optics took as its point of reference, given that it was entitled *Paralipomena ad Vitellionem* ('Commentary on Vitello's work'). Kepler's commentary on a treatise that stood optics on its head was a turning point worthy of note in itself.[7]

the back of the eye thanks to the projection onto the retina of a duplicate of the image generated by the natural lens known as the lens of the eye. Before Simon, many studies on vision in Antiquity by respected Greek scholars deemed that concept to be an unquestionable natural fact and implicitly included it in their reading of Antique opticians.

7 See the paragraph entitled 'Visio: *pictura* or *imago rei*? Johannes Kepler,' in Duden, 2007, pp. 498–501.

The re-emergence of elements from Antiquity's ethics of the gaze down to Kepler's time

Everything occurred as if, down to Kepler's time, something that allowed for the preservation of the gaze's ethical nature had emerged, had disappeared again, only to arise once more in a different shape within the new optics science. As Illich wrote in an unpublished note, Kepler in 1604,still drew a clear distinction between 'the physical and physiological optical phenomena in the eye and the primacy of perception.' Kepler envisaged light as a messenger that brought news of the world to the soul, and held that in an optical tool the image of the thing seen had to enable the viewer to locate the actual position it occupied.[8] The fact that some of moral optics' postulates have managed to be either preserved or reinvented after the inversion of the ray up to the time of the first optical tools could possibly lend weight, substance and hope to the project of developing an ethics of the gaze suited to the age of virtual reality, interfaces, and on-screen *shows*.

It might be claimed that, after Kepler, all of scientific optics' developments were achieved to the detriment of its moral sense of old. Illich did not simply mean to carry out a reckoning of those losses. His plan was far more ambitious: namely, to lay the foundations of ethics of the gaze suited to contemporary times.

> Antique optics is concerned with preparing a virtuous way of seeing and making you aware of the pitfalls into which your visual ray can fall. I think that a contemporary optics ought to do the same—to make me aware of what happens when I establish the habit of consorting with the seductive non-entities that are constantly being conjured up all around me and of how this preponderance of the virtual affects my everyday intercourse with others (Illich, 2005, p. 119).

8 In a text that was not meant for publication, Illich wrote: 'With his distinction between observing by means of a *pictura* and the ecologically-based act of seeing an *imago rei*, Kepler meant to explain optics mathematically without rejecting at the same time the tradition of *opsis*... The clarity with which he turned the gaze into a fundamental topic that optical theory can partially contribute to elucidate... was to become once again an object of research only in the twentieth century, thanks to Merleau-Ponty, Gibson, and others.'

Being able to tell an image from a 'show'

Illich intended to develop his proposal in full awareness of the fact that optics had dissociated itself from the marriage between vision and image for which Kepler had stepped in as best man, at first slowly after the end of the nineteenth century, and then quite speedily after the end of the 1980s. That divorce was marked out by such a far-reaching transformation of the concept of image that what the word 'image' eventually ended up designating had very little to do with what it had meant in the sixteenth and seventeenth centuries. In those days, an image was understood as a duplicate of reality such as it would have appeared to a draftsman or a painter applying the rules of perspective. Perspective creates a space in which the apparent size of the same object decreases in proportion to the increment of its distance from the viewer's eye. Vision is subjective, in the sense that it portrays what the draftsman or the painter has seen and encourages viewers to place themselves within real space in approximately the same position previously occupied by the draftsman. The space taken up by the object is in a relation of apparent continuity with the space in which viewers find themselves. The object, which is situated within a geometrically built space whose vanishing points ('points at infinity') are in turn placed at a finite distance, is in a relation of proximity to the viewers, who often have the impression of being actually able to touch it. Moreover, a perspectival view places the feet of those who see it in a clearly defined spot.

Leonardo da Vinci never tired of telling his apprentices that only what had been *drawn* could be *seen*. Leonardo's lesson anticipated the predominant thought of the seventeenth century, which developed the concept of *objectivity* in a much more practical fashion by establishing an increasingly close association between reality and its objective representation, or its image. The body became what it had first appeared to be to a draftsman who applied the rules of perspective, and who marked its most noteworthy details with the letters A, B, C, etc. Modern science began with the interpretation of drawings. Yet, it was still a kind of representation that placed the draftsman at the center of the image, albeit invisibly, by means of the rules of perspective.

The early nineteenth century witnessed the emergence of a new way to conceive images as the representation of physical reality, rather than just of what anatomists or artists saw: by discarding perspective representation and the kind of objectivity it entailed, scientific treatises began to show objects in their actual size with increasing frequency. The kind of objectivity associated with that 'image' (which strictly speaking was no longer such, as it no longer provided a point of view) has been defined as 'a-perspective objectivity.'[9] The draftsmen who applied it generated a virtual space in which they placed objects as they were, rather than as they saw them, and they encouraged viewers to look at those objects in a space that had become inaccessible, given that it was situated at an infinite distance from their eyes (*cf.* Illich, 2005, p. 118).[10] That space was not defined by perspective, but was rather a space bereft of vanishing points that reminded one of a picture taken with a telephoto lens.

Another kind of virtual space which became widespread in state-run schools in the first half of the twentieth century was the stereoscope. What that instrument showed was not situated at an infinite distance from its viewers, but rather in a space whose tridimensionality was highlighted, thereby disrupting any form of continuity with the space occupied by its viewers. According to Jonathan Crary, stereoscopes were the forerunners of 'those non-local, *virtual spaces* that have now become so ubiquitous' (Illich, 2005, p. 119, emphasis added).

> Something that has made a great impression on me is the speed with which, in the second half of my seventy years of life, vir-

9 *A-perspective objectivity* (Daston, 1999).

10 The space built to contain those objects is an isometry (an axonometry) that places them at an infinite distance from the viewers. Already at the end of the eighteenth century, William Hunter, a manufacturer of plaster models for medical schools, used to hire a number of artists to make drawings of the organs contained within the corpses he obtained from the morgues. In order to enable the workers of his plaster models-producing workshop to derive the appropriate measurements from the drawings, he imposed on them the application of the rules of isometry instead of the rules of perspective. The 'farther shore' on which isometry placed the represented objects encouraged their contemplation in an inaccessible and uninhabited space. Those drawings were the forerunners of the fourth scopic regime (see footnote 151).

> tual spaces, 'images' and other objects shown within virtual spaces have become generalized. There are currently many respected thinkers who claim that the most profound changes of the past twenty-five years include the ubiquity of the virtual spaces within which, and from which, we are asked to draw our knowledge (Illich, 2000, Italian translation, p. 72).[11]

In the passage quoted above, I have placed the word 'images' between quotation marks, because the way they are seen changed radically at the beginning of the 1980s. Without a point of view, or continuity between the viewers' space and that in which they are seen, those 'images' have become part of a show, a pageant that locks viewers up in the virtual world.

> The difference between image and 'show' contained in the act of seeing them is of course subtle, yet of fundamental importance for any critical analysis of the sensual 'you-me' relationship... The way I see it, a 'show' leads back to the transducer or the program that allows systems to interact, whereas 'image' has been adopted to indicate the entity produced by the imagination. A 'show' conjures up the momentary condition of a cybernetic program, whereas an image is never deprived of *poiēsis*. In this sense, image and 'show' designate two heterogeneous categories of mediation (Illich, 2004, pp. 188–189, footnotes 25 and 26).

Before that recent change, and for many centuries,

> ...'seeing' [had] become synonymous with 'visualizing.' The act which consist[ed] in 'creating an image' in the brain's eye [had] been interpreted as a neurological fact. The identification of vision with inner visualization must be acknowledged as one of European modernity's crucial experiences. Once that has been understood, it becomes possible to see how the duplicative interiorisation deriving from the interaction with a 'show' is something that is wholly unique (Illich, 2004, p. 188).

11 Illich was here referring to the years between 1975 and 2000.

Around 1980, many of our contemporaries shifted from visualizing the world to reducing the world to a 'show.' To them, the formation of the gaze was nothing other than a technical improvement on their pace of digital digestion. It is appropriate to stress here that, according to Antique optics, the formation of the gaze consisted in protecting the eye from the delusions occasioned by desire. In the present era of virtual 'realities,' the establishment of new moral optics is an especially pressing issue.

A very instructive precedent: the re-emergence of the 'moral eye' after Al-Haytham

Peter of Limoges, a Franciscan scholar who practiced medicine and who had become familiar with the Latin translation of Al-Haytham's treatise soon after its circulation, wrote a treatise he entitled *De oculo morali*. Peter intended to train good preachers by means of edifying examples. His audience included high-ranking prelates belonging to the Church in Avignon, to whom he submitted a theory of vision that integrated the inversion of the ray with Antique optics' ethical postulates.

'The treatise *De oculo morali* is a historical testimony that comes in handy in a number of ways: the eye is at the center of the analysis, ...the center of an optical space in which it becomes a "tool" that allows for the examination and reckoning of refraction's physiological and geometrical aspects' (Duden, 2007, p. 490).

At the same time, Peter of Limoges broke new ground, and focused his attention on what was behind the eye: the optical nerves as the source of visual strength and a renewed concept of *sensus communis*, understood as an instance of moral judgment located at the point of entrance of the eye's *visibilia*. His conception of that organ seemed to combine Al-Haytham's revolution with some of Antique optics' characteristic features: a moral eye that stood guard at the light rays' point of entrance and sent out an equivalent number of visual rays. *De oculo morali* essentially integrated two theories of the gaze that were, strictly speaking, altogether incompatible. To put it differently, Peter of Limoges wished to consider the gaze as *hexis*, a suitable behavior that justified the *custodia oculorum*. However, he wished to do so *scientialiter*, within the framework of the new optics.

The history of scopic regimes[12]

I would like to stress once again that, for Illich, the history of the gaze represented a chapter in the overall history of the body. I would also like to point out that Antiquity conceived the gaze in carnal terms, as a temporary organ which the eye projected onto the *visibilia*, or things, in order to see them. Optics, in the sense Euclid understood *ta optikà* (the things pertaining to the gaze), was an ethical discipline in itself that entailed the acquisition of good habits concerning the act of seeing, in the same way that it is desirable to acquire good habits as regards listening or extending hospitality to one's friends.

In keeping with Barbara Duden's approach to the study of various forms of the self-perception of one's body, each of which was associated with a clear-cut historical age, Illich identified four separate *scopic regimes* in the Western history of the gaze, from Antiquity to late modernity. In a conversation with David Cayley, Illich stated that his attempt at a subdivision of the history of the gaze, which he documented throughout its 2,500-year-long evolution, had required at times skills that were more akin to a novelist's than a historian's.[13]

Rather than their degree of conformity to modern optics, what really characterized those scopic regimes was the moral attitude, the hexis which viewers could acquire as a disciplined habit. In the period between Antiquity and the beginning of the second millennium, concerns about 'the good gaze' held sway in the reflections made by the philosophers who took an interest in the topic. That long period corresponded to the regime of the radiant gaze, when the gaze was the pupil's erectile organ that stretched out towards objects, absorbed their colors and carried

12 Illich borrowed the concept of scopic regimes, which he later expanded, from Martin Jay, whose essay on 'modernity's scopic regimes' (1988) he was familiar with.

13 The writing in which Illich outlined in more detail the 'epistemological rifts' in the history of the gaze was 'Guarding the Eye in the Age of Show' (in Illich, 2004, pp. 177–215): the first scopic regime, pp. 192–201; the second scopic regime, pp. 201–205; the third scopic regime, pp. 205–208; and the fourth scopic regime, pp. 208–215.

them back to the eye. Since the gaze was conceived as a somatic activity, its ethical nature was readily apparent. In a historical perspective, that regime corresponded to the age of the *organon*, during which the gaze was one of the 'tools' that helped human beings to fulfill their essence.

Around the year 1000, an Arab scholar turned the cone of vision upside down, and by extension also inverted the meaningful ray's direction. The light ray now directly penetrated the eye and was no longer a mere agent that brightened colors up. It was thus that the second scopic regime began, the *regime of the radiating object*. The gaze ceased to be eminently active and therefore lost its immediate ethical nature. In his *De oculo morali*, Peter of Limoges developed morals that suited the second scopic regime.

The regime of the radiating object cannot be separated from the *causa instrumentalis*, a kind of sub-category of Aristotle's *causa efficiens*, which first emerged between the eleventh and the twelfth centuries. The instrumental cause did not depend on the cosmic circumstances surrounding concrete beings endowed with a gender and a specific cultural affiliation: it could be activated for any conceivable intention. This notwithstanding, the instrumental cause, which was now separate and autonomous from the subjects' intentions, still possessed a rather limited range of action: it did not spread out in an abstract and universal space, but rather in a space which some medievalists see as compartmentalized, or to be more precise, in concrete places that are 'compartmentalized' in the sense that they do not constitute a continuous set. In consequence of the absence of a universal space, the objects portrayed by the painters of the time were not illuminated by a central light source, and consequently hardly cast any shadow. They seemed to irradiate a light of their own and were seldom shaped by their own shadow. Medieval miniatures exemplified the sense of a local light source that was peculiar to, and inseparable from, the objects they portrayed.

During the Renaissance, images became conceptually incorporated into the visual process. That marked the beginning of the regime of the *gaze mediated by the image*, which was to predominate until the nineteenth century. It was the regime under which perspective and optics became branches of science, no longer concerned with the gaze, but rather with light rays. It witnessed the emergence of a new concept of images as mediators of vision, which possessed the following characteristics: a clearly defined position for the painter's or draftsman's eyes and feet (a subjective point of view that highlighted the point in space where the image was created in perspective); a proportional relationship between the object's size and the viewer's; and contiguity between the space of the viewer and that of the object.

Illich proposed to call this third scopic regime the *regime of the humiliated gaze*, which ended up entailing the predominance of the willingness to turn the gaze into an image-capturing tool that was a forerunner of video cameras. It was the age in which the world became visualized within a universal space, while concrete, local perceptions began to wane. This space, which was built in accordance with the rules of perspective, was the background against which painters and draftsmen set their objects, the fixed backdrop around which every era after the fifteenth century was to arrange the setting for its dramas.

> Henceforth the truth will not be what the eye has seen, but rather the observation's outcome. The use of the word 'observation' is a novelty: it designates vision in relation to a given tool. That entails the concomitant lowering and raising of the gaze; the eye itself will progressively be reduced to a means of observation. Sight will become separate from synaesthesis,[14] and vision, which will have consequently become independent from both touch and taste, will be cherished as the means of observation par excellence. The eye loses the co-naturalness it shares with objects the moment it is allowed to gain the upper hand over the other senses (Illich, 2004, p. 289).

Between the end of the eighteenth century and the present time, a fourth scopic regime, which Illich called the age of the 'show,' began to impose itself, at first extremely slowly. Imag-

14 Translator's Note: *Synaisthēsis*: a synaesthesis, i.e., the fusion of the various senses' perceptions.

es were no longer images,[15] and the 'images that were no longer such' began to vie with one another to stand out, even for just a second, from the equally incessant and numbing 'visual din' that Illich called the 'show.' They no longer represented the point of view of a localized observer, and the latter's size was no longer proportional to that of the observed object, which could either be a molecule or a galaxy, or even an abstraction endowed with 'dislocated concreteness.'[16] The 'show' began to progressively invade contemporary visual perceptions.

Many words have been suggested to differentiate non-localized 'pseudo-images,' whose flow is threatening to drown us all, from the images reproduced by painters—or photographers—whose feet rest on a clearly defined spot. One such word, which was proposed by Uwe Pörksen, is 'visiotype' (Pörksen, 1997).

Interfaces are not to be mistaken for images

After the Florentine fifteenth century, images became so closely associated with the acts of seeing and gazing that it became impossible to understand the latter without the former. The fourth scopic regime marked the beginning of the progressive dissolution of that union. Illich almost appeared to be preaching in the desert when he claimed that said rift had been one of Western history's most dramatic instances of an epistemic collapse. Had I not been thoroughly convinced that he was right, I would not have written the present book, even though I still do not really have high hopes that it may actually help to redress the balance in favor of Illich's thought.

The text mentioned above was read at a conference which Illich gave in Hamburg on 19 January 1993. Its main topic concerned interfaces. By way of introduction, he immediately made the following statement:

> As a medievalist, I am fish out of my water in this crowd that

15 See the images produced by William Hunter's draftsmen (see footnote 10 on p. 123), from which it was possible to derive measurements since parallel lines never met.

16 See footnote 17 on p. 80.

> studies informatics and communication. Despite being a layman, I have been asked to speak about *das Bild*, a German word which designates both a 'picture' and an 'image.' I shall do so by comparing image that befits interface with the image I know from the past. By presenting a historical mini sketch of the notion of image, I intend to clarify concepts that I believe relevant to ethics (Illich, 2004, pp. 178–179).

Since he was only too aware that most of his audience availed themselves of virtual reality and its 'shows' as their main source of knowledge, he began by defining two of their relevant key concepts: *information* and *interface*. As far as the first was concerned, one was dealing with a plastic word, which had developed a large number of connotations but which did not possess any specific denotation for most people, with the possible exception of an inner circle of specialists for whom it designated an entity whose quantifiable unity, known as 'bit,' was the equivalent of a 'yes/no' question. As for the impact force of the word information in terms of connotations, it could be claimed that it corresponded to what the linguist Uwe Pörksen called 'the tyranny of a modular language' (Pörksen, 1995).[17]

The word *interface*, for its part, was first coined in 1962 by Marshall McLuhan, with the meaning of 'a means or place of interaction between two systems' (McLuhan, 1962). Given the present generalization of the word system, interface has now come to designate almost everything and anything: 'The interface between physics and music is of direct interest… to the psychological effects of hearing,' or 'the issue of madness as a defense strategy in criminal matters… stands at the interface between medicine, law, and ethics' (Illich, 2004, p. 178, footnote 3). As late as 1975, Jean-Pierre Dupuy was still able to define interfaces as the most basic information required by a subsystem in order to work within the system.

The main topic of the Hamburg conference was 'the im-

17 According to a turn of phrase coined by a famous French biologist, Henri Atlan, computer scientists handle information in the same way postmen handle letters: they take them to their destination without opening them. *Bits* and *bytes* are not units of knowledge.

age at the time of digitalization.' Had the organizers meant to imply that the regime of the 'show' and digitalization had modified the images' status, Illich might have countered that their statement constituted an understatement. As was the case with the transformations affecting 'tools,' those which turned images into something quite different from what they had been for five centuries was the outer sign of an unprecedented epistemic upheaval.

Although Illich left to historians the task of defining precisely how the 'show' differed from what is known as an image, he stressed the fact that the development of the ethics of the gaze required first and foremost distancing oneself from the all-pervasive 'show.' In other words, his history of optics (or rather its historical *opsis*), from Antiquity to late modernity, which was conceived right from the start as an overview of the present given from the past, was aimed at one's self-distancing from the present itself. Conversely, the functional adjustment to the systems and the 'show' required the unconditional acceptance of their basic postulates. Taking one's distance from a present which Illich unwaveringly examined in the perspective of various past eras was also meant to represent a clean break with our acceptance of a visual perception that is now taken for granted. Once the necessary distance has been kept, the question one ought to ask is 'How can I survive the "show"'s environment?' rather than 'How can the show's enterprise be improved?' (Illich, 2004, p. 180).

Illich concluded his conference on how to keep one's gaze under surveillance in the age of the 'show' with the following sentence: 'We are threatened by the emergence of an epoch which takes the "show" for the image' (Illich, 2004, p. 215).

For a historical *opsis*

> Historians of scopic regimes are people who concentrate their attention on the ethology of sense activities in different cultures and epochs. If I had to come up with a name for their discipline, I would settle for historical *opsis*, to distinguish it from the history of optics… *Opsis* is a verbal noun that in Greek designated the gaze. It bespeaks a human activity—

> gazing—that is analogous to other such activities: speaking, walking, eating and listening. To gaze is a widespread action… My concern is to make clear the distinction between an earlier and contemporary gaze: the European gaze wedded for several centuries to the image, and the gaze of today, absorbed in interface with the 'show' (Illich, 2004, pp. 182–183).

There is at least one thing that is certain: neither Ivan Illich nor Barbara Duden intended to contribute to the history of optics' development. Their interest revolved more around the history of the progressive loss of the ability to speak ethically (in a fashion that was not merely allegorical) about the gaze and vision in the period that ranged from Kepler's time to the present, which I would describe as the *age of ethical vacuum* in optics' history. The last four centuries have witnessed the advances made by projection and imaging devices, while the last hundred years or so have seen a prodigious development of video-recording technology; the creation of inaccessible spaces in which to observe and measure objects that do not share the size of those perceived by human senses; the elimination of any proportional relation between the viewers' size and the objects'; and the scanning of images that bring to the fore worlds located light years away, or else of molecular structures made 'visible' by 'scanning tunneling microscopes.' All of the above has led to the generalization of a kind of 'objectivity' that dispenses with viewers located in a clearly defined space, and by extension with any object that the senses can experience directly.[18] Each of those phases of the 'images' martyrdom' helped to undermine the foundations of the 'world's visualization' which after the seventeenth century determined objectivity's criteria for natural sciences and medi-

18 Until the eighteenth century, objectivity was associated with perspective, which presented the object 'from a specific point of view' (which was thus subjective), a proportional relation between the object and the painter, the draftsman or the photographer that produced the image, and contiguity between the space occupied by the object represented and the observer's. The objectivity that characterized the fourth scopic regime, which presented measurable objects in inaccessible spaces, in relation to which it was impossible to place the image's author, constituted a kind of objectivity in which there was neither an object that could be perceived by the senses nor an author. It was a kind of objectivity that forced the viewer to appropriate the construction rules of uninhabitable spaces, and encouraged him to contemplate a world located on a 'farther shore,' as Illich wrote, i.e., 'at an infinite distance.'

cine. What Lorraine Daston has called *a-perspective objectivity* (Daston, 1999) could possibly designate the legitimization of virtual spaces of observation in which 'objects' inaccessible to the senses may be measured.

Illich described what had been neglected during the centuries of scientific optics' ethical silence, even though it kept being practiced outside science itself, as follows:

> It is too often forgotten that the gaze was traditionally considered to be a free, wholly human and *virtuous* activity, provided that it was also disciplined. The invitation I received to give one of the opening speeches before a large gathering of technicians, psychologists, and communication specialists to evoke the impact which screen images have on our society was a welcome chance to address the ethics of the gaze by calling to mind the thousand-year-long tradition of ocular ascesis, the *custodia oculorum* which has been practiced to this day (Illich, 2004, p. 177, footnote 1).

The West's unease in the presence of images

By following in the footsteps of the historian Alain Besançon (1994), Illich studied the Western gaze's specificity.[19] What marked it out from all the other kinds of gaze attested throughout history was the sense of unease it experienced in the presence of images. According to Besançon, philosophy arose from a feeling of perplexity, and then of skepticism, towards images, the second of which was contemporary with the first diffusion of the alphabet, about two centuries before Plato. It was still a long way from what was to become, in the fifteenth century, the images' assimilation to the visual process. The image (*eikōn* in Greek) was still carved in marble, cast in bronze or painted on vases. In Archaic Greece, which was not yet literate, it usually portrayed a God or a hero. The God's physical presence coincided with his carved or painted representation. Then, around the sixth century

19 On Greek thought's specificity and on philosophy as the alphabet's offspring, see Ong, 1982.

BC, it looked as if an already literate society had suddenly started shifting its focus from images to concepts. The statue of Aphrodite no longer presented the goddess but rather symbolized Love, the one of Poseidon evoked Water, the one of Ares War, and the one of Helios the luminous Center and Light. This shift from concrete images to words and concepts was the starting point of the *ikonoskepsis* (the diffidence, doubt and censure in the presence of images) that characterizes Western thought.

'Christianity, at its origin, enters a world in which the image has been rejected, overcome, and transcended by philosophers; …it enters it, at first, as a sect of Judaism, a crucial point because the Jews maintained an extraordinarily radical attitude towards images. "Thou shalt not make unto thee any graven image or any likeness of anything that is in heaven above, or that is in the earth beneath, or that is in the water under the earth (Exodus, 20,4)"' (Illich, 2005, p. 112).

The Jewish proscription of images represented a dilemma for the disciples and the first Christians, who 'felt they had seen the Son of God' and considered the Word made flesh as God's own image. In open defiance of the Jewish Commandment, they began to portray the object of their worship. It is quite surprising that the Church of the early centuries never drew a parallel between Christian images and pagan statues: until the eighth century, it rejected pagan images without ever questioning the Christian ones.

> The tension between the Old Testament proscription of images and the New Testament account of Christ as the image of the Father came to an explosive head in the year 726. It was fifty years before the birth of Charlemagne, a time already well into the Middle Ages, when expanding Islam had become a major threat to the continued existence of Byzantium. Leo III was then the Emperor of Byzantium… and he had won a battle in which he had stopped the iconoclastic, image-destroying Muslims… Right after his victory over these notoriously iconoclastic Muslims, the Emperor went to the bronze main gate of his palace and removed the image of Christ that was above it and replaced it with a simple symbol: a cross.

> With this ceremony, he started a fierce debate that raged for several generations. Its issue was, can Christians bow and pray before an image? For the first time the question of iconoscepsis—which caused the Greeks to doubt the desirability of speaking of love only in terms of the beautiful deity—became an occasion of civil war... A true and pretty bloody war began about the gaze (Illich, 2005, pp. 113–114).

That war pitched *iconodules*, who upheld the legitimacy of the cult of images, against *iconoclasts*, who demanded their destruction by invoking the second commandment. In 787, a Council (the Second Nicene Council), which was summoned at the emperor's behest, decided that the cult of images was legitimate.

The icon of Christ found once again its place above the bronze door. How was that controversy solved? St. John of Damascus, who was the first to analyze in depth the difference between contemplating an image and looking at the face of a person in the flesh, expressed the consensus reached by the majority of the Council Fathers. According to his doctrine, an icon was the threshold on which the inspired artist laid a reflection of the glory he had glimpsed beyond it: as St. John wrote, it was a typos of the prototypos that was in heaven. Icons were a window on eternity, where Christ and his mother reincarnated in heaven were already sharing in the angels' glory. Those who prayed by kneeling before the iconostasis (the 'wall' of icons that conceals the altar from the faithful) drew inspiration from the beauty created by the painter to devoutly reach, through the typos, the prototypos: although they prayed before an image, the latter actually reflected the real flesh of those who had already been incorporated into the body of Christ. When the faithful applied themselves with devotion and fervor to performing that expression of respect, St. John explained, they did not merely touch with their eyes what lay beyond the threshold represented by the icon, but their gaze actually reverted to them after mingling with the flesh of the Risen One, thereby enabling them to partake in the construction of the Church as an authentic body of flesh (*cf.* Illich, 2005, pp. 114–115).

> We are, therefore, here again, at a point where an enormous, extraordinary belief—namely, belief in the flesh already in eternity, and accessible to the gaze of faith which reaches from darkness into eternal light—led to the acceptance of the cult of images. This decision, as I understand it, was thoroughly in line with the Christian spirit, in the way it links the visible and the invisible worlds. But it also laid the foundation for the world which now surrounds us, the world of iconomania. And this is what I call the *perversio optimi*, the perversion of the best, in which a first, perfectly innocent step leads eventually to the digitalized, interactive TV screens, and on to ever newer and stranger developments in a long, drawn-out martyrdom of the image (Illich, 2005, pp. 116–117).

Chapter 7: The Cultural History of the Alphabet

The alphabet, elixir and poison

In 1984, Ivan Illich began to write, in a number of languages, eight texts (essays, books, lecture notes) on the social history of the alphabet. That history had its inception more than 2,600 years ago, in the context of the celebrations during which *aoidoi* and *rhapsodes*[1] sang of the Achaeans' heroic deeds in Troy around 1100 BC, and of the journey undertaken by one of them, Odysseus, to return to the island of Ithaca. The culture of the alphabet in modern times, Illich wrote, was threatened with extinction caused by the din of communication.

Between those two extremes, Illich situated the joys which the alphabet had given to humanity and the destructive potential it harbored within itself, which is nowadays clearly identifiable 'in the bulldozer hidden in every computer.'

The alphabet deprives the sphere of hearing of what has been said and transfers it to the sphere of seeing. Right from the beginning, it snatched the winged words of conversations and epic songs and deposited them, static and frozen, on some kind of material support (a codex, a scroll, a page or a screen). The alphabet was the first form of writing whose signs were (almost) entirely phonetic.

> The protocol of writing by means of wholly phonetic signs delivers for the first time the spoken word to a shore where history splits into two periods. The scribe steals from the fleeting instant what is being said, and seals what he has heard in the lasting space of language. Thus is born a 'text,' that is to say, a 'woven textile.' In the other dimension, namely that of orality, there is no 'content' that may be differentiated from what has been heard (Illich, 1984, p. 25).[2]

1 Singers of epic deeds.

2 For a list of the essays which Illich devoted to the social and cultural history of the alphabet, see pp. 140–141 below.

The alphabet in its many variants (Greek, Latin, Cyrillic, etc.) was the only form of writing among the numerous documented ones to pose a threat to oral expression. Studying the history of the alphabet necessarily entails studying the history of the relationship between a unique form of writing and orality. It implies studying the history of the power to transform orality possessed by the alphabet, a history which was slow in coming to light.

Let us consider the Mycenaean syllabic script known as Linear B, which was deciphered by Ventris and discarded in the twelfth century BC, to examine the reasons why it could in no way compromise orality:

- Its use was limited, confined to the great palace that stood as a small town of sorts within the city of Mycenae, and it was employed to compile registers and write down religious formulae.
- It consisted of about a hundred syllabic signs which could not be learned by just anyone, since the process required specialized training. It may be surmised that writing itself was a secret to which only the world within the palace had access.

I believe that complicated forms of writing such as the Chinese or the Japanese ones managed to spread among the common folk, starting no later than the nineteenth century, because of the imposition of compulsory schooling on the one hand, and subtle phoneticization[3] on the other. The Japanese language possesses two syllabic scripts, which in theory allow for the phonetic transcription of virtually anything, whereas the use of ideograms (*kan-ji*) is associated with prestige. My Chinese and Japanese friends are only too aware that their form of writing is at risk, threatened as it has been first by pens and later by computers, which consign to oblivion the gestures linked to a way of writing performed by means of a paint brush. The great Belgian sinologist Pierre Ryckmans (also known by the pseud-

3 Translator's Note: The adoption of signs that match the uttered word, rather than the object which it designates.

onym Simon Leys) has highlighted the difference between the mental processes involved in the reading of Chinese ideograms and those at play in the reading of alphabetic writing.

In this chapter, I endeavor to understand the nature and the various historical forms of the manifestation of the alphabet's power, which at the beginning of the third millennium has moved well beyond 'instrumentalization.' The historians of the alphabet seek to understand how orality, once it was exposed to the alphabet's impact, came to be a metaphor for the transformation of one kind of 'matter' at the hands of a 'technology.' In a way, the alphabet was the primeval 'technological phenomenon' (*cf.* Ong, 1982) that (in the digital age in which there are no longer any tools as such) is now becoming outdated. This notwithstanding, just as the material culture of a so-called 'primitive' society can manage to hold out for a long time against Western development's assaults, so can oral culture hold its own against alphabetization. New forms of resistance may be devised. One of these is the preservation of a plurality of ways of reading.[4]

Walter Ong has suggested (in reference to the Western world) that philosophy, like all sciences, relies heavily on alphabetic writing: '...they are produced not by the unaided human mind but by the mind making use of a technology that has been deeply interiorized, incorporated into mental processes themselves. The mind interacts with the material world around it more profoundly and creatively than has hitherto been thought. Philosophy, it seems, should be reflectively aware of itself as a technological product...' (Ong, 1982, p. 172) However, the alphabet is not an artifact whose distality (the distance that establishes a relationship with the user's body) and material nature may be analyzed, as is conversely the case with tools. Faced with a material tool, one is always free to decide whether to take it or leave it. Those who have interiorized the alphabet, on the other

4 Illich proposed the following example: in the twelfth century, various ways of reading were replaced by the *lectio scholastica*, the silent and interpretative reading which, as will be shown below, has exerted a monopoly of sorts ever since. To preserve something of the art of reading in the digital age, it would be necessary to safeguard a different way of reading. For my part, I was involved for ten years in the initiative of running a read aloud group.

hand, can no longer leave it, because the latter has become the mold that shapes their thoughts and horizons.

A transcultural invention

Although it is undeniable that the alphabet was a unique invention attributed to the Greeks of the Homeric age, it is too often forgotten that they did not achieve it on their own. The alphabet was the outcome of the relations which the Greeks entertained with a Semitic people, in all likelihood the Phoenicians. It drew its origin from transcultural interactions in which the former's wish to learn and the latter's readiness to teach went hand in hand with innovative misunderstandings, such as the 'discovery' of what Phoenician letters lacked in order to write down the Greek language. It may be added straightaway that it was vowels. The Phoenician form of writing, which was purely based on consonants, included gutturals that did not exist in Greek. It was those Semitic gutturals that Greeks allegedly perceived as vowels.

Of all the essays that Illich wrote on the alphabet, the one that thrilled me the most was the first, which was published in 1984. To support the sometimes bold theories that I am going to present in this chapter, I would like to include here documentation that may be useful to those who wish to embark on a research path.

Ivan Illich's works on the social history of the alphabet

On this topic Illich wrote the books, essays, and lecture notes which are listed below:[5]

1. *Schule ins Museum. Phaidros und die Folgen* ('The school in the museum. Phaedrus and the consequences,' Illich, 1984).
2. *A Plea for Research on Lay Literacy*, a conference held at the general assembly of the American Education

5 Translator's Note: For the relevant bibliography, see the references at the end of the book.

Research Association, San Francisco, August 1986 (in Illich, 1992, pp. 159–181).

3. *Computer Literacy and the Cybernetic Dream*, a speech given at the 'Science, Technology and Society' second national conference on the topic of 'Technological Alphabetization,' Washington 1987 (in Illich, 1992, pp. 202–207).
4. *Schriften lesen im 12. Jahrhundert: das Disdascalicon Hugos von Sankt Viktor* ('Reading texts in the twelfth century: Hugo of Saint Victor's *Didascalicon*,' Illich, 1987; *cf.* Illich, 1991).
5. *ABC, The Alphabetization of the Popular Mind* (Illich and Sanders, 1988, also available in French).
6. *In the Vineyard of the Text. A Commentary to Hugh's Didascalicon* (Illich, 1991).
7. *Text und Universität. Zur Idee und Geschichte einer einzigartigen Institution* ('The text and university: the idea and history of a unique institution,' Illich, 1991a, also available in English and French).
8. *Lectio divina dans la haute Antiquité et l'Antiquité tardive* ('The *Lectio divina* in High Antiquity and in late Antiquity,' 1993, reissued in Illich, 2004, pp. 157–176).

A first criticism of the alphabet's destructive powers

The *Phaedros* recounts how Socrates, who was having a conversation with a young man by the same name that drew his arguments from a text he had learned off by heart, the scroll of which he kept hidden under his tunic, chided him for behaving like a sophist, one of those pedants who claimed to do philosophy in writing. Socrates maintained that the alphabet put in jeopardy the very backbone of philosophy, which was oral improvisation in the *symposion* (or banquet) under the guide of an expert in *maieutics* (literally, the midwives' art).[6] Plato, one of Socrates' students, used writing to deliver to posterity Socrates' criticism of writing.

6 Translator's Note: A teaching method adopted by Socrates: by means of dialogues and debates, his disciples were encouraged to 'give birth' to the truth.

Plato's *Dialogues* display a passion for writing and a criticism of its use. The y present the alphabet as a *pharmakon*, which is concomitantly an elixir and a poison. The pupils of Athens' schools at the time of Plato had become extremely skilled in the use of alphabetic writing.

For many centuries after the invention of writing, most of the men who took part in Greece's assemblies were hardly able to scribble their own names on a clay shard: their writing skills did not go beyond that. The alphabet remained, for a long time, an island in a sea of orality.

Four centuries after the invention of the alphabet, thanks to the increase in the literacy rate, a first reflection was undertaken on the transformational power it possessed.

While it is undeniable that the Greeks, who 'invented' the alphabet, were intelligent, it was not necessary for them to have recourse to any superpower to do so. The reason is that they did not develop it on their own.

Accomplished scribes right from the outset

The current theories on the origin of the alphabet have led to the acknowledgment that shortly after its invention there were extremely skillful scribes who were capable of transcribing the *aoidoi*'s and *rhapsodes*' oral improvisations by essentially keeping pace with their singing. Whenever scribes were about to transcribe one of Homer's cantos, it may be surmised that they simply asked him to sing more slowly than usual, or else to introduce longer pauses.

That hypothesis is a necessary requirement to explain the existence of *Urtexte*, namely original texts that do not descend from earlier ones, but are, in fact, the transcription of oral epic songs, as, for instance, the Iliad and the Odyssey, Beowulf,[7] the *Chanson de Roland*, or the hymns that celebrated Quetzalcoatl, which were transcribed by Sahagún's assistants[8] on the highlands of Mexico half a century after the conquest.

7 Translator's Note: The earliest known Anglo-Saxon epic song.

8 Translator's Note: A sixteenth-century Spanish missionary and historian.

In 1928, the US linguist and Greek scholar Milman Parry published at the Sorbonne a revolutionary dissertation written in French, in which he contended that the Iliad and the Odyssey were not the compositions of a writer of genius, but rather oral improvisations written down by scribes who were already being trained in a relatively fast form of writing shortly after the introduction of the Greek alphabet.[9]

Milman Parry's students have subsequently employed the term 'Urtext' to designate a text with no antecedents. The songs which underlie such texts may be sung many times, but they are never performed twice in the same way. The concept of 'the first transcription' of an oral improvisation was initially applied to Homer's cantos, then to Serbian songs, and subsequently to songs from all the world regions where a tradition based on oral epic singers had lingered on. The basic unit of those songs is never the word, as is the case with written poetry (suffice it to consider the search for the *mot juste*), but rather the formula or the epithet (Illich, 1984, pp. 33–34).

As the criteria that enable the distinction between the transcriptions of oral improvisations and written compositions are improved, fresh controversies arise among scholars. This notwithstanding, it is still necessary to go back to Parry and his colleagues' main intuition: what occasioned the Iliad's 27,000 hexameters was not a poetic composition but an improvisation, whose core elements were not words, but rather the speech formulae which *aoidoi* and *rhapsodes* derived from the repertory people employed to describe their circumstances, or else borrowed from other *rhapsodes*. It is important to understand that 'Homer' did not fetch them from the reservoir of a generic 'memory:' it was something quite different from a mnemonic technique. To actively 'remember,' *rhapsodes* had to be in the state of 'en-thusiasm,'[10] which their interaction with their audience brought about.

9 *Cf.* Parry, 1928, as well as other writings by the same author, which have been collected and published by his son Adam (Parry, 1987).

10 Translator's Note: In the etymological sense of the word: feeling a god within oneself, and being possessed by a god's essence.

> I am not aware of a better way to understand what the activity of 'remembering' was like in a time that preceded the birth of memory and of its bastard child, information. But our understanding of cultural continuity without the mediation of texts relies on the dominant and a-critical concept of teaching, which accepts as natural the concept of information transmission (*ibid.*)

Neither epics nor their written transmission contain or convey 'information.' After Shannon and Turing, the concept of information designates what is to be found inside computers: bits. Perhaps those who label a form of knowledge with the word information mean to say that, in their view, every form of knowledge may be stored in a 'memory,' be it human or mechanical.

> The notion of a form of knowledge, of a piece of information that can be stored in a memory as if it were a reservoir, could only arise after the winged words of orality were pinned down in writing. This idea seems nowadays to be so self-evident that one can hardly conceive the perceptions and experiences from eras in which acts and the memory of them were not stored in a warehouse (Illich, 1984, p. 33).

Illich repeatedly pointed out how much he owed to Milman Parry, the young linguist from California who died in an accident at thirty-three. After publishing his dissertation at the Sorbonne (Parry, 1928), Parry was given the chance to set up a team of researchers which included Albert Lord and Bela Bartok, who confirmed his core theory on complex oral improvisations by recording epic Serbian songs.

> It does not happen very often that a fundamental concept which has hitherto never been questioned becomes relativized. It is my belief that Milman Parry's relativization of our fundamental concepts on what memory is represents an achievement on a par with Einstein's first formulation of the theory of relativity (Illich, 1984, chapter III, p. 33).

Most of the texts known to us, be they modern or ancient, had their original source in other texts with which they were associated as either copies or commentaries, unless they were compositions pieced together word by word by an author. We have now become literate to such an extent that it is quite difficult for us to conceive a text that has neither been copied nor devised by an author. A text that does not have its source in another one, and which has not been claimed by any author, could not be anything other than the first transcription of an oral improvisation.

Alphabet and power

In Antiquity and in the early Middle Ages, the ability to write sometimes went hand in hand with an aristocratic form of power. The rhetoric to which young Romans of noble birth were initiated was part of the learning process for the acquisition of the language of power. In the early Middle Ages, the knowledge which monks drew from their polyptychs, the ledgers that listed the abbeys' properties and the services due by the farmers who tilled them, was, in the latter's eyes, just as mysterious as the 'Domesday Book.'

In the eighth century, for instance, the monks from Prüm Abbey (now in the diocese of Trier) used to travel through their territory (which was as large as a mid-sized European country) by following a spiraling path that had the abbey at its center. In every inhabited place they came across, they assessed the local *mansi* (roughly the equivalent of modern 'small holdings'), which could be whole- or half-sized, free or servile, and established the criteria by which they determined, through an elaborate calculation, the amount and the nature of the services and salt taxes their farmers owed them. All of the above was written down in their polyptychs.

In a subsequent journey, the monks referred to the polyptych associated with 'their own' *mansus* and reckoned the amount of 'their own' tax. What is more, in the case of Prüm Abbey, the polyptychs were a Latin 'translation' of an earlier land survey carried out in Old High German. The farmers had no access to the logic underlying those erudite calculations. The distance between the monks' knowledge and the farmers' prevented the latter from appropriating the monks' (alphabetic) type of knowledge.

The case of Prüm Abbey's polyptychs is a significant example. A host of distances 'protected' the farmers, who were rooted in orality, from the alphabetic knowledge possessed by those monks who seemed to 'know everything' about them. Those distances placed the farmers in a condition of relative disadvantage but prevented them from being transformed by the monks' alphabetic knowledge. The rulers' power remained external to them, and while it put them under certain obligations, it did not change them from within.

In the Antique world, the alphabet was not long in revealing the nature of its power on society. In the Greek and Roman *oecumene*, that power was put at the service of the expression of different ideals and of the education of various *elites*.

> Both the ideal of the city-state's *paideia* and the Roman ideals of *docentia* and *disciplina*, which are very different and centered on the *magister*, are impossible to translate.[11] This notwithstanding, all three are employed to literally impose the strict observance of a number of precepts on a specific category of youth who are destined to occupy positions of power. In either case, they are a means to turn adolescence into the initiation to a tradition of alphabetic writing, and to base power on written culture (Illich, 1984, p. 31).

All that changed in the thirteenth century, when a kind of 'lay alphabetization' began to spread that was prompted by the discovery, made by 'illiterate' people, that writing could bestow a power of sorts also on those who had not mastered its technique.

A new relationship between orality and the alphabet, as well as a new perception of the powers that the latter could confer, began to develop, and later defined the outline of the mentality that became associated with *Europe*. It may even be

11 Translator's Note: Greek *paideia* and Latin *docentia*, which are usually translated as 'education' and 'teaching,' relied on an approach to those two activities which did not correspond to the meaning they are nowadays given.

ventured that the period in question celebrated the alphabet's wedding with Europe and, in more general terms, with the West.

After the thirteenth century, a change in the essence of social relations obtained north of the Alps: trust, property, power, and the role one played daily began to be defined against something that was written.

Writing (which had previously been the mysterious source of the Word of God) became the tool for the transmission of immanent relations. In the late Middle Ages, the domains of daily life, which had earlier been regulated by oral customs, became subjugated to a kind of 'legal alphabetization' that reflected a new experience: before they could be owned, objects had to be described (Illich, 1984, p. 53).

The thirteenth century has bequeathed us thousands of topographical descriptions in which some demarcation lines were defined in great detail. In those documents, the world, which theologians portrayed as one of God's books that man had to decipher, was turned into a collection of objects that could be appropriated by describing them. Before natural science seized it as its own, the description of reality was first and foremost a legal approach.

There were three pivotal moments that defined the relationship between Europe and the alphabet at the dawn of the second millennium:

- the *revolution* of the 'technology of writing;'[12]
- the *revolution* of the ethology of reading in the twelfth century;
- the emergence of *bookish texts* and the diffusion of silent reading after the thirteenth century.

The reading of lines with unspaced words is quite different from that of texts displaying clearly spaced words. In the

12 *Cf.* Ong, 1982. Illich wrote: 'I would like to draw your attention to a possibility that was only became feasible thanks to this technical revolution: namely, the production of a text that was essentially visible. If my considerations are pertinent, at least as a first approximation, it then becomes necessary to admit that the *invention* of a text's visible, typographical layout is an achievement that has historically been underestimated' (Illich, 1991a).

first case, the reader's voice pronounces the lines *before* they have been understood: their understanding occurs after they have been heard. The text is akin to a musical score that has first to be sung. Reading it in silence is extremely difficult, if not altogether impossible. The reading of spaced texts, conversely, allows for their understanding to precede their aural reception, thereby making silent reading feasible. A shift from a *phonic* to a *typographical* order has taken place, which has transferred the page onto the plane of what is *visible.* Readers store up in their memory the image of thousands of individual words, which they recognize in the same way they would recognize a thousand faces.

When Illich spoke of the 'revolution of the written page,' he was referring to a change that had affected both the technology of writing and the ethology of reading.[13] On the one hand, the text's material support became lighter (sheepskin or calfskin, and later paper), and a number of innovations in the page layout began to spread, such as marginal notes and especially spacing, which by separating words ultimately made them visible. In a way, the book that 'I own' and have borrowed somewhere in the neighborhood loses its uniqueness and becomes part of a series of books that quote one another in their notes, and of which there are copies available in libraries. By borrowing one of George Steiner's expressions, Illich stated that books had become 'bookish texts,' meaning that above each of their pages hovered a sort of text that was ideal, immaterial and 'referential.' Once books adopted the format they still have today, it became possible to describe them as 'manuals' (i.e., something that can be held in a hand).

After the first half or the twelfth century, the 'technology' of book production underwent a number of transformations, which gave the books a closer resemblance to the first printed books than to the huge manuscripts of the early part of

13 *Cf.* Illich, 1991a. That essay includes an excellent introduction to the writing technology's 'revolution' in the twelfth century, and to the fashion in which it paved the way for the emergence of the mentality, the various kinds of knowledge, and the blindness that were to characterize what was subsequently called *Europe*, and later still *the West.*

the century. Illich held that the printing press had made possible the reproduction of the object created by the revolution of the page layout in the twelfth century. In the social history of the alphabet, the emergence of bookish texts was of far greater importance than the invention of the printing press halfway through the fifteenth century, which led to the duplication in a great number of copies of an object whose shape had been established three centuries before.

Illich went as far as proposing a periodization of the history of the alphabet that relied on three main events:

1. Its invention around 750 BC;
2. the emergence of bookish texts at the start of the thirteenth century;
3. the invention of movable type printing around 1450.

The association of the alphabet with schools

The text to which I shall be referring to address this topic was originally presented at a conference given by Ivan Illich for the inauguration of the School Museum in Ichenhausen, in Bayern, on 16 July 1984. That museum presentation of the interdependence between schools and the history of the alphabet was meant to encourage a new perspective on both of them. *Schule ins Museum* (Illich, 1984) was published thirteen years after *Deschooling Society* (Illich, 1971), is still unavailable in either French or Italian, and, unlike the 1970s criticism of industrial society's three main service institutions (education, transportation, and the health system), it did not focus on the school's counterproductivity, but rather examined its history within the much wider framework of the history of the alphabet. After providing a historical excursus encompassing more than 2,600 years, Illich examined, concomitantly, the damage wrought by the alphabet and the joys it brought to mankind. The first chapter of the book I am presently discussing is entitled 'The threatening and threatened alphabet.' Just as George Steiner and others had done before him, Illich hoped that something of the alphabetic culture could be salvaged from the disaster he saw looming ahead: the extinction of alphabetic culture at the hands of the chitter-chatter of robots equipped with speech.

The association of the alphabet with schools is a specifically European phenomenon. It may even be ventured that after the thirteenth century this association was the mold that shaped European culture and, beyond that, what is generally meant by words such as 'the West' and 'modernity.' Since then, in a slow and gradual fashion, it has become mandatory to attend schools regularly, as well as to subject oneself to the increasingly uniform and universal ritual of alphabetization. One of the surprises contained in that book is the development of a theory concerning the cultural history of what is nowadays known as 'Latin America,' which allegedly witnessed a farther-reaching kind of 'lay alphabetization' than was the case in Europe.

In the early 1970s, Illich denounced the counterproductivity of compulsory schooling, a holy cow that it was necessary to discard. At the time, the fact that schooling was an institution of *compulsory alphabetization* was taken for granted. In 1984, Illich widened the perspective of his analysis, and came to see alphabetization as an activity for which schools had not always been, nor would always be, either the main place or the means.

The history of Europe is so closely linked to that of the alphabet that it is impossible to discuss one without also mentioning the other. The alphabetized civilization has the presumption to dominate the world, and that dominance coincides with the one which Europe later exerted over other continents. Should those who nowadays speak of 'decolonization' not perhaps see their project as an effort to grasp what the alphabet has done to Europe, with Europe, and ultimately with all Westernized cultures? And to also grasp what the alphabet is still doing to those cultures that have come to resist the worldwide alphabetization movement? The dominance which the alphabetized culture imposes rests on a form of blindness that leads to the establishment of a specific kind of knowledge of what memory, language, conscience, and perception are, a kind of 'knowledge' that is infectious.

Before compulsory alphabetization, a form of 'lay alphabetization'

One of Ivan Illich's original contributions was his being able to understand that in Europe, as had been the case in its colonies, the age of schooling and of compulsory alphabetization was first preceded, and then accompanied, by a form of 'lay alphabetization,' which was carried out by 'illiterate' people who understood the social power the alphabet bestowed on those capable of employing it even without possessing the technical expertise to handle it.

Illich called *lay alphabetization* (Illich and Sanders, 1988) the selective appropriation of the alphabet on the part of people who were technically incapable of reading, but who could still ask somebody to read or write a letter for them. In the years he spent in Puerto Rico, Illich came to the realization that a form of alphabetization encouraged by still illiterate people affected Latin American colonial culture much more deeply than any other element. Illich' profound knowledge of that culture, which he acquired in Puerto Rico and in Mexico, and later also in Brazil and in Peru, prepared him to understand a culture that was still partially illiterate, but nonetheless well-disposed towards the alphabet due to its belief in the latter's benefits and in the power of written documents.

In Puerto Rico (where he sat on several school boards), Illich witnessed, with a certain degree of amazement, the first formulations of development theory's 'dog Latin.'[14]

Development theory was presented as a new kind of social anthropology that believed schools to be the only gateway to the Land of Plenty; the great amount of credibility it enjoyed among the people took Illich aback. In Latin America, he subsequently witnessed the emergence of a category of people who had not attended any schools and were technically outside the world of letters, but who were aware at the same time of writing's

14 In the 1960s, Puerto Rico became a sort of laboratory of new ideas which the US government allowed to be tested on the 'natives.' The debates concerning the discourse on development, which began to be addressed in the 1940s, greatly amazed Illich for the equally redeeming and scientific impact they made at the time. Since he was unable to take them seriously, he described them as something akin to 'dog-Latin.'

power and could avail themselves of it by proxy.

> My intuitions concerning this fundamental ambiguity of writing became stronger the more I became acquainted with Central America and South America. I understood that the section of population which my colleagues on the Board of Education described as 'illiterate' was in fact made up of individuals who had mastered writing better than most of the educated proletariat. Just as Charlemagne had resorted to a secretary whenever he wanted to have something written down, they dictated to a colleague, a relative, or a neighbor, in full knowledge that writing could still be employed even without knowing how to handle it in first person (Illich, 1984, p. 18).

Illich formulated the possibility of a popular culture imbued by the alphabet and possessed by illiterate people, and endeavored to present it to his colleagues on Puerto Rico's Board of Education. However, the latter only accepted that the radio, the television, and even political activism could succeed in spreading alphabetization just as schools did, but they could not really go much further. In other words, they went as far as admitting that schools were not the only place and means for effective alphabetization, but criticizing alphabetization *per se* was beyond the scope of their abilities, as is usually the case with most alphabetized people. Europeans, Westerners, 'modern' or alphabetized people are so bogged down in alphabetic culture that they are utterly incapable of examining it from the outside.

> This reflection was aimed at developing a history of the schools' monopoly on education, and especially on written culture. I would like to define the present period of that history as *the age of compulsory schooling,* in opposition to the *postmedieval era of a popular culture imbued with an alphabetic mentality* (*ibid.*, the italics are mine).

The grounding of schools in a popular culture imbued with the alphabet

Ichenhausen's School Museum, which is affiliated to the Bavarian National Museum, testifies on the one hand that traditional European schools are rooted in orality, and on the other that the alphabet permeates popular culture. That complementary reciprocity deserves proper consideration at a time when the din caused by the *communication* between cybernetic systems threatens with extinction an alphabetic culture the beginnings of which date back to more than 2,600 years ago, which has shaped Europe, given mankind literature and science, destroyed most oral cultures, and which is now on the brink of self-destruction.

Bookish reading: A medieval phenomenon unknown to the Antique world

The Antique world was familiar with books and libraries, but was unacquainted with *bookish texts*, 'the texts that seem to hover above the pages' of an actual book. After the thirteenth century, books began to adopt that characteristic feature. Bookish texts lend themselves to what Steiner called 'bookish reading' (1988, p. 754).[15] The text that hovers above the actual book in my hand potentially summons all of the other books to my act of reading. According to Steiner, bookish reading paved the way for novels and science. After the thirteenth and fourteenth centuries, chivalric romances (such as for instance *Amadis of Gaul* and its imitations) began to mix together their subject lines and appeared to entertain a dialogue with one another. René Girard (1961) demonstrated that, even before Cervantes, a common subject (that of triangular or mimetic desire, according to Girard) seemed to be woven through each individual romance. As for science, the interconnections between individual works and disciplines are too apparent to require any comment.

15 See also another book by Steiner entitled *After Babel: Aspects of Language and Translation*, which was first published in 1975 and subsequently re-issued in a revised and expanded edition in 1992.

Text means textile. Equipped with alphabetic indexes and marginal glosses, bookish texts establish a fabric of relations with all the extant books by means of networks of archives and libraries where copies and translations may be obtained. Given their 'referential presence' in multiple places, bookish texts anticipated the ubiquity that was later to become a distinguishing feature of printed texts. Its diffusion entailed a mentality, a form of conscience and sensitivity that colonized thinking, thereby reducing reality to the textual level and dampening one's sense of what was real. In Illich's view, the emergence of bookish texts in the thirteenth century was of far greater import than the invention of the printing press for mankind's journey to modernity, to the extent that the history of the latter's consequences may in fact be seen as a sub-chapter in the history of bookish texts.

These historical considerations could potentially lead to permanently discarding any optimistic conception of progress, but they remain unpopular because they also occasion a self-critical reflection on the mutually constitutive link between alphabetic writing and Europe (or the West). As Ong claimed, if the alphabet is the prototype of technology, the progress of alphabetic culture is the model for the progress of technology, and their present drift towards the processing of information by robots capable of reading is just as disquieting as the mix-up between images and interfaces. If such reflection were tacked with courage, it would include a history of the weakening of perceptions and of reality's density, the latter of which is increasingly being replaced by virtuality. In other words, the social history of the alphabet forces Europeans to do what they find hardest: to face the undeniable historical fact that they themselves are a product of the alphabet, that they cannot conceive their existence without it, and that they are now threatened by the potential dissolution of alphabetic culture in the desert of the communication between machines and systems.

For a specific history of alphabetic writing

It will be impossible to grasp anything of the alphabet's uniqueness as long as it keeps being seen as just one of the world's many forms of writing. That (almost) purely phonetic type of writing constitutes in fact an exception among them, in the same way that motor vehicles are an exception among means of transport or microphones among megaphones. It was one of those innovations that marked a 'radical subversion,' or an *Umstülpung*, as Illich would often say in German.

The alphabet stands out among all other forms of writing (including the Western Semites' consonantal writing system from which it descends) because it reproduces, by means of two dozen graphic signs, only the basic phonemes of a language and *nothing else*. That is the alphabet's ingenuity, which became a real possibility more than 2,600 years ago. According to Ivan Illich and Barry Sanders (1988), it was that feature which anticipated the subsequent transformation of speech into language and, later still, the ultimate reduction of language to a means of communication.

In a historical perspective, the emergence of the alphabet is one of those events that seem to be unthinkable before they occur, and without which it is no longer possible to think once they have occurred.

In examining the eversion which the alphabet represented, I decided not to go farther back than the thirteenth century. Nonetheless, I believe that the considerations I made on digitalization in Chapter 6 could equally apply to what has been left unsaid in the present one.

Each stage of that eversion witnessed a rift between the portion of society that had already been subverted (alphabetized) and the *conditio humana* of the time.

Those of us who are alphabetized can no longer conceive of thinking if we leave the alphabet's orbit. It is impossible for us to revert to a pre-alphabetic condition. The alphabet's presence within a given culture may have a transformational effect comparable to that subversion. Of all the possible forms of writing, the alphabetic one is the only one to generate a kind of conscience that has its model in books. This notwithstanding, the emergence of that 'bookish mentality' is not a phenomenon of Antiquity, but rather a medieval one.

The alphabet as the outcome of a Semitic people's interaction with the Greeks

The beginning of the second millennium BC saw the appearance in the Mediterranean basin of two incomplete types of phonetic writing, in the sense that readers needed to have a clear idea of the subject at hand in order to be able to read them correctly: Crete's Linear A and Mycenae's Linear B, two syllabic scripts of which only the second has been deciphered. Linear B managed to achieve a high degree of simplicity and rationality due to the decision of transcribing only open syllables, i.e., those that end in a vowel (*ba be bi bo bu*), which reduced the number of signs that had be learned to about a hundred. Linear B was discarded in the twelfth century BC.

The North-Western Semitic peoples, for their part, were experimenting with purely consonantal writing systems made up of only about twenty signs. The alphabet was unquestionably invented in a region where contact between Greeks and Semites was a frequent occurrence (Cyprus? The port of Athens with its Phoenician merchants who took orders in writing, to the Greeks' great astonishment?). A conversation between a Greek customer and a Phoenician merchant might have run as follows: 'What are you doing with that hard tip, scratching signs that mean nothing to me on a wooden tablet?' 'I'm writing down that you want me to bring you thirty blankets on my next trip.'

'And what's this "writing" supposed to be?' Whenever the Greek's curiosity was matched by the Phoenician's willingness to divulge the secret of writing (which consists in snatching winged words from the fleeting time that lasts only as long as the voice resonates, and in transplanting them, once their wings have been clipped, into the lasting durability of visible evidence), the Greek participant in the conversation would conceivably end up being busy carving the twenty-two signs of the Phoenician script. Was he hoping to use them to write Greek? That would have been a waste of energy. The Greek language was thoroughly impervious to being transcribed in Semitic characters, as they lacked the 'a-e-i-o-u' vowels.

In hindsight, it may be surmised that the alphabet owed its existence to a proper examination of the human vocal apparatus, which can produce two kinds of sound: those that make the vocal chords vibrate and are modulated by the voice, and those which are not issued by the vocal chords but are rather caused by a smack of the lips, a click of the tongue, or a tap of the tongue against the palate. They are the vowel and consonant sounds: the former are sustained and vibrate, whereas the latter briefly announce the voice's arrival on the scene or its departure from it.

The language manuals for learning Arabic, for example, state that to pronounce the *ain* sound, one ought to think of a camel rasping its throat. That sound undoubtedly involves a partial contribution from the vocal cords, but it is also possible to attempt to pronounce a completely non-vocalized *ain* sound.

Perhaps the Greeks thought that certain consonants were in fact badly pronounced vowels, and it was that 'creative misunderstanding' that led to the birth of the Greek alphabet. The names of the Greek consonants still bear traces of their Semitic origin.

Some maintain that the Greek people, 'the most intelligent of all ancient peoples,' discovered by means of pure logic what the Semitic characters still needed, in order to write down the Greek language. Once they had appropriated the unique artifact represented by the alphabet, they proceeded to invent written philosophy, geometry and its theorems, grammar, and formal logic. That explanation would of course confirm the Greeks' reputation as the masters of Western thought, but it is a phony one. First, the Greeks did not discover the secret of alphabetic writing by virtue of their extraordinary intellectual skills: it was rather a series of coincidences that enabled them to take stock of what Semitic consonants lacked to be suitable for writing Greek. According to Walter Ong, the alphabet was a technology of which the Greeks' later intellectual achievements were a mere consequence (*cf.* Ong, 1982, p. 80).

Why were North-Western Semitic peoples (especially the Phoenicians) able to read lines made up of mere consonants?

North-Western Semitic peoples form their words based on triconsonantal roots. In Arabic, for example, the *ktb* root always refers to a book. Its subsequent vocalization (*kitab*, *keteb*, etc.) specifies whether it is a book as such, the place where it is read, or the place where it is stored. Since Hebrew and Phoenician are Semitic languages, both of their vocabularies were also developed based on three consonants.

> A 'normal' Hebrew word is essentially formed by three consonants, which are written down and visually transmitted to posterity, and by a few vowels, which are not written but rather learned and transmitted exclusively through oral tradition, and which confer on the root (and on its generic meaning) the precision of a clear concept (Illich, 1955, p. 15).

The root *kds*, for instance, refers to the generic concept of something separate or cut off. In early Biblical times, that root designated first and foremost God's otherness, his radical 'non-worldliness,' in contrast to his opposite, the lay world. Once it was vocalized as *kadosh*, in the Old Testament that same root took on the meaning of 'sacred.' A 'sacred' creature is removed from its lay environment and keeps belonging 'to God' despite its impurity. That was true of Adam and David after they committed their sins, but also of Israel, 'the sacred people,' after their adultery with other gods.

Jewish readers see the act of reading as giving flesh to the tiny bones which Hebrew characters seem to represent by letting their breath flow into them, just as in the Book of Ezekiel God lets his *ruah* (his breath his spirit) flow into the bones of the dead (Ezekiel, 37, 5).

The alphabet was born at a time when the Greeks had long forgotten the Mycenaean syllabic script. The time gap between Linear B's demise and the appearance of the alphabet has (erroneously) been described as the Greek Dark Ages. In fact, it was a period in which oral culture blossomed, with celebrations during which *aoidoi* and *rhapsodes* celebrated the Achaeans' adventures in Troy centuries after the actual events. 'Homer' was the prototype of the epic singers of the seventh century BC. Milman Parry advanced the hypothesis that the singer of the Iliad and the Odyssey had lived at a time when the alphabet already enabled a few skilled scribes to transcribe long songs, and that Homer's literary corpus was the product of such transcriptions (*cf.* Parry M., 1928; Parry A., 1987).

It is to Parry that we also owe several critical concepts that allow for a proper distinction between oral improvisations and written compositions, that is to say, epic songs without an underlying text on the one hand, and poems on the other.

Both the Iliad and the Odyssey possess oral characteristics which are not to be found in later texts, which would seem to indicate that they were originally transcription drafts that made visible those oral songs which kept being improvised over and over again on the basis of *formulae* employed by the Ancient Greeks to describe their circumstances and their feelings.

Popular speech formulae and stylistic speech formulae

Orality-based populations do not quite see speaking as a matter of forming sentences by means of words. Their basic speech unit is not the word, as is the case with alphabetized populations, but rather the formula. All members of an oral culture have at their disposal a veritable 'library' of formulae, each of which can portray a specific existential situation. Indeed, it is no coincidence that farmers tend to speak in proverbs: 'You snooze, you lose,' 'better an egg today than a hen tomorrow.' Orality-based populations form very few sentences. They prefer to describe their circumstances and their feelings by resorting to the mass of formulae extant in their culture.

The hexameters sung by the aoidoi were rhythmic and assonant formulae, of the same kind as the formulae they employed in their daily speech. There was consubstantiality between the formulae found in common parlance and the formulae on which the *aoidoi*'s improvisations relied. The latter resorted to the formulae of daily life to recount the feats of the Achaeans in Troy or those of Odysseus/Ulysses on his way back to Ithaca many centuries before Homer did. Thanks to their rhythm and assonance, which allowed everybody to remember them with greater ease, the formulae of the hexameters sung during the celebrations could once again reach daily life and stay there. Oral epic narratives' essential feature is the improvisation based on a wide yet limited range of possibilities. Conversely, alphabetized poets compose their works, search for the *mot juste*, and contribute to generate a potentially infinite set of possibilities (*cf.* Queneau, 1961).[16]

The Italian language is just as capable of giving meaning to a series of consonants of variable length as Greek was. What does *L bfn vn d ntt cn l scrp ttt rtt* mean? It is the consonantal transcription of the opening line of a well-known nursey rhyme: *La Befana vien di notte con le scarpe tutte rotte* ('The Befana comes at night, her shoes all broken and worn out'). It would be impossible to give any meaning whatsoever to such a series of characters in any Indo-European language. The reason is self-evident: those languages do not possess the triconsonantal roots that are typical of Semitic languages.

It is, however, quite unlikely, as mentioned above, that the Greeks were able to identify the reasons behind the infeasible application of Semitic characters to their language by means of logical analysis, since the solution to that problem presented itself well before its logical formulation. Among the approximately twenty Semitic consonants, there are about half a dozen that to a Greek ear sound neither like consonants nor like vowels. These are the 'guttural' consonants. The discovery of what Semitic characters lacked to effectively transcribe the Greek language must have been the consequence of a fortunate misunderstanding rather than of logical analysis: the five or six Semitic consonants that could not be pronounced in Greek became the Greek vowels. The invention of the alphabet would therefore amount to the discovery, which was more empirical than theoretical, of what the Semitic characters lacked in order to write down the Greek language.

16 'Ten sonnets are here presented to the reader with the invitation to explore the one hundred thousand billion ways in which they may be rearranged on the basis of the one hundred thousand billion possibilities suggested by the title.'

The 'revolution of writing' and the emergence of bookish texts

As a period in the social history of the alphabet, the Middle Ages was an era of far-reaching transformations. First of all, there was the revolution of the page layout in the twelfth century, and later, in the thirteenth, there was the *popular* discovery of the power which writing can bestow even on those who have not mastered its technique. The use which the elites of the Antique world made of writing to impose their dominance was expanded in the Middle Ages with the addition of further uses, which were still aimed at the preservation of the rulers' power. In this regard, Illich took special interest in 'the alphabetization carried out by illiterate people.' Before the revolution of the written page in the twelfth century and its consequence, namely the generalization of silent reading after the thirteenth century, reading required a synesthesia, a merger of the perceptions of all the senses. It was akin to strolling along the rows of vineyard while picking and noisily swallowing their fruit. In the following century, silent readers were only guided by their eyes. Every form of synesthesia was eliminated, and there began the long process of disincarnation culminating in the information age which now threatens to destroy alphabetic culture.

After the thirteenth century, the progressive disincarnation of the page was matched by the growing passivity of the gaze. As discussed in the previous chapter, the metaphor of the eye as a passive receptor of light rays preceded and anticipated the metaphor of cameras. The quest for the *ethics of the gaze* for the digital age is thus suitably complemented by the *ethics of reading*.

Epilogue

The word *techno-logy*, according to the two Greek words from which it derives (*technē* and *logos*), literally means: a discourse on ability, deftness, 'technics.'

Illich's proposal for 'techno-logy' was radical, in the sense that it harked back to the roots of every Western discourse on technics: the emergence, in the twelfth century, of a new concept of tool.

The French language (as well as the Italian one) often speaks of *les techniques* in the plural. However, Jacques Ellul has spread the use of the expression *La Technique* to indicate a general inclination on the part of industrial society to cast every issue in such a way as to provide an answer that matches the offer of service tools, appliances, and institutions available at that particular moment. Ellul claimed that if Marx had lived in the twentieth century, his criticism would not have focused on the economy but rather on *La Technique*. The English language has forgotten that the word *technology* designates a discourse on technics, and has started using it as a *synonym* for technics.

Why did Illich choose to speak of *tools* to refer to that domain that is usually designated by the words 'technics' and 'technology?' As a historian, he wanted to examine tools in light of the history of the body (of *historical somatics*, to use the expression he proposed himself). Any use of a tool establishes a relationship between the latter and its user's body. The history of the tools could be subdivided into periods based on the kind of relationship they have with the body of those who use them. There are allegedly three ages that followed hard upon one another:

- The age of the organic tool (the Greeks' *organon*), from Antiquity to the beginning of the second millennium AD.
- The age of the tool as an instrumental means (which is inseparable from the age of Western hegemony), of which industrial society represented the epilogue.
- The age of the post-instrumental tool, which was bereft of most of the features that define classical tools.

In Antiquity, and until the beginning of the second millennium, in the areas where the Greek language was spoken, every artifact that helped human beings to fulfill themselves was called *organon* (an organ). For instance, a hammer was an organ, just as much as the hand that held it or the hand without it was. The hand was 'the organ of all organs,' and the 'tool' (which may be called an organic tool) could not be conceived in any way other than as dependent on the hand. The organ was part of the body, and the tool was an organ.

In the early twelfth century, a new concept was developed, namely that of *instrumentum*, which was originally given a theological meaning: priests, for instance, were tools in the hand of God. Soon, however, the immanent meaning of the word *instrumentum* gained the upper hand on its transcendental meaning. The tool became conceptually separate from the body. The distance between the tool and its users' body, on which their mutual relationship relied, was given the name of *distality* by Illich.

The instrumental age associated the tool with the intentions enshrined in it. The body and its tool were in a face-to-face relationship. A fifth cause, the instrumental cause, was devised to define the kind of causality introduced by the tool. The instrumental cause does not possess an intention of its own but can absorb the intention of the tool's user. After the fourteenth century, the historian Illich claimed to have identified, within Europe's 'techno-logical' landscape, a plethora of intentions, including that of riding a self-moving tool or producing images mechanically.

At the end of the twentieth century, the 'tool' (which is often designated as 'technology') established a new kind of relationship with the body, one without distality. It would, however, be a mistake to believe it meant going back to the ancient *organon*. Through the hand that held it, the *organon* was previously part of the body. Now, on the other hand, it was the body's turn to become part of a new relationship, which Illich later defined as a *system*. In that relationship without distality, the *system* swallowed up the body, absorbed it, made it become part of itself, and turned it into a sub-system. The new 'technological object' defined as a system lost all the characteristic features of the classical tool. Systems are not distal in relation to a body but actually 'swallow them up.' The word designates the behavior of an entity that consists of relations represented by arrows and knots, and which can absorb weaker entities and turn them into sub-systems. Since they do not acknowledge any of the traditional boundaries, systems can potentially expand throughout the whole of space. *A systemic relationship is bereft of any external space whatsoever*. It is a conceptual amoeba that devours any weaker relationship and subjects itself to any stronger system by becoming integrated into it.

The category labeled 'technics' or 'technology' allows for the placement in the same box of things as different as a hammer and a computer. A hammer may be taken at will, for instance to hammer a nail, and may be put back into the box. Those who position their fingers on a keyboard, conversely, usually end up becoming dependent on it in a matter of weeks. Even though I am unable to trace a clear demarcation line between the instrumental use of my computer (it is an enhanced typewriter) and its constant presence on my desk (it is the gateway to a system of relations that requires unwavering attention on my part, if I wish to go on 'existing' in the 'networks' into which it has plunged me), I feel and know that my computer is not a mere tool, and I experience it as such. Computers as 'typewriters' and typewriters proper are almost identical. The relationship between the computer that gives me access to an unlimited number of connections and my old typewriter is of a wholly different kind, or rather wholly other. Grasping the difference between what is 'almost similar' and what is 'radically other' is of paramount importance to understanding what Barbara Duden has described as Ivan Illich's 'second period' (Duden, 2010).

Another sign of Illich's shift into that 'second period' was his explicit reference to ethics, which in the first period had remained implicit, as if the tools' appropriate measure or gender complementarity already contained their ethic principle within themselves. The subject of ethics pervaded each of this book's first chapters: there is no ethics of *doing* that does not also take into account the means to act, as represented by the tools.

It would be hard to reconstruct Illich's path towards a criticism of the industrial mode of production without also mentioning what he learned in his Mexican village. His immersion in *vernacular gender* made him comprehend that the disintegration of 'mutually constitutive dissymmetric complementarity' between the male and female domains was irreversible.

A possible *remedy* (which actually does not mean restoration) could be the development of ethics suited to an age that denies gender and demands that men and women speak the same language, avail themselves of the same tools (or be in the service of the same machines), be subjected to the same labors, feel the same emotions, and be capable of mutual envy.

The need to define ethics for the digital age became especially pressing when Illich began to take an interest in the 'disincarnation' of the gaze, of the voice, and of the body in an age when machines can read and robots can speak.

Chapter 6 examined the visual stimuli of the digital age, 'which are no longer images.' So what are they? At first glance, they are 'almost similar' to the images, which the Renaissance taught us to create and the twentieth century to multiply by means of cameras. However, they are also 'interfaces' that impose the visual perceptions that will eventually enable the systems' users to become integrated into them without a glitch. As such, they fall into the category of what is 'radically other.'

The alphabetic culture, whose history up to the thirteenth century was outlined above (see Chapter 7), is nowadays threatened with extinction by the clicking sounds of the machines' communication, to the extent that reading from a screen requires the adoption of systemic behaviors. The relationship between a printed text and a textbook on Scholasticism is of the 'almost similar' kind, whereas the emergence of hypertexts is of the 'radically other' one.

The cases listed above are those in which it is important to identify a demarcation line between what appears to be a continuation of the past and what constitutes a radical break leading to the sphere of those realities without a past that occupy an ever-growing amount of space in late modernity.

Ivan Illich possessed special antennae when it came to distinguishing what was almost the same from what was wholly different. In the hope of clarifying any misunderstanding on the matter, I would now like to address once again, and with different words, the example on the difference between bookish texts (be they printed or not) and the texts that can be read from a screen. Printed texts, which began to be multiplied at will in the 1450s, were somehow 'almost the same' as the products of thirteenth-century *scriptoria*, which developed bookish texts with a referential presence in a multitude of archives and libraries. Conversely, what is performed by a search engine, which I ask to supply all the references to all the texts containing a given adjective and associated with a specific author, belongs to the 'wholly other' sphere.

I am convinced that what enabled Illich to preserve that fundamental distinction was his decision to discuss tools in practical terms, including their relationship with physical hands and bodies, rather than focusing on technology. By contrast, one thinker on technology, one of the most widely read French writers in the field worldwide, envisaged the world of digital communication as follows:

> Digital proliferation makes us come face-to-face with a device that is seriously beginning to look like a planetary nervous system. We finally have at our disposal the means to make real, visible and material the network of connections that were previously invisible, or which only existed in people's minds… These are only the first steps of the expansion of a partially serious nervous system, which replaces 'on paper' information systems that, for their part, used to be quite slow… We are in the process of building that planetary nervous system, and although it is still in its infancy, it nonetheless frees us from localism (Latour, 2018, pp. 163, 164, 166; quoted in Cérézuelle, unpublished text, p. 6).[1]

1 It would be quite difficult to discern the least ethical intuition in Latour's writings, or indeed in any of the authors he often quoted as his masters, including Teilhard de Chardin, whenever they discussed technology.

As for the language of the systems' world, which consists of words that have few synonyms, it is a language that eliminates verbs, and especially the verb 'to be' (the *copula*, which states what something is), and prioritizes nouns, which are more suited to concealing what something *is* and hiding it under numerous *could be*s. Uwe Pörksen, a linguist and a friend of Ivan Illich's, has identified hundreds of instances of said drift towards a language without a copula, without the verb 'to be:' 'The Federal Republic (of Germany) as an information society.' 'The postal system's duties in the information age.' There is no verb. In our minds, we complete such sentences as follows: 'The Federal Republic *is becoming* an information society.' '*In the present age*, the postal system *has* specific duties.' These verbless formulae, however, do not display any need for a copula. In fact, they act as imperatives. 'What they need is for us to accept the idea that, in the information age, every human being is a creature that needs information' (Pörksen, 1995, p. 44).

The intentions that can be read in a system cease to be personal and clearly defined. Systemic discourse presents probabilities rather than facts. The computer on which I am transcribing the present chapter still acts in accordance with my will: it behaves like an improved typewriter. But it also does many other things, such as, for instance, appropriating my personal data and spying on my choices. An artifact-that-is-no-longer-a-tool (which we call a system) imposes on its user the perceptions that will subsequently enable him to act as a sub-system.

The choice of discussing tools rather than technology allows for the identification of the historical turning points when what was almost similar became radically different, *other*. The objects that became 'other as opposed to tools' or 'other as opposed to images' have built a world that witnesses the proliferation of artifacts without a past.

The absence of a past in a number of realities which have become familiar to most of our contemporaries is, for a limited number of them, a source of anxiety, which is the price for rejecting all illusions. In our psychoanalyzed society, anxiety cannot manifest itself without also opening the doors to anxiety therapists. Suffice it to consider what happened when Illich addressed the topic of vernacular gender in Berkeley in 1982. By presenting 'economic sex' as the present time's predominant relationship between men and women on the one hand, and 'vernacular gender' as a relic of the past on the other, he instilled a sense of unease in his audience: sex is a reality without a past. A few years later, a group of Californian feminists came up with a soothing treatment for that anxiety. They stated: 'Let us call the relationship between men and women "gender," thereby agreeing that it is a generic term for a relationship that has always existed, and let us call "sex" the modern form of that relationship. Gender will thus become the past of sex, which in this way will lose its nature as a reality without a past.' The same operation was carried out for the 'realities without a past' represented by systems and visual interfaces, in which we are encouraged to see the images' avatars.[2]

And what about the din occasioned by the communication between speaking robots, which drowns out the conversation between alphabetized people who struggle to understand one another beyond the limitations of alphabetic conceptualization?

One of the consequences of the systemic thought's emergence after the Macy Conferences[3] held in the immediate post-war years (*cf.* Dupuy, 1985) was the modification of the concept of causality: the finalization of concepts such as program, *input-output*, *through-put* and *feedback* ousted the *causa instrumentalis*. This notwithstanding, those new concepts did not sweep through common parlance before the 1970–1980 years. A movement of long duration such as the instrumental age met its death, after eight centuries, on the last strands of the twentieth century, and lends itself to a new narrative. Only too often has it been presented in a 'continuist' perspective, which Jacques Ellul described as follows:

> The image of a modern society that is basically nothing other than the traditional society *cum* technics keeps popping up

2 Translator's Note: See footnote 18 on p. 82.

3 They were meetings of scholars from various disciplines debating the future of science and technology, which were held in New York at the Josiah Macy Jr. Foundation in the 1940s and 1950s.

> constantly, even among the most progressive minds... It is very difficult to accept that we live in fact in a society that has nothing in common with the societies that went before it (Ellul, 1977, p. 102, quoted in Cérézuelle, unpublished text, p. 6).

The 'continuist' vision criticized by Ellul is generally based on evolutionist metaphysics, which is expressed by slogans such as Teilhard de Chardin's ('everything that rises must converge,' the 'Law of Complexity-Consciousness'), or else by a few sentences by the same writer (such as the one below) that take issue with the complete separation we have introduced between what is natural and what is artificial:

> It is due to the influence of the same ill-boding premise that we have uncomprehendingly stood by for years while the extraordinary network of land, sea and air routes, postal services, wires, cables, and ethereal pulses, which day after day increasingly envelop the face of the earth, was taking shape under our very eyes (Teilhard de Chardin, 1957, pp. 87–88, quoted in Cérézuelle, unpublished text, p. 11).

Between the past and the present, there was allegedly an acceleration of the processes, but no radical rift. 'Digital proliferation' highlights something that had long been in the works within technology, an abstract word that opens all doors and conceals the concrete dimension of the concept of tool. The demise of the concept of tool has represented the greatest epistemological landslide ever. Moreover, it has also been matched by a new concept of the body, which Barbara Duden defined as follows:

> The 1980s marked a turning point in historical somatics. While medicine lost its power to define the body, it paradoxically began to impose on patients' perceptions that conformed so much to the new systemic conceptions as to induce them to start seeing themselves as sub-systems of the biomedical system. Before the 1980s medicine had disseminated the image of a body in constant need of treatment, but after that turning point the image evolved into that of a 'human being'

> capable of self-generating inasmuch as it was a component in a complex cybernetic program. Illich then devoted himself to freeing his perception and his friends' from the trap represented by cybernetic concepts disguised as common sense. Medicine, which had induced its patients to see themselves as iatrogenic constructs, now required them to personally take decisions that were to turn them into sub-systems of the biomedical system (Duden, 2007).

If I were asked to point out what has *not yet* been understood of Illich's message after the 1980s, I would propose the following:

In the twelfth century, it became necessary to redefine the concept of tool (the *instrumentum*) in its physical relationship with the body. Tools, which were still kept at a distance, began to absorb their users' private intentions. For example, plows, as the instrumental cause of tillage, replaced the personal efficient cause represented by farmers. The instrumental cause paved the way for the concept of productive force. The latter prospered philosophically during the Industrial Age, when there was an exponential growth in the number of instrumental devices that did not display their ties to the body. The post-instrumental age that seems to loom after the end of the twentieth century has witnessed the disappearance of the distance between the body and the 'tool,' which is no longer handheld and which has become a system: the body has been swallowed up by the system, of which it has now become a sub-system.

All I ask is to be allowed to present this theory as a possible hypothesis, which I acknowledge has to work its way through a hostile environment. It relies on foundations that the modern mentality strives to ignore. However, when the concept of instrumental cause loses its strength, there arises the possibility of finding new perspectives, as, for instance, a rediscovery of gratuitousness, or *Umsonstigkeit*, as Illich would often say in German: what is done 'without a purpose,' simply because it is a good or a fitting thing to do (*cf.* Illich, 2005, p. 227).

Without indulging in preaching, Illich presented his horizon without any subterfuge: it was that of a Christian who firmly believed in the Incarnation of the Word. His reflections on the tools seem to have led him to an 'apocalyptic' (understood in its literal meaning of 'revealing') vision of the relationships between bodies and the artifacts that they use and by which they are increasingly being used. It is, moreover, necessary to consider the times and the spaces in which these relationships occur. I believe it is appropriate to see those relationships, times, and spaces in light of the Incarnation—or, rather, in the shade of their progressive disincarnation.

The theorists of technology who publish their studies in France generally espouse a point of view that is the exact opposite of Illich's distinctions. Especially noteworthy among them are the supporters of a tradition that harks back to Teilhard de Chardin, according to whom technics is a medium that mankind has been granted to be able to play its part in creation. That Jesuit thinker saw the explosion of the atomic bomb in Hiroshima as the manifestation of the 'spiritualization of matter.' The distinction between what was 'almost similar' and what was 'radically other,' to which Illich's gaze had become accustomed, was of little importance in the face of Man's elevation as co-creator of the world.

> Echoes of Teilhard's theology are to be found in the thought of the Dominican friar Marie-Dominique Chenu (1895–1990), who held that men were called upon to continue God's work, namely the transformation of the whole of nature by means of technics, a task whose ultimate goal was the spiritualization of matter and the suppression of the material world's otherness, considered to be ontologically defective. Chenu had therefore no hesitation in repeatedly stressing that through technics man became a 'co-creator of the world' (Cérézuelle, unpublished text, p. 9, quoting Chenu, 1960, p. 164).

Emmanuel Mounier, the founder of the personalist movement, was among the first to promote such a spiritualist interpretation of the meaning of technics, partially to assuage the unease felt by 'Gascon personalists'[4] such as Bernard Char-

4 Translator's Note: Literally, 'the inhabitants of Gascony.' That word is employed

bonneau (1910–1996) and Jacques Ellul (1912–1994), who in the 1930s had started questioning all kinds of technophile optimism (*cf.* Cérézuelle, unpublished text, p. 9; Cérézuelle, 2005; 2018; 2019).

The epilogue of a long essay should not be taken as an excuse to correct what has not been properly stated earlier on. In fact, it may provide me with the chance (at least in the present case) to better clarify the perspective in which I have attempted to retrace the itinerary followed by a thought that was so alive it was even capable of questioning itself. It was no coincidence that I mentioned Illich's plan to subvert universities, and to shift their center of gravity from their classrooms to private rooms, well-stocked with spaghetti and wine of decent quality, which he considered to be part of his teaching methods.

> I was inspired by the Symposium of Plato. Plato's idea of philia, of love, as the way into knowledge has been a challenge because, from decade to decade, I have had to interpret it in new ways. But one conviction remained constant: friendship can never mean the same thing to me as it does to Plato. In the Greek city, virtue was understood as fitting behavior. It was the ethos, or ethics, appropriate to a certain ethnos, or people. And such virtue was the foundation of friendship, what made it possible. Friendship was the flowering of civic virtue and its crown. It was only as virtuous Athenians that the guests at Plato's sym-posium—literally, 'drinking party'—could love one another. This has not been my destiny as a wandering Jew and Christian pilgrim. I have not been able to seek friendship as something arising from a place and the practices appropriate to it. Rather, the ethics that developed around the circle of my friends arose as a result of our search for friendship and our practice of it. This is a radical inversion in the meaning of philia. For me friendship has been the source, condition, and context for the possible coming about of commitment and like-mindedness. For Plato, it could only be the result of practices befitting a citizen (Illich, 2005, p. 147)

in France to designate people who are somewhat bold and daring, both in a positive and negative sense.

Illich confessed it openly: throughout the controversies in which he engaged with 'teaching' institutions, he always endeavored to convince them to focus on scholarly friendship, of the kind that is ready to discard all teaching categories.

References

Works by Ivan Illich

Illich, I. *Œuvres complètes*, vol. 1. Fayard, Paris, 2003.

Illich, I. *Œuvres complètes*, vol. 2. Fayard, Paris, 2005.

Illich, I. *Obras reunidas*, vol. 1. Fondo de Cultura económica, México, 2006.

Illich, I. *Obras reunidas*, vol. 2. Fondo de Cultura económica, México, 2008.

Illich, I. (1955) "Sacred Virginity," in *The Powerless Church and Other Selected Writings, 1955–1985*. The Pennsylvania State University Press, University Park, 2018.

Illich, I. (1971) *Deschooling Society*. Harper & Row, New York.

Illich, I. (1971a) *Celebration of Awareness: A Call for Institutional Revolution*. Calder & Boyars, London.

Illich, I. (1973) "Energy and Equity," in *Towards a History of Needs*. Equinox Publishing, Sheffield, 2026.

Illich, I. (1973a) *Tools for Conviviality*. Harper & Row, New York.

Illich, I. (1975), *Limits to Medicine: Medical Nemesis and the Expropriation of Health*. Marion Boyars, London, 1995.

Illich, I. (1977) "Disabling Professions," in Illich, I., Zola, I. K., McKnight, J., Caplan, J. and Shaiken, H., *Disabling Professions*. Marion Boyars, London, pp. 11–39.

Illich, I. (1978) *The Right to Useful Unemployment*. Marion Boyars, London.

Illich, I. (1981) *Shadow Work*. Marion Boyars, London.

Illich, I. (1982) *Genere. Per una critica storica della disuguaglianza*. Neri Pozza Editore, Vicenza, 2013 (*Gender*, Marion Boyars, London, 1982).

Illich, I. (1984) *Schule ins Museum. Phaidros und die Folgen*. Klinckhardt, Bad Heilbrunn.

Illich, I. (1985) *H_2O and the Waters of Forgetfulness: Reflections on the Historicity of Stuff*. Heyday Books, Berkeley.

Illich, I. (1987), *Schriften lesen im 12. Jahrhundert: das Disdascalicon Hugos von Sankt Viktor*. FernUniversität, Hagen.

Illich, I. (1991), *In the Vineyard of the Text. A Commentary to Hugh's Didascalicon*. Marion Boyars, London, 2022.

Illich, I. (1991a) *Text and University*. Online: https://www.pudel.samerski.de/pdf/TEXTANTL.pdf

Illich, I. (1992) *In the Mirror of the Past: Lectures and Addresses, 1978–1990*. Marion Boyars, London.

Illich, I. (1999) "The End of Science, Technology and Society Programs: Report on a Conversation with Ivan Illich," *Science, Technology and Society*, n. 121–122.

Illich, I. (2000) *The Corruption of Christianity*. Radio Program, Canadian Broadcasting Corporation.

Illich, I. (2004) *La perte des sens*. Fayard, Paris (*La perdita dei sensi*, G. Pucci, Libreria Editrice Fiorentina, Firenze, 2009; *The Loss of the Senses*, Equinox Publishing, Sheffield, 2026).

Illich, I. (2005) *The Rivers North of the Future: The Testament of Ivan Illich as Told to David Cayley*. Anansi Press, Toronto.

Illich, I. (2010) "L'énergie, un objet social," in Paquot, Th. and Robert, J. (eds.), *Actualité d'Ivan Illich, Esprit*, agosto-settembre, pp. 211–227.

Illich, I. and Cayley, D. (2005) *La corruption du meilleur engendre le pire*. Entretiens traduits de l'américain par Daniel de Bruycker et Jean Robert, Actes Sud, Arles, 2007.

Illich, I., Hoinacki, L. and Groeneveld, S. (1990) *Declaration on Soil*. Online: http://davidtinapple.com/illich/1990_declaration_soil.pdf

Illich, I. and Sanders, B. (1988) *ABC, The Alphabetization of the Popular Mind*, Marion Boyars, London.

Duden, B., Hoinacki, L., Illich, I., Rieger, M. and Trapp, S. (1997) *Schriften Bremen 1994–1997*, vol. III. Bremen.

Duden, B., Hoinacki, L., Illich, I., Rieger, M., Samerski, S., Trapp, S. and Beck J. (1999) *Schriften Bremen 1997–1999*. Bremen.

Other Works Cited

Bowles, Gloria (1983) "Beyond the Backlash: A Feminist Critique of Ivan Illich's Theory of Gender," *Feminist Issues* 3 (1), pp. 3–6.

Agamben, G. (2006) *What is an Apparatus? & Other Essays*. Stanford University Press, Redwood City.

Arney, W. R. (2016) "The Age of Systems." Lecture presented at the Ivan Illich Symposium, Cuernavaca, México.

Arney, W. R. (1991) *Experts in the Age of Systems*. University of New Mexico Press, Albuquerque.

Becher, U. and Rüsen, J., eds. (1989) *Weiblichkeit in geschichtlicher Perspektive*. Suhrkamp, Frankfurt am Main.

Beck, H. (2017) *Otra modernidad es posible. El pensamiento de Ivan Illich*. Malpaso, México.

Besançon, A. (1994) *L'image interdite: une histoire intellectuelle de l'iconoclasme*. Fayard, Paris.

Bonfil, G. (1987) *México profundo: una civilización negada*. Grijalvo, México.

Caillé, A. (1988) "L'emprise du marché," in Aymard, M. et al., *Lire Braudel*. La Découverte, Paris, pp. 93–132.

Castoriadis, C. (1975) *L'institution imaginaire de la société*, Seuil, Paris (*The Imaginary Institution of Society*, MIT Press, Cambridge, MA, 1987).

Cayley, D. (1992) *Ivan Illich in Conversation*. Interviews with Cayley, D., Anansi Press, Toronto (*Conversazioni con Ivan Illich*, S. Stogl, Eleuthera, Milano, 1994, 3rd edition).

Cayley, D. (2015) "Review of Todd Hartch, *The Prophet of Cuernavaca: Ivan Illich and the Crisis of the West*," Oxford University Press, Oxford. Online: https://www.davidcayley.com/blog/2015/4/20/a-review-of-todd-hartchs-the-prophet-of-cuernavaca-ivan-illich-and-the-crisis-of-the-modern-west

Cayley, D. (2021) *Ivan Illich: An Intellectual Journey*. Penn State Press, Pennsylvania.

Cérézuelle, D. (2005) *Écologie et liberté: Bernard Charbonneau précurseur de l'écologie politique*. Parangon.

Cérézuelle, D. (2018) *Bernard Charbonneau ou La critique du développement exponentiel*. Le passager clandestin.

Cérézuelle, D. (2019) "Une nouvelle théodicée? Remarques sur la sociologie des techniques de Bruno Latour," Revue du MAUSS permanente. Online: https://journaldumauss.net/?Une-nouvelle-theodicee-Remarques-sur-la-sociologie-des-techniques-de-Bruno

Chenu, M.-D. (1960) "Vers une théologie de la technique," in *La Technique et l'homme, Recherche et débats*, n. 31, pp. 157–166.

Collectif des amis de Brème (2005) *Ivan Illich, Bibliographische Sammlung*, Universität, Bremen.

Daston, L. (1999) "Objectivity versus Truth," in Boedeken, H. H. et al. (eds.), *Wissenschaft als kulturelle Praxis*. Veröffentlichungen des Max-Planck-Instituts für Geschichte, Vandenhoeck & Ruprechtpp, Göttingen, pp. 17–32.

Dodwell, C. R. (1961) *Theophilus, Presbyter: The Various Arts*. T. Nelson, New York.

Douglas, M. (1970) "The Two Bodies," in *Natural Symbols. Explorations in Cosmology*. Barnes and Jenkins, New York, pp. 64ss (Routledge Classics, London, 2003).

Du Plessix Gray, F. (1971) *Divine Disobedience. Profiles in Catholic Radicalism*. Knopf, New York.

Duden, B. (1987) *Geschichte unter der Haut. Ein Eisenacher Arzt und seine Patientinnen um 1730*. Klett-Cotta, Stuttgart.

Duden, B. (1991) *Der Frauenleib als öffentlicher Ort: Vom Mißbrauch des Begriffs Leben*. Luchterhand, Hamburg/Zürich (*Il corpo della donna come luogo pubblico. Sull'abuso del concetto di vita*, Bollati Boringhieri, Torino, 1994).

Duden, B. (2002) "The Quest for Past Somatics," in Hoinacki, L. and Mitcham, C. (eds.), *The Challenges of Ivan Illich*. State University of New York, Albany, pp. 219–230.

Duden, B. (2007) "'De oculo morali:' Ivan Illich zur Blickgeschichte und dem bedrohten Blicken heute," in Wimböck, G. et al. (eds.), *Evidentia. Reichweiten visueller Wahrnehmung in der frühen Neuzeit*. Litt Verlag, Berlin, pp. 481–503.

Duden, B. (2010) "Illich, seconde période," in Paquot, Th. and Robert, J. (eds.), *Actualité d'Ivan Illich, Esprit*, agosto-settembre, pp. 136–157.

Dumouchel, P. and Dupuy, J.-P. (1979) *L'enfer des choses. René Girard et la logique de l'économie*. Seuil, Paris.

Dupuy, J.-P. (1985) "L'Essor de la première cybernétique (1943–1953)," in Dupuy, J.-P. (ed.), *Histoires de cybernétique*. École Polytechnique, Centre de Recherche Épistémologie et Autonomie (CREA), Paris, pp. 7–139.

Dupuy, J.-P. and Robert, J. (1975) *La trahison de l'opulence*. Presses universitaires de France.

Ellul, J. (1954) *La Technique ou l'enjeu du siècle*. Armand Colin, Paris (*The Technological Society*, Vintage Books, 1964].

Ellul, J. (1977) *Le Système technicien*. Calmann-Lévy, Paris (*The Technological System*, Continuum Books, 1980).

Ellul, J. (1988) *Le bluff technologique*, Hachette, Paris (*The Technological Bluff*, William Eerdamanns Publishing, 1990).

Fortier, M. (2016) "Illich et la méthode peirastique. Petit manuel de déboulonnage de l'irrationalité des modernes," in Fortier, M. and Paquot, Th. (eds.), *Ivan Illich, l'alchimiste des possibles*. Lemieux Éditeur, Paris, pp. 73–136.

Fortier, M.. and Paquot, Th., eds. (2016) *Ivan Illich, l'alchimiste des possibles*. Lemieux Éditeur, Paris.

Fox-Keller, E. (1985) *Reflections on Gender and Science*. Yale University Press, Yale.

Gimbutas, M. (1956) *The Pre-history of Eastern Europe. Part I: Mesolithic, Neolithic and Copper Age Cultures in Russia and the Baltic Area*. Peabody Museum, Cambridge, MA.

Girard, R. (1961) *Mensonge romantique et vérité romanesque*.

Grasset, Paris.

Grönemeyer, M. (2012) *Wer arbeitet sündigt. Ein Plädoyer für gute Arbeit.* Primus Verlag, Darmstadt.

Gross, R. (2009) "The Pre-patriarchal Hypothesis: An Assessment," in *A Garland of Feminist Reflections: Forty Years of Religious Exploration.* University of California Press, San Francisco, pp. 156–170.

Hartch, T. (2015) *The Prophet of Cuernavaca: Ivan Illich and the Crisis of the West.* Oxford University Press, Oxford.

Harvey, D. (2009) *Social Justice and the City.* The University of Georgia Press, Athens, GA.

Hoschchild, Arlie (1983) "Illich: The Ideologue in Scientist's Clothing," *Feminist Issues* 3 (1), pp. 6–11.

Jay, M. (1988) "Scopic Regimes of Modernity," in Foster H. (ed.), *Vision and Visuality.* Dia Art Foundation, Seattle, pp. 3–27.

Kaller-Dietrich, M. (2007) *Ivan Illich (1926–2002). Sein Leben, sein Denken*, Verlag Bibliothek der Provinz edition seidengasse, Wien (*Vita di Ivan Illich. Il pensatore del Novecento più necessario e attuale*, ediz. dell'Asino, Roma, 2011).

Latour, B. (2018) "La technique, c'est la civilisation elle-même," in *Revue internationale et stratégique*, n. 2., pp. 163–171.

Lemoine, M. (1991) *Hugues de Saint-Victor. L'Art de lire. Didascalicon.* Cerf, Paris.

Litt, Th. (1963) *Les corps célestes dans l'univers de saint Thomas d'Aquin.* Publications Universitaires, Louvain–Béatrice-Nauwelaerts, Paris.

Marshall, L. (1976) *The !Kung of Nyae Nyae.* Harvard University Press, Cambridge.

McLuhan, M. (1962) *Gutenberg Galaxy. The Making of Typographic Man.* University of Toronto Press, Toronto.

Mitcham, Carl (2018) "Teaching with and Thinking after Illich on Tools," *International Journal of Illich Studies*, 6 (1), pp. 172–178.

Nora, F. (2011) *Historien public.* Gallimard, Paris.

O'Gorman, E. (1958) *L'invention de l'Amérique. Recherche au sujet de la structure historique du Nouveau monde et du sens de son devenir.* Presses de l'Université Laval, Québec, 2007.

Ong, W. (1982) *Orality and Literacy, the Technologizing of the Word.* Methuen, London and New York.

Paquot, Th. (2012) *Introduction à Ivan Illich.* La Découverte, Paris.

Parry A., ed. (1987) *The Making of Homeric Verse: The Collected Papers of Milman Parry.* Clarendon Press, Oxford.

Parry, M. (1928) *L'Épithète traditionnelle chez Homère*. Les Belles Lettres, Paris.

Percovich, L. (2012) "Culture di pace." Introduzione al Convegno Culture Indigene di Pace, Donne e Uomini Oltre Il Conflitto, organizzato dall'associazione Laima, Torino. Online: https://cartesensibili.wordpress.com/2013/09/24/segni-fuori-dal-tempo-la-vita-e-lopera-di-marija-gimbutas-luciana-percovich/

Polanyi, K. (1944) *The Great Transformation*. Holt, Rinehart & Winston, New York (*La Grande Transformation*, Gallimard, Paris, 1983).

Pörksen, U. (1995) *Plastic Words: The Tyranny of a Modular Language*. Pennsylvania State University Press, University Park (*Plastikwörter*, Klett-Cotta, Stuttgart, 1988).

Pörksen, U. (1997) *Weltmarkt der Bilder. Eine Philosophie der Visiotype*. Klett-Cotta, Stuttgart.

Pörksen, U. (2014) *Camelot in Grünewald Szenen aus dem intellektuellen Leben der achtziger Jahre*. Beck, Munich.

Queneau, R. (1961) *Cent mille milliards de poèmes*. Gallimard, Paris.

Rahnema, M. and Robert, J. (2008) *La puissance des pauvres*. Actes Sud, Paris.

Reimer, E. (1971) *School is Dead: Alternatives in Education*. Penguin, New York.

Rey, O. (2014) *Une question de taille*. Stock, Paris (*Dismisura. La Marcia infernale del progresso*, Controcorrente, Napoli, 2016).

Robert, J. (2009) *La Crise: el despojo impune. Como evitar que el remedio sea peor que el mal*. Universidad de la Tierra (Chiapas)–Cl de Cl (Las Casas).

Sachs, W., ed. (1992) *The Development Dictionary*. Zed Books, London.

Samerski, S. (2005) "Il mito della scelta informata e dell'autonomia. Come le decisioni personali e libere diventano illusione in un mondo dominato dal rischio," in Ivan Illich, *"Le 'paz' dei popolari:" Una rivisitazione del pensiero del grande intellettuale*, Cooperativa L'Altrapagina, collana Quaderni. Online: https://www.provincia.lucca.it/sites/default/files/16_maggio_2005.pdf

Samerski, S. (2015) *The Decision Trap: Genetic Education and its social consequences*. Imprint-Academic, London.

Samuel, S. (2010) "Le rôle des professions," in Paquot, Th. and Robert, J. (eds.), *Actualité d'Ivan Illich, Esprit*, agosto-sett., pp. 185–192.

Scheper-Hughes, N. (1983) "Vernacular Sexism: An Anthropological Response to Ivan Illich," *Feminist Issues* 3 (1), pp. 28–37.

Simon, G. (1988) *Le regard, l'Être et l'Apparence dans l'optique de l'Antiquité*. Seuil, Paris.

Smeed, R. J. (1964) *Road Pricing: The Economic and Technical Possibility* (Smeed Report). Her Majesty's Stationery Office, London.

Steiner, G. (1975) *After Babel: Aspects of Language and Translation*. Oxford University Press, London, 2nd edition, ampliata, 1992.

Steiner, G. (1988) "The End of Bookishness," *Times Literary Supplement*, July, pp. 8–14.

Teilhard de Chardin, P. (1957) *La Vision du passé*. Œuvres, vol. 3, Seuil, Paris (*La visione del passato*, Jaca Book, Milano, 2016).

Wagner-Hasel, B. (1989) "Das Private wird politisch. Die Perspektive 'Geschlecht' in der Altertumswissenschaft," in Becher, U. and Rüsen, J. (eds.), *Weiblichkeit in geschichtlicher Perspektive*, Frankfurt a. M., pp. 11–50.

About the Author and Translator

Jean Robert

Jean Robert (1937–2020) was born in a farming village in the Swiss Jura. Partly self-taught, he began university studies relatively late. At the age of twenty-three, he learned that the École Polytechnique Fédérale in Zurich offered people without a high school diploma the opportunity to study at the university. He was chosen, along with two others, from among the twenty candidates who had applied for the exam. Having graduated in architecture, he began working as an architect in the town of Neuchâtel.

One day, by pure chance, he read an article about CIDOC, the Intercultural Documentation Center of Cuernavaca in Mexico, and about the singular character who was its director: Ivan Illich. That article came to mind years later, when he moved to Mexico with his Mexican wife, Sylvia. With a scholarship, she was the one who began attending CIDOC. He became a regular visitor, soon establishing a friendship and intellectual collaboration with Illich that was destined to last a lifetime.

Fluent in many languages and comfortable in diverse cultural settings, Jean Robert has authored numerous books and articles on a vast array of subjects, ranging from architecture to Zapatista politics. A representative sample of his writings are available in two collections (2018; 2021), published in the *International Journal of Illich Studies*, available online.

Edoardo McKenna

Born and raised in a bilingual Scottish-Italian family, he graduated as a conference interpreter and translator from the renowned SSLMIT at the University of Trieste. After completing two further Master's degrees in 'Human Rights and Conflict Management' (Scuola Sant'Anna, Pisa) and 'Language Policy and Planning for Minority Languages' (University of Aberdeen, Scotland), he devoted himself to his lifelong passion for historical linguistics and obtained a PhD from the University of Aberdeen. He is currently based in Italy, where he works as translator, subtitler, and (online) English teacher. In his spare time, he pursues his interest in play-writing and performs regularly as a multilingual trad musician. He is also a keen supporter of the Scots language, into which he has translated and published various international poems and short stories.

Index